MISSION  T

MISSION IN
THE NEW TESTAMENT

FERDINAND HAHN

SCM PRESS LTD

Translated by Frank Clarke from the German
Das Verständnis der Mission im neuen Testament
(Wissenschaftliche Monographien zum Alten und Neuen
Testament 13)
Neukirchener Verlag, Neukirchen-Vluyn, 1963

Translation © SCM Press 1965

266

334 01023 3 ⎰ 20028820

First published in English 1965
by SCM Press Ltd

58 Bloomsbury Street London WC1
Second impression 1981

Printed in Great Britain by
Richard Clay (The Chaucer Press) Ltd,
Bungay, Suffolk

TO MY WIFE

CONTENTS

PREFACE

THIS book was written in 1962 and published in German at the end of 1963. In it I meant to show the basic problems as well as the connecting links in the New Testament view of the Christian mission, its task and significance. Many special questions would have merited a much more detailed analysis. However, particular parts of the subject have been sufficiently discussed elsewhere, whereas few books attempt to treat it as a whole.

The different New Testament views on mission reflect to a high degree the history of the early Christian Church. This I had to consider in writing the book; it was comparatively easy to work out for the period starting with St Paul and ending in the sub-apostolic age, but much more difficult for the period of the beginnings of the Christian mission. I am prepared to meet with disapproval of my treatment of the missions in the earliest days of the Church. But the biblical pronouncements on the subject are so full of tensions that they are best explained by supposing completely different views on missions in the earliest Christian communities. Moreover, I have sought to understand this diversity as a result of Jesus' own attitude to the Gentiles. Nevertheless the chapter on Jesus is purposely short, and the discussion on the Old Testament presuppositions even more so, since there is a Christian mission in the true sense of the word only after the resurrection of Jesus.

In using the work of other scholars I have confined myself mainly to exegetical researches. Works on mission itself are introduced only occasionally, except in the concluding section. I am aware of this deficiency. I am aware that much more literature from other countries could have been used in more detail, but I wanted to deal in the first place with the New Testament's own contribution. What consequences may arise from this in the study of missions and in the missionary work of the Church itself will be better judged by others than by myself.

I am glad that the book is now to be published in English. In this way it will find new readers, including, I hope, some additional serious critics, whose contributions will be helpful in the discussion of the problems involved. If my research takes the discussion a little further, it has fulfilled its task. My book is not meant to be conclusive; in it I have merely sought to take up the questions arising out of the New Testament texts and to make some suggestions in trying to answer them.

Kiel   FERDINAND HAHN
April 1965

ABBREVIATIONS

AThANT	Abhandlungen zur Theologie des Alten und Neuen Testaments, Zürich
BEvTh	Beiträge zur evangelischen Theologie, München
BFchrTh	Beiträge zur Förderung christlicher Theologie, Gütersloh
BHTh	Beiträge zur historischen Theologie, Tübingen
BWANT	Beiträge zur Wissenschaft vom Alten und Neuen Testament, Stuttgart
BZ (NF)	*Biblische Zeitschrift* (Neue Folge), Paderborn
BZNW	Beihefte zur Zeitschrift für die neutestamentliche Wissenschaft, Berlin
EMM	*Evangelisches Missionsmagazin*, Basel
EMZ	*Evangelische Missionszeitschrift*, Stuttgart
ET	English translation
EvTh	*Evangelische Theologie*, München
FRLANT	Forschungen zur Religion und Literatur des Alten und Neuen Testaments, Göttingen
HbNT	Handbuch zum Neuen Testament, Tübingen
JBL	*Journal of Biblical Literature*, Philadelphia/Pennsylvania
JThSt (NS)	*Journal of Theological Studies* (New Series), Oxford
KommAT	Kommentar zum Alten Testament (ed. E. Sellin), Leipzig
KommNT	Kommentar zum Neuen Testament (ed. T. Zahn), Leipzig

KrEnKommNT	Kritisch-Exegetischer Kommentar über das Neue Testament, Göttingen
NovTest	*Novum Testamentum*. International Quarterly for New Testament and related Studies, Leiden
Nt.Abh.	Neutestamentliche Abhandlungen (ed. M. Meinertz), Münster
NTD	Das Neue Testament Deutsch, Göttingen
NtForsch	Neutestamentliche Forschungen (ed. O. Schmitz), Gütersloh
NTSt	*New Testament Studies*, Cambridge
RechScRel	*Recherches de Science religieuse*, Paris
R*GG*³	*Die Religion in Geschichte und Gegenwart*, 3rd edn., Tübingen
RHPbR	*Revue d'Histoire et de Philosophie Religieuses*, Strasbourg-Paris
SAH	Sitzungsberichte der Heidelberger Akademie der Wissenschaften, Heidelberg
SBT	Studies in Biblical Theology, London
SNT	Die Schriften des Neuen Testaments neu übersetzt und für die Gegenwart erklärt, Göttingen
StTh	*Studia Theologica*, Lund
Suppl. to *NovTest*	Supplements to *Novum Testamentum*, Leiden
ThBüch	Theologische Bücherei, München
ThBl	*Theologische Blätter*, Leipzig
TheolViat	*Theologia Viatorum*, Berlin
ThEx (NF)	Theologische Existenz heute (Neue Folge), München
ThForsch	Theologische Forschung, Hamburg-Volksdorf
ThHdKomm	Theologischer Handkommentar zum Neuen Testament, Leipzig-Berlin

ThLZ	*Theologische Literaturzeitung*, Leipzig-Berlin
ThR (NF)	*Theologische Rundschau* (Neue Folge), Tübingen
ThSt	Theologische Studien, Zürich
ThWb	*Theologisches Wörterbuch zum Neuen Testament*, Stuttgart
ThZ	*Theologische Zeitschrift*, Basel
TU	Texte und Untersuchungen zur Geschichte der altchristlichen Literatur, Berlin
Unters.z.NT	Untersuchungen zum Neuen Testament (ed. H. Windisch), Leipzig
VetTest	*Vetus Testamentum*, Leiden
WMANT	Wissenschaftliche Monographien zum Alten und Neuen Testament, Neukirchen-Vluyn
ZAW	*Zeitschrift für die alttestamentliche Wissenschaft*, Berlin
ZKG	*Zeitschrift für Kirchengeschichte*, Stuttgart
ZNW	*Zeitschrift für die neutestamentliche Wissenschaft und die Kunde der älteren Kirche*, Berlin
ZThK	*Zeitschrift für Theologie und Kirche*, Tübingen

INTRODUCTION

THE question of the right theological basis of the Christian mission has not rested since the beginning of the great modern missionary movement. Its clarification is all-important for the Church's existence and service; and it cannot be answered without objectively examining and judging the biblical report, especially that of the New Testament. As mission can be based only on the living word and witness of the Scriptures, we must constantly strive to understand rightly the biblical pronouncements on mission.

Notwithstanding certain constant elements, the earliest Christian view of mission is by no means homogeneous, and is not easy to grasp in its historical and practical differentiation. Thus the interpretation of biblical missionary pronouncements is very varied. The exegetical questions have been studied thoroughly by missiologists, and New Testament research has not avoided them either, although there the subject is not yet given its due importance. About the turn of the last century there was an intensive basic discussion, since when the question has been handled mainly piecemeal. For the presentation of the mission problem as a whole and a comprehensive collection of the material about the expansion of Christianity in the initial period we still have to go to Adolf von Harnack's work.[1] It is particularly unfortunate that New Testament studies have often concentrated one-sidedly on the disputed problem of Jesus' attitude to the Gentiles.[2] The danger in such isolation is that essential points may be overlooked or inadequately judged. It should be remembered that mission was first of all a

[1] Adolf von Harnack, *Mission und Ausbreitung des Christentums in den ersten drei Jahrhunderten* (1902¹), 1924⁴ (ET of 1st ed., *The Expansion of Christianity in the First Three Centuries*, 1904–5, not cited). Rudolf Liechtenhan, *Die urchristliche Mission. Voraussetzungen, Motive und Methoden* (AThANT 9), 1946, is very brief. The only other comprehensive presentation that need be mentioned is Karl Georg Kuhn's important essay, 'Das Problem der Mission in der Urchristenheit', *EMZ* 11 (1954), pp. 161–8.

[2] Max Meinertz, *Jesus und die Heidenmission* (*Nt.Abh.* 1/1–2) (1908¹), 1925²; Friedrich Spitta, *Jesus und die Heidenmission*, 1909; Bengt Sundkler, 'Jésus et les païens', *RHPhR* 16 (1936), pp. 462–99, also in *Arb.u.Mitteil.a.d.nt.Sem.z.Uppsala* VI (1937), pp. 1–38; Helene Stoevesandt, *Jesus und die Heidenmission* (Diss. Göttingen, 1943, typescript); T. W. Manson, *Jesus and the Non-Jews*, 1955; Joachim Jeremias, *Jesus' Promise to the Nations*, ET (SBT 24) 1958; David Bosch, *Die Heidenmission in der Zukunftsschau Jesu* (AThANT 36), 1959.

problem of the early Church. Of course, Jesus' own attitude plays an important part in this, but in the nature of our tradition we can frequently get enlightenment about Jesus himself only by arguing back from the efforts of the primitive Church. For this reason, in considering our judgment of Jesus' attitude, we might well prefer in all circumstances one that explains at the same time the very divergent conceptions of the missionary problem.

For the early Church it was a matter of course that the gospel had to be proclaimed, and that therefore mission was a necessity.[1] The Church was, in the initial period, a missionary Church in the best sense; it lived through the mission and for the mission. We cannot now form anything like an adequate picture of the vitality and effectiveness of the early Christian mission. The people who spread the gospel were in most places certainly not specially distinguished missionaries; the good news was simply carried farther and farther, spreading like wildfire and forming churches which were at first small and then grew rapidly. A more or less systematic mission, such as that undertaken from Antioch or in Paul's own missionary work, was probably a special case. But even Paul was content on each occasion to carry the gospel to the centres of a district and to trust that the message would spread out from there.

The fact that in early Christianity the mission was a matter of course does not mean that it had no problems. We need only think of the stock phrase 'Jews and Gentiles' to remind ourselves how great was the contention as to how the mission was to be understood and how it was to be carried through. The unrestricted right to a mission to the Gentiles, and the indissoluble unity of Jews and Gentiles in the Church, were clarified and put into

---

[1] Of course, the fact strikes one that the idea of 'mission' does not appear in the New Testament. The noun ἀποστολή, derived from the verb ἀποστέλλειν, is connected with the special apostolic office, which is determined by the unique transition from the historical activities of Jesus to the founding of the Church. So the office is unique. The verb ἀποστέλλειν has not been fixed terminologically in the same way; it has kept a wider meaning, and relates, as is shown, e.g., in Matt. 10, to the sending of the disciples and the community generally. But we must consider that in the New Testament this verb does not stand in the foreground in connection with sending; it serves mostly as a secondary description of the procedure, while the real expression of sending is characterized by the formulation πορευόμενοι (-θέντες) κηρύσσετε (Matt. 10.7; Mark 16.15; cf. Matt. 28.19). The Latin tradition has used beside the verb *mittere* the noun *apostolatus* (cf. Vulgate). The noun *missio* in the sense that is current with us does not appear till the sixteenth century (with the Jesuits, Carmelites, and the *congregatio de propaganda fide*); cf. Thomas Ohm, *Machet zu Jüngern alle Völker*, Theorie der Mission, 1962, pp. 37ff.

practice only after long and strenuous discussions. Indeed, in the New Testament the subject of Jews and Gentiles involves the question of the significance both of the Old Testament covenant and of the universal reality of salvation.

The present investigation aims only at showing essential relationships, setting out important boundary-posts in the history of the early Christian mission, and outlining the theological conceptions that must be known if the individual attitudes to the mission are to be fully understood. Above all, the presentation concentrates on the history of the way in which the mission was understood, while discussions about missionary methods and preaching,[1] about the position of missionaries and the newly formed churches,[2] are left aside, as is also the whole complex of the spread of Christianity in the New Testament period.[3] The Old Testament and Jewish presuppositions need be touched on only briefly and be defined on some of their main points. Clarification is specially needed of Jesus' attitude in relation to the Gentiles, and of the beginnings of the mission, as well as the co-existence of different lines of thought up to the Apostolic Conference. The Pauline view of the mission presents fewer difficulties, and need be considered only in its fundamental features, especially as the subject penetrates the whole texture of Paul's theology, and would in other circumstances have to be treated in great detail. For the Synoptic Gospels and Acts the missionary points of view have to be specially worked out. Lastly, for the post-Pauline and the Johannine tradition the recession of direct missionary activity, the greater emphasis on consolidating the existing churches, and in that connection the separation of sending and gathering, but also on the other hand the fidelity to the universal commission, have to be made clear. Thus we arrive at the sketch of how the mission was understood in the first century. In the conclusion an attempt has been made to put the results, finally summarized, into relation to some fundamental questions that concern the understanding of the mission and of its task in our Church of today.

---

[1] Harnack, *Mission und Ausbreitung* I[4], pp. 111ff., 390ff.; Albrecht Oepke, *Die Missionspredigt des Apostels Paulus* (Missionswiss.Forsch. 2), 1920.

[2] Harnack, *op. cit.* I, pp. 332ff.

[3] Harnack, *op. cit.* II, pp. 528ff.; Karl Müller and Hans Frhr. von Campenhausen, *Kirchengeschichte* I/1, 1941[3], pp. 126ff.; Hans Lietzmann, *The Beginnings of the Christian Church*, ET, rev. ed., 1949, pp. 131ff.

I

THE OLD TESTAMENT AND JEWISH PRESUPPOSITIONS OF THE EARLY CHRISTIAN MISSION

1. THE OLD TESTAMENT

A FUNDAMENTAL element of missionary thought and action is the universalist understanding of God. Although Israel's faith was particularist from the outset, it took on a universalist aspect very early—as early as the contact with the idea of celestial gods in the area of Canaan.[1] Even if the existence of other gods was not denied, the superiority of Yahweh to all other deities was yet consistently asserted,[2] and the exclusive claim of the jealous God of Israel stressed.[3] Accordingly the history of the nations is already brought by the Yahwist into connection with the activity of Yahweh, and still more so, in an entirely changed political situation, in the prophetic books; not only do all the nations come from Yahweh, but they are used by him as an instrument and must bow to his judgment.[4]

To this universal idea is joined another important one: for the nations, too, there is salvation through Yahweh. In Gen. 12.3, after the story of the Tower of Babel, the Yahwist has already

---

[1] Cf. Otto Eißfeldt, 'Partikularismus und Universalismus in der israelitisch-jüdischen Religionsgeschichte', *ThLZ* 79 (1954), cols. 283f.; Gerhard von Rad, *Old Testament Theology* I, ET 1962, pp. 23ff.

[2] That foreign nations are under the power of other gods, and indeed are given up to them, is a familiar Old Testament thought; cf., e.g., Deut. 32.8ff.; Jer. 46.25; Isa. 24.21; from these there come later the national angels, first mentioned in Dan. 10.13, 20f.; 12.1. But behind such ideas is the concept, expressed in Ps. 82, that all foreign gods are dependent on Yahweh. The same is true for the passages where the gods are described as 'no gods'; it is not their existence but their power that is denied in the Old Testament. On this cf. Walther Eichrodt, 'Gottes Volk und die Völker', *EMM* 86 (1942), pp. 129–45, especially pp. 133ff.

[3] On the significance of the first commandment cf. v. Rad, *Theology* I, pp. 207ff.

[4] Cf. Albrecht Alt, 'Die Deutung der Weltgeschichte im Alten Testament', *ZThK* 56 (1959), pp. 129–37; Hans Walter Wolff, 'Das Geschichtsverständnis der alttestamentlichen Prophetie', *EvTh* 20 (1960), pp. 218–35, especially pp. 227ff. Therefore all the nations, too, can be exhorted to extol the power of Yahweh, as, e.g., in Ps. 117.

uttered a promise for the nations without giving it a precise interpretation: mediated through Abraham and the chosen people
whose history is now beginning, there stands as the final goal,
behind the judgment of Gen. 11, the supremacy of the divine
blessing for all nations. Since Isaiah this promise has been resumed
in conjunction with Yahweh's eschatological action in a clearer
form. The idea of the nations' pilgrimage to Zion in the last days
emerges for the first time, and from then it is fairly constant in the
Old Testament tradition.[1]

A third idea must also be taken into account: the idea, particularly evident in Deutero-Isaiah, of Israel's bearing witness before
the nations. In earlier research the view has been put forward in
one way or another that here we already have a declared basis for
mission.[2] But there is an absence of any idea of going out to the
nations. Israel is God's witness solely by reason of its existence
and of God's salvation which is given to it. As this saving activity
takes place in the midst of the nations, and Israel (or the servant
of the Lord) bears witness thereof with thanks and praise before
Yahweh, it is the light of the nations, so that they come and
acknowledge Yahweh as the one God.[3] 'Thus the nations come
to the people of God. They experience what Israel experienced,
and acknowledge what Israel acknowledges—their Judge and
Conqueror is their only Saviour.'[4] Nor can the Trito-Isaianic

---

[1] Cf. Gerhard von Rad, 'Die Stadt auf dem Berge' in *Gesammelte Studien zum
Alten Testament* (ThBüch 8), 1958, pp. 214–24; Hans Wildberger, 'Die Völkerwall-
fahrt zum Zion Isa. II, 1–5', *VetTest* 7 (1957), pp. 62–81; Robert Martin-Achard,
Israël et les nations (Cahiers théologiques 42), 1959, pp. 55ff.; Jeremias, *Jesus' Promise*,
pp. 57ff.; Bosch, *Heidenmission*, pp. 23ff. For pre-exilic evidence we may mention Isa.
2.1–4 par. Micah 4.1–4; Isa. 18.7; Jer. 3.17; 16.19; Micah 7.12 (later addition); main
representatives of the view are then Deutero- and Trito-Isaiah (cf. only Isa. 45.18–
25; 60.1–22); from the post-exilic period come Zeph. 3.8–11; Hag. 2.6–9; Zech. 2.10–
13; 8.2, 20–23; 14.16; Isa. 25.6–8; there are later echoes of these in Ps. 68.29, 31;
86.9; 96.8, 10. Other ideas about the salvation of the Gentiles are very rare; cf.
Isa. 19.18–25; Zeph. 2.11.

[2] I mention merely Alfred Bertholet, *Die Stellung der Israeliten und der Juden zu den
Fremden*, 1896, pp. 117ff.; Max Löhr, *Der Missionsgedanke im Alten Testament* (Samml.
gemeinverständl. Vorträge 5), 1896; Ernst Sellin, 'Der Missionsgedanke im Alten
Testament', *Neue Allg. Missionszeitschrift*, 1925, pp. 33–45, 66–72; Paul Volz, *Jesaja II*
(KommAT IX/2), 1932, pp. 149ff., especially pp. 168f. Similarly H. H. Rowley,
The Missionary Message of the Old Testament, 1944 (repr. 1955). For a contrary view
(perhaps the first) see Joachim Begrich, *Studien zu Deuterojesaja* (BWANT IV/25),
1938, p. 110.

[3] Cf. especially Hans Walter Wolff, 'Israel und die Völker bei Deuterojesaja',
EMZ 8 (1951), pp. 1–14; Martin-Achard, pp. 13ff.; also Gerhard von Rad, *Theologie
des Alten Testaments* II, 1960, p. 263.

[4] Wolff, *EMZ* 8 (1951), p. 13.

text Isa. 66.18f. and the Book of Jonah be regarded as evidence
for a mission in the Old Testament;[1] for in the one case it is the
'survivors' of the Gentiles themselves who are Yahweh's witnesses
among the nations, and in the other it is a question of the freedom
of divine dealings with the Gentiles.[2]

We may therefore say that in the Old Testament there is no
mission in the real sense. There is an absence of a divine commission for the purpose and of any conscious outgoing to the Gentiles
to win them for belief in Yahweh. Nevertheless, there are given
here decisive basic features for the New Testament understanding
of mission: belief in the God who is the Lord of all nations and
directs their history, knowledge of the eschatological salvation
of the nations, and the perception that witness must be borne
before the Gentiles in view of God's accomplished act of salvation,
even if this witness still has, in the Old Testament, an entirely
passive character.[3]

[1] Explicitly Sellin, *op. cit.*, pp. 33f., 67ff., who here sees accomplished what is
recognized in principle already in Deutero-Isaiah. The Book of Jonah was even
described on occasion as 'a tendentious document written in the interests of the
mission to the Gentiles'; cf. Wilhelm Bousset and Hugo Gressmann, *Die Religion
des Judentums im späthellenistischen Zeitalter* (HbNT 21), 1926[3], p. 82.

[2] Cf. Martin-Achard, pp. 45ff.

[3] Cf. the concluding reflections by Martin-Achard, pp. 69ff. Johannes Hempel,
'Die Wurzeln des Missionswillens im Alten Testament', *ZAW* 66 (1954), pp. 244–72,
emphasizes beside the prophetic word the idea of suffering and the insertion of the
'redeemer myth' in Deutero-Isaiah; but here both comparative religion and exegesis
cause some hesitations. Johannes Blauw, *Gottes Werk in dieser Welt. Grundzüge einer
biblischen Theologie der Mission*, 1961, brings forward various noteworthy considerations about the position of the nations in Old Testament thought, about the relation
of universalism and particularism, as well as about the choice of Israel as a summons
to service (referring to Th. C. Vriezen, *Die Erwählung Israels nach dem Alten Testament*,
1953); he then deals with the eschatological expectation of an acknowledgment of
Yahweh by the nations, showing rightly that there is no idea of a call and a going
out to the nations, but only of the coming of the nations as an answer to God's deeds
in Israel' (p. 43). He does not feel able to question that this eschatological hope has a
missionary character, and he therefore distinguishes between a missionary consciousness of a centripetal and of a centrifugal kind (p. 36), only the former being manifest
in the Old Testament. But not much is gained with this distinction, because there is,
in fact, no real mission in Israelite thought. Even the Wisdom literature (pp. 66ff.)
cannot be understood to imply that Israel had become 'increasingly conscious of its
missionary calling'; on the contrary, even Prov. 1–9 is concerned merely with the
question of Yahweh's dealings with the nations and of the special position of Israel.
It is quite erroneous to connect with the problem of the mission the considerations
of the Old Testament expectation of a Messiah—quite apart from the inappropriate-
ness of drawing parallels between the idea of the Messiah, of the servant of God, and
of the Son of man (pp. 47ff.) Very problematic, too, is the concept of the *Heilsgeschichte* as a purely temporal course of affairs with progressive actions by God, by
which the author tries to grasp the facts and expectations of the Old Testament itself
(p. 40), as well as the continuity between the Old Testament and the New (pp. 71ff.);
he actually speaks of a '*heilsgeschichtlich* founding of the mission' (p. 15). Of course,

2. LATER JUDAISM

In later Judaism we come to a picture that has been in many respects transformed, and yet Old Testament ideas have been preserved as regards essentials. The extent to which the acknowledgment of the one God played a part is shown by the custom, which had taken firm root in the meantime, of reciting the *shema*‘ every day. The eschatological expectation of the nations' pilgrimage still remained alive, though its importance was now restricted.[1] We may see an Old Testament heritage, too, in the fact that for wide circles of later Judaism there was no missionary inclination. This cannot be attributed entirely to increasingly narrow nationalism and particularism which was certainly in part characteristic of the Judaism of that period; it has deeper roots. It is interesting that we find no evidence, either in apocalyptic or in Qumran writings, of winning over and converting the Gentiles.[2] Even within the rabbinic tradition the attitude is by no

---

one must not delete temporal elements from biblical thought; it is, however, extremely characteristic of the Old Testament, and completely so of the New, that the line of time is again and again broken into and spanned by God's revelation. In the background of this concept we have Oscar Cullmann, *Christ and Time* (ET 1962[2]), who, however, takes care not to place a one-sided emphasis on the temporal structure of the *Heilsgeschichte* itself, and as is shown particularly in the introductory chapter to the new edition (pp. xviiff.), would like to work out the tension of 'already fulfilled' and 'not yet completed', the determination of which is, in fact, of decisive importance. But this does not dispose of the question whether his *heilsgeschichtlich* sketch is not primarily oriented on Lucan theology, thus missing the common ground of the New Testament as a whole; apart from that the question is less of the relation of time and eternity than of the fact that the New Testament view of time is itself inwardly broken and of many strata. Cf. the excellent research by Walter Kreck, *Die Zukunft des Gekommenen. Grundprobleme der Eschatologie*, 1961, and below, ch. IV, pp. 103ff.

[1] Sverre Aalen, *Die Begriffe 'Licht' und 'Finsternis' im Alten Testament, im Spätjudentum und im Rabbinismus* (Skrifter utgitt av Det Norske Videnskaps-Akademi i Oslo II. Hist.-Filos. Klasse, 1951, no. 1), 1951, pp. 202ff., especially pp. 228ff. and 299ff.; and Jeremias, *Jesus' Promise*, pp. 61f.

[2] That apocalyptic, with all the comprehensive breadth of the historical concept, did not by any means know a universalistic idea of salvation has been excellently demonstrated by Albert Schweitzer, *The Mysticism of Paul the Apostle*, ET 1931, pp. 177f.; cf. further Dietrich Rössler, *Gesetz und Geschichte. Untersuchungen zur Theologie der jüdischen Apokalyptik und der pharisäischen Orthodoxie* (WMANT 3), 1960, pp. 64f. The coming of the Gentiles in the last days appears, then, only rarely and marginally, thus, e.g., II (4) Esdras 13.12f.; on this cf. Nils Alstrup Dahl, *Das Volk Gottes* (1941), 1963[2], p. 87. The occasional echoes of Deutero-Isaiah in the Ethiopic Book of Enoch are compiled from quite a different point of view; on this see Stoevesandt, *Jesus und die Heidenmission*, pp. 132ff. Further cf. Bousset and Gressmann, *Religion des Judentums*, pp. 234f.; Bosch, *Heidenmission*, pp. 35f. For Qumran cf. Karl

means unvarying, the Shammaites at least opposing in many cases the acceptance of Gentiles.[1] It is only if this negative evidence is given due weight that the efforts that were undoubtedly made in the other direction, to win Gentiles for the Jewish religion, can be rightly judged.

Extensive and intensive recruiting for the Jewish faith was obviously undertaken by Hellenistic Jews.[2] There the meaning of 'proselytes', and the corresponding 'God-fearers', was terminologically fixed.[3] When this movement set in cannot be said for certain, but it was certainly well under way in the second century BC. Even if the Septuagint, the greater part of which originated as early as the third century BC, arose in the first place from the needs of the Jewish community itself, the fragmentary survivals of the literature of Hellenistic Judaism since the second century BC show how markedly Diaspora Judaism turned towards the Gentile world, not only to defend its own faith with apologetics, but even more to commend it to the people in a time of religious uncertainty.[4] The continually recurring basic ideas are monotheism, with a conception of God closely assimilated to philosophic tradition, the spiritualizing of the *heilsgeschichtlich* and cultic tradition,[5] polemics against the vices of paganism, the demonstration of the high ethics of Judaism—in which rationalizing and pragmatizing were not avoided—and finally the consciousness of having been a chosen people ever since the remote past. Eschato-

---

Georg Kuhn, *EMZ* 11 (1954), pp. 161–8, there pp. 163f.; Hempel, *ZAW* 66 (1954), pp. 245ff.: 'Therefore, to undertake a mission is to say the least not a matter of course' (p. 248).

[1] Cf. Jeremias, p. 16.
[2] On this see especially Dieter Georgi, *Die Gegner des Paulus im Zweiten Korintherbrief* (WMANT 11), 1963, pp. 51ff., 83ff.
[3] Cf. Karl Georg Kuhn, art. προσήλυτος, *ThWb* VI, pp. 727–45, especially pp. 730ff.
[4] Cf. Otto Stählin, 'Die hellenistisch-jüdische Literatur' in W. von Christ, *Griechische Literaturgeschichte* II/1, 1921[6], pp. 588–624; Bousset and Gressmann, pp. 24ff.; Peter Dalbert, *Die Theologie der hellenistisch-jüdischen Missionsliteratur unter Ausschluß von Philo und Josephus* (ThForsch 4), 1954, pp. 27ff.; also Hartwig Thyen, *Der Stil der Jüdisch-Hellenistischen Homilie* (FRLANT 65), 1955, pp. 7ff. That the Septuagint later became of considerable importance for the expansion of Judaism is rightly emphasized by Blauw, *Gottes Werk*, pp. 64f., though his treatment of later Judaism is quite inadequate. On the place of the Septuagint in Jewish propaganda cf. Georg Rosen, Friedrich Rosen, and Georg Bertram, *Juden und Phönizier. Das antike Judentum als Missionsreligion und die Entstehung der jüdischen Diaspora*, 1929[2], pp. 35ff., especially pp. 48ff.
[5] On this cf. Hans Wenschkewitz, *Die Spiritualisierung der Kultusbegriffe Tempel, Priester und Opfer im Neuen Testament* (Angelos-Beiheft 4), 1932.

logical expectations play only a marginal part, mainly in the
threat of God's future judgment.[1] Even though it may have been
an extremely vital movement, often borne along by genuine
enthusiasm,[2] yet it can hardly be spoken of as a 'mission'. For
there is no question here of a real mission—nowhere is any claim
made to a special divine commission—nor does the Old Testament eschatological basis of the conversion of the Gentiles play
a decisive part. The limits of the whole far-reaching effort as to
non-Jews are shown especially in the consciousness of superiority,
so much stressed and persistently recurring in literature, as well
as in the fact that no more was usually attempted than to induce
the Gentiles to acknowledge the one God and follow the fundamental ethical demands of the Old Testament.[3] Besides the many
σεβόμενοι τὸν θεόν ('God-fearers') there were, it is true, also
προσήλυτοι (proselytes), who accepted circumcision and undertook
to observe fully the Jewish law and rites; but, as is shown not
least by the inscriptions, these may well have remained only a
small circle in the Diaspora's sphere of influence.[4]

We meet with a very different attitude wherever, in Palestinian
Judaism, efforts to win the Gentiles over were approved of and
supported. As far as we can see, this probably did not come about
till towards the end of the first century BC, and is associated with
the name of Rabbi Hillel. There are good reasons to suppose that
in general it was only an effect of the already extensive and
successful activities of the Hellenist Jews among the Gentiles.[5]
It is beyond question that in the first century AD intensive efforts
among the Gentiles were being made in the rabbinic schools that
owed their origin to Hillel; this can be seen also in rabbinic
writings, though with the Jewish war a reaction had already set
in.[6] But it is characteristic of this group that adopted an open

---

[1] Cf. Bertholet, *Stellung den Israeliten . . . zu den Fremden*, pp. 257ff.; Bousset and
Gressman, pp. 76ff.; Dalbert, *op. cit.*, pp. 124ff.

[2] Cf. Rom. 2.17–20; *Sibylline Oracles* III, 195, 582.

[3] Cf. Kuhn, *EMZ* 11 (1954), p. 162; *id. ThWb* VI, p. 731.

[4] Kuhn, *ThWb* VI, p. 733. On the position of the proselytes see further Jean
Juster, *Les Juifs dans l'empire romain* I, 1914, pp. 253ff.

[5] Cf. Kuhn, *EMZ* 11 (1954) pp. 162f.; he actually speaks of a 'corrective movement' (with inverted commas) in face of the efforts of Diaspora Judaism.

[6] Cf. Jeremias, pp. 13f., 16f.; Bousset and Gressmann, pp. 83ff.; (H. L. Strack
and) Paul Billerbeck, *Kommentar zum Neuen Testament aus Talmud und Midrasch*, 1922–8,
I, pp. 924ff.; IV/1, pp. 353ff.; Joseph Klausner, *The Messianic Idea in Israel*, 1956,
pp. 470ff., esp. pp. 476ff.; also Hans Joachim Schoeps, *Paulus. Die Theologie des
Apostels im Lichte der jüdischen Religionsgeschichte*, 1959, pp. 232ff.

attitude towards the Gentiles that they were in no circumstances satisfied with gaining 'God-fearers', but were consistently out to recruit proselytes. The Old Testament idea of the *gēr* or the *tōšāb*, the stranger who had settled in the land, had meanwhile been re-fashioned; the 'God-fearer' was described as merely *gēr tōšāb*, in contrast to the *gēr ṣedeq*, who accepted circumcision and the law. Here it is characteristic that a distinction from birthright Jews should be consistently maintained.[1] It is instructive to recall the well-known story of the conversion of the royal house of Adiabene to the Jewish faith, where the Hellenist Jew Ananias had at first said that the king could worship God without circumcision; but the Palestinian Jew Eleazar successfully pressed for circumcision, obtaining the complete conversion.[2] Thus what occurred only occasionally in Diaspora Judaism, and was indeed not even specially striven for, was the real aim of that group of Palestinian Judaism; that is clear from Matt. 23.15a.[3] But even this proselytizing cannot be described as mission in the real sense; for, apart from the fact that there is again no divine commission, what is finally decisive is not that the Gentiles worship the true God and make the right faith their own, but that they become Jews; the aim is their 'naturalization'.[4]

Thus we must distinguish all Jewish efforts to win over the Gentiles from mission in the real sense.[5] On the gaining of 'God-fearers' it is best to speak of religious propaganda,[6] and

---

[1] On this see Kuhn, *ThWb* VI, pp. 728ff., 736ff., 740ff.; Joachim Jeremias, *Jerusalem zur Zeit Jesu* IIB, 1958², pp. 191ff.; Bosch, *Heidenmission*, pp. 34f.

[2] Jos.*Ant.* XX (17ff.), 34-48; on this see Kuhn, *ThWb* VI, pp. 731, 735.

[3] It is a question of a logion that comes from the early Church in Palestine; cf. Jeremias, *Jesus' Promise*, pp. 17f., n. 4.

[4] Jeremias, *Jesus' Promise*, p. 17: he speaks of 'the inseparable connexión between religion and national custom'.

[5] This distinction necessarily follows from any attempt based on the New Testament to define the missionary idea. Without giving here and now a comprehensive definition (see below, p. 173), we may point out that the directions given by Jesus are of decisive importance for the New Testament. Indeed, in the New Testament view of the mission it is not a matter of merely 'arranging a mission' (Warneck); rather are Jesus' injunctions determined by the eschatological hour that has now dawned through his own words and works. But it is just this eschatological promise and presence of salvation, from which the commission and the service to the nations result, that is completely absent from the Old Testament and from later Judaism.

[6] Thus already Karl Axenfeld, 'Die jüdische Propaganda als Vorläuferin und Wegbereiterin der urchristlichen Mission' in *Missionswissenschaftliche Studien* (G. Warneck-Festschrift), 1904, pp. 1–80; more recently Bosch, *op. cit.*, pp. 31ff. This, however, is justified only if it is distinguished from the recruiting of proselytes. Moreover, it may indeed be open to question whether the Diaspora Jews took the

on the efforts to obtain a complete conversion, of a recruiting of proselytes. The success of these efforts was not small, and it is beyond doubt that they paved the way in large measure for the first Christian mission.[1]

'propagandist drive' with them from their native land. It may, however, be true that their success is to be attributed, not to the literary activity of individuals, but to the assimilative power of the communities with their living religion. So Axenfeld, pp. 31, 34f.

[1] On the spread of Judaism in the New Testament period cf. Emil Schürer, *Geschichte des jüdischen Volkes im Zeitalter Jesu Christi* III, 1911[4], pp. 1ff. (ET of 2nd ed., *A History of the Jewish People in the Time of Jesus Christ* II, 2, 1885, pp. 220ff.); v. Harnack, *Mission und Ausbreitung* I, pp. 5ff.

II

JESUS' ATTITUDE TO THE GENTILES

As has been shown, the Judaism of Jesus' time made considerable efforts to win the Gentiles over; but these efforts, however distinctive in detail, were throughout 'not supported by an eschatological emphasis'.[1] In sharp contrast to this, the conversion of the Gentiles and their worship of the true God is understood again in the whole of the New Testament, as in the Old, from the point of view of the eschatological expectation.

The New Testament's view of the mission is most deeply rooted in Jesus' message that 'the Kingdom of God is upon you'. This was largely overlooked, or at least wrongly interpreted, by nineteenth- and early twentieth-century research.[2] The basic insights of Johannes Weiss and Albert Schweitzer had to bear fruit[3] before an adequate judgment could be reached on the problems of the early Christian mission. In present-day research the eschatological point of departure is on the whole approved of, but there is still much dispute over the question how far Jesus himself wanted, brought about, or even directly ordered the mission among the Gentiles. Jesus' attitude to the Gentiles must therefore be investigated before it can be shown how the mission was understood in the earliest Christianity.

Four attempted solutions play a prominent part in the recent discussion:

(*a*) Adolf von Harnack was of the opinion that the mission to the Gentiles lay entirely outside Jesus' horizon, even if his preaching with its concern for humanity in general at once led

---

[1] Kuhn, *EMZ* 11 (1954), p. 163.

[2] This holds good for New Testament research as well as for the study of missions; I mention only G. Warneck, *Evangelische Missionslehre* I, 1897[2], pp. 6off.

[3] Johannes Weiss, *Die Predigt Jesu vom Reiche Gottes*, 1892 (1900[2]); Albert Schweitzer, *The Mystery of the Kingdom of God: the Secret of Jesus' Messiahship and Passion*, ET 1913 (repr. 1950); *Geschichte der Leben-Jesu-Forschung*, 1913[2] (1951[6]), pp. 39off.; cf. *The Quest of the Historical Jesus*, ET 1954[3], pp. 351ff.

logically, after his death, to the early Church's missionary activity among the Gentiles.[1]

(*b*) Friedrich Spitta, on the other hand, supported the view that because of the accounts of his having stayed several times in Gentile territory, and of the various reports of his accepting non-Jews, we must allow for a positive attitude of Jesus towards the Gentiles; he had taken them into the new community of the saved, and may himself be regarded as the first missionary to the Gentiles.[2]

(*c*) Max Meinertz, while recognizing that Jesus' activity during his lifetime had been confined to Israel, thought that he had already envisaged a future inclusion of the Gentiles, and that after his resurrection he had commanded his disciples to undertake a universal mission.[3]

[1] Von Harnack, *Mission und Ausbreitung* I, pp. 39ff.: Jesus' message was directed to the Jews; he appealed, not to the liberal, but to the orthodox circles; but he contended against all selfish and self-righteous piety, and achieved an inner detachment from the national attitude—a detachment that was seen especially in his contesting all reliance on kinship with Abraham, and in his basing divine sonship 'on the pillars of repentance and humility, faith and love' (p. 39). Indeed, men found here 'a love of God and men which may be described as an implicit universalism' (p. 48). Jesus gave no instructions for a world mission. 'But we may certainly say that the world mission was bound to proceed from Jesus' religion and spirit, and that its originating without any direct word from Jesus—in fact in apparent contradiction to some of his words—is a stronger testimony to the nature, force, and greatness of his preaching than if it had been the carrying out of a definite instruction. The tree is known by its fruit, but one must not look for the fruit at the root' (p. 40). Similarly Maurice Goguel, 'Jésus et les origines de l'universalisme chrétien', *RHPhR* 12 (1932), pp. 193–211.
[2] Friedrich Spitta, *Jesus und die Heidenmission*, esp. pp. 72ff., 109ff. The mission to the Gentiles was in Jesus' mind and heart from the very first; it is not an idea that he has just conceived, but he resists the Pharisees' caricature of the mission. In the mixed population of Galilee, Jesus was constantly in touch with Gentiles, but he also went beyond the borders. 'It was therefore quite impossible for him to have no influence on the Gentiles' (p. 81). Jesus did not first turn to the Gentiles after his failure among the Jews, nor can we say that he had previously confined himself to Israel (pp. 83ff.). Spitta supposes that Matt. 28.18 implies a direction given to a larger circle of co-workers for a mission to the Gentiles during Jesus' lifetime (pp. 61ff.).
[3] Max Meinertz, *Jesus und die Heidenmission*, especially pp. 84ff., 114ff., 159ff.; *id.*, 'Zum Ursprung der Heidenmission', *Biblica* 40 (1959), pp. 762–77. Although Jesus confined his own activities to Israel, the critical words to Israel show 'a genuine presupposition of Jesus' concern for the Gentiles' ('Zum Ursprung . . .', p. 764). His awareness of being the messianic servant of God coincided with the intensive universalist idea of salvation. Already in his lifetime he pointed to the future exertions on behalf of the Gentiles (now the intensive universalism becomes explicit; cf. *Jesus und die Heidenmission*, pp. 49ff., 80ff.). Mark 13.10; 14.9, and other sayings lead to Matt. 28.18ff. 'What had hitherto been spoken only occasionally and with his eyes on the future became reality in this universal commission' (*ibid.*, p. 771). Similarly

(d) Lastly, Joachim Jeremias strongly emphasized that Jesus had confined to Israel both his own activity and that of his disciples, and had reserved the bringing in of the Gentiles for God's own action in the last days; it was not till Jesus' resurrection that the mission to the Gentiles was brought within the horizon of the disciples with the dawn of the eschatological hour and the happenings of the last days already coming to pass.[1]

The first of these attempted solutions, while emphasizing the contrast between Jesus' own attitude and the early Church's missionary activity, tries to show their inner connection; but it pays much too little regard to the eschatological factor, and thus fails to recognize the decisive basis for understanding Jesus and his Church. The second interpretation rightly emphasizes Jesus' unreserved attitude towards Gentiles, but from that it draws unwarranted conclusions; there is no justification at all for speaking of a real missionary activity by Jesus himself among the Gentiles. The third solution likewise aims at setting out Jesus' open attitude towards the Gentiles, but seeks to avoid premature

---

Heinrich Schlier, 'Die Entscheidung für die Heidenmission in der Urchristenheit' in *Die Zeit der Kirche*, 1956, pp. 90–107, who regards the resurrection and exaltation of Jesus as the presupposition of the mission to the Gentiles; further Thomas Ohm, *Machet zu Jüngern alle Völker*, pp. 243ff. Cf. also Bosch, *Heidenmission*, pp. 76ff., 93ff., 184ff., especially 193ff.: 'A mission to the Gentiles is not possible till after Jesus has by his call to repentance brought the Israelite people to a decision, after he has died for the "many" and been raised from the dead, and after he has sent his Holy Spirit as "missionary" into the world at large' (p. 194); moreover, there is an attempt here to take more account of Jesus' eschatological view.

[1] Jeremias, *Jesus' Promise*, pp. 38f., 55ff., 70ff.: in contrast to the preceding argument, the resurrection and the interval up to the parousia are not regarded as lying within Jesus' field of view; rather does the raising of Jesus from the dead bring an anticipation of the events that are expected with the parousia. These characteristic qualities of Jesus' own attitude had already to some extent been dealt with by Albert Schweitzer, *Mysticism*, pp. 177ff.; he contrasts the 'universalism of the old eschatological expectation' that characterizes the Old Testament and Jesus with the 'missionary universalism' of the Pharisees, and emphasizes 'that Jesus is universalistic in his thinking and Jewish-particularistic in his action' (p. 180); and here he points expressly to the idea of the nations' pilgrimage. These thoughts are carried further by Bengt Sundkler, *RHPhR* 16 (1936), especially pp. 485ff., 491ff.; he also brings in the idea of the centre of the earth (first in Ezek. 38.12), and with regard to Jesus he tries to proceed from the cleansing of the temple as the beginning of the eschatological renewal of the world. Also worthy of consideration is Helene Stoevesandt, *Jesus und die Heidenmission*, esp. pp. 141ff., who likewise disputes the idea of Jesus' mission to the Gentiles, on the ground that he had expected their eschatological coming; the Church took in hand the mission to them, because it thought that the new creation had already dawned in Christ.

conclusions; the significance of Jesus' resurrection is also brought more firmly into the foreground, the eschatology remaining relatively unstressed, and the result is an accommodation between the various elements of the tradition, with no critical analysis undertaken. The advantage of the fourth proposed solution is that it puts in the centre of the investigation the question of the eschatological expectation of Jesus and the early Church. Nevertheless, this one-sided judgment cannot satisfy us either. For, quite apart from the question of the authenticity of some of the logia, even if the guiding thought in the nation's pilgrimage to God's mountain had been, as is here represented, the decisive element in Jesus' promise to the Gentiles, it would be incomprehensible how an active missionary effort of the Church could begin at all after Easter. We may at first leave aside Matt. 28.18ff., as it has its own complicated history in the tradition; and moreover, the text in this form as an instruction from the Lord going directly back to Easter would make inexplicable the strongly particularist attitude of the early Church. The words in Matt. 10.5b, 6; 10.23; 15.24 cannot without a closer examination be regarded as the Lord's authentic sayings,[1] but must also be put later. Even if Jesus' resurrection had been generally regarded as the dawning of the eschatological hour, it would still remain unexplained why, after Jesus had expected that God himself would take action to bring in the Gentiles, it could come about that the disciples should now go out to the nations at all. In my opinion the statement: 'The Gentile mission is God's own activity'[2] masks rather than solves the difficulties that arise here. We must therefore take a slightly different road, where the views expressed in the other attempted solutions will also be given due consideration.

There is no doubt that Jesus directed his work in the first place to Israel. He laid a claim to God's people as a whole. In this he

[1] Matt. 10.5b, 6; 10.23; 15.24 are regarded as authentic by v. Harnack, *Mission und Ausbreitung* I, pp. 41f., 43 n. 3; Meinertz, *Jesus und die Heidenmission*, pp. 114f.; Bosch, *op. cit.*, pp. 84f.; A. Schweitzer, *Mysticism*, pp. 179f.; Jeremias, *Jesus' Promise*, pp. 19ff., 22ff., Stoevesandt, *op. cit.*, pp. 24ff. Spitta, on the other hand, *op. cit.*, pp. 41ff., regards them as unauthentic. Matt. 28.18 is attributed by Meinertz, *op. cit.*, pp. 116ff.; Bosch, *op. cit.*, pp. 184ff.; Jeremias, *op. cit.*, pp. 38f., to the risen Lord; by Spitta, on the other hand, *op. cit.*, pp. 61ff., in its original form to the earthly Jesus; but v. Harnack, *op. cit.* I, pp. 45f. and Stoevesandt, *op. cit.*, pp. 37ff., regard it as a later production of the Church. These texts are discussed in detail in ch. III below.

[2] Jeremias, *Jesus' Promise*, p. 74; similarly Bosch, *op. cit.*, pp. 195ff.

followed John the Baptist, who likewise addressed himself to all Israel, summoned them to repentance, and warned them of God's judgment. But whereas John's ministry was dominated by the preaching of judgment, Jesus was concerned with a great new promise of salvation. He did not turn back to the idea of gathering the holy remnant, as was the widespread tendency in the Judaism of that time, but took up again the Old Testament concept of God's people.[1] For that reason he appointed the twelve as representatives of God's newly established covenant with the tribes of Israel, once more numerically complete.[2] For that reason, too, the conventional boundaries within Israel, as they had been drawn by devout Jews of all shades of opinion, no longer existed for him: neither to the sick who were segregated on cultic and ritual grounds, nor to the prostitutes and sinners who were boycotted on moral grounds, nor to the tax-collectors who were excluded on religious and nationalist grounds, did he refuse contact, help, and fellowship. But it is obvious that his claim went still further,[3] for it may have been precisely because of his commission to all Israel that he also turned to the Samaritans and tried to break down the existing prejudices.[4] This appears from the parable Luke 10.30–37, as well as in the narrative Luke 17.(11), 12–19, and in the tradition behind John 4.1ff. In my opinion it is highly probable that this reflects a real effort of Jesus to reach the Samaritans;[5] and yet to judge by Luke 9.51ff., the Samaritans may have gone so far as to reject him completely.[6]

[1] Cf. Joachim Jeremias, 'Der Gedanke des "Heiligen Restes" im Spätjudentum und in der Verkündigung Jesu', *ZNW* 42 (1949), pp. 184–94; Anton Vögtle, *Das öffentliche Wirken Jesu auf dem Hintergrund der Qumranbewegung* (Freiburger Universitätsreden NF 27), 1958; otherwise Sundkler, *RHPhR* 16 (1936), pp. 475ff.

[2] Doubts as to the historicity of the circle of the Twelve are in my opinion unfounded. Against this again quite recently Philipp Vielhauer, 'Gottesreich und Menschensohn in der Verkündigung Jesu' in *Festschrift für Günther Dehn*, 1957, pp. 51–79, there pp. 62ff.; Günter Klein, *Die Zwölf Apostel. Ursprung und Gehalt einer Idee* (FRLANT 77), 1961, pp. 34ff. The repeated reference to Judas as 'one of the twelve' would, however, be inexplicable if the Twelve had been an institution created by the early Church.

[3] Liechtenhan, *Die urchristliche Mission*, p. 34, has very appositely pointed out that Jesus, by turning to sinners and tax-collectors, has already broken through the religious particularism of Judaism, and that it is then 'a necessary further step for the door also to be opened to the Samaritans and Gentiles'.

[4] Jeremias, *Jesus' Promise*, pp. 42f., has shown that the relation between Jews and Samaritans had improved somewhat in the first century BC, but that the antagonism then became more acute again.

[5] Disputed by Stoevesandt, *op. cit.*, pp. 98ff.; Bosch, *op. cit.*, pp. 103ff.

[6] Notwithstanding Rudolf Bultmann, *The History of the Synoptic Tradition*, ET

Jesus, however, crossed the boundaries of the Judaism of that time—in so far as it still kept to the worship in the temple in Jerusalem—not only towards Samaria, but also in the northern and eastern region of Galilee. Both form-criticism and literary and historical criticism have clearly shown that we have not to deal with a full-scale 'northern journey' of Jesus; but that does not get over the fact that in connection with a whole series of traditional details we have statements about places which can hardly be explained by reference to later tradition or to editorial work, and which thus indicate that Jesus occasionally stayed in those Gentile territories.[1] This cannot be based on the idea of a withdrawal into solitude or of avoiding Herod,[2] nor, of course, is it permissible on the other hand to speak at once of Jesus' missionary activity among the Gentiles.[3] In any case the view that Jesus sought 'outposts of Israelite nationality and Jewish religion' in those territories[4] deserves consideration. But this is only one side of the matter. For even if Jesus extended his activity only over the whole of ancient Israel, it would not be possible for him to avoid frequently coming into contact with Gentiles; and that could certainly happen on occasion in Galilee as well as in Judaea.

As we know from the gospel tradition, non-Jews did actually turn to Jesus and ask him for help. The narrative, preserved in various forms in Matt. 8.5–10, 13 par. Luke 7.1–9 and in John 4.46–53, about the centurion at Capernaum, as well as the story about the Syrophoenician woman in Mark 7.24–30 par., have been kept and handed on as paradigms of unconditional confidence in

---

1963, it is unlikely that Luke 9.51ff. reflects only the missionary experience of the Church. On the contrary, it may well indicate that Jesus rejects the hostile attitude towards the Samaritans that was shared also by the disciples. The text is judged rather differently by Hans Conzelmann, *The Theology of St Luke*, ET 1960, pp. 65f.

[1] This holds good particularly for Mark 7.24; 8.27, and also for the various reports of a journey over to the region east of the Jordan; cf. in detail Willi Marxsen, *Der Evangelist Markus. Studien zur Redaktionsgeschichte des Evangeliums* (FRLANT 67), 1959², pp. 41ff.
[2] The former, e.g., in Stoevesandt, *op. cit.*, pp. 17ff.; Bosch, *op. cit.*, p. 97; the other thesis is supported mainly by Julius Wellhausen, *Evangelium Marci*, 1902², pp. 44ff., esp. pp. 48f.: 'Jesus auf unsteter Wanderung'.
[3] Spitta, *op. cit.*, pp. 109ff.
[4] Thus Albrecht Alt, 'Die Stätten des Wirkens Jesu in Galiläa territorialgeschichtlich betrachtet' in *Kleine Schriften zur Geschichte Israels* II, 1953, pp. 436–55, esp. pp. 450ff. (quotation from p. 455); similarly earlier Gustav Dalman, *Sacred Sites and Ways*, ET 1935, pp. 205f., and now Jeremias, *Jesus' Promise*, pp. 35ff.

Jesus. Let us proceed from the last-mentioned narrative, which has been well preserved in its original form, apart from the additions in vv. 24b and 27a. The description is free from all specifically theological abstraction.[1] There may well be related here, in a compact form and substantially unchanged, a historical incident in which Jesus, with the familiar allusion to the contrast between Jews and Gentiles as children and dogs, emphasizes the exceptional position of Israel, but nevertheless grants the request of the woman who sets her hope on him and will not take No for an answer.[2] Similarly the story of the centurion at Capernaum in Matt. 8.5–10, 13 par., although in all the versions handed down to us it bears traces of a certain bias, lets us see in its essentials a readiness on Jesus' part to respond promptly to the trustful entreaty of a Gentile.[3]

[1] Matt. 15.21–28 is undoubtedly secondary. Verses 22–24 are a later addition, the request in v. 25 is transposed, in v. 28 a formularized answer is used, by which the concept of πίστις could be brought in and stressed. Apart from v. 21 and small additions in v. 22, this form of the narrative was taken over by Matthew from his special material, and is not traceable to a free editorial revision. I have tried to prove in my book *Christologische Hoheitstitel. Ihre Geschichte im frühen Christentum* (FRLANT 83), 1963, pp. 81f., that in Mark 7.28 the κύριε form of address does not yet imply any title of sovereignty.

[2] Bultmann, *Synoptic Tradition*, p. 38, and Martin Dibelius, *Die Formgeschichte des Evangeliums*, 1961[4], p. 53 n. 1 (ET, *From Tradition to Gospel*, 1934, omits); p. 261 (ET, same page), emphasize the closeness of Mark 7.24–30 to the verbal tradition, and consider whether it is not a case of a dialogue that was at first handed down only as part of a speech, and was not given its present setting till later. But there is no mistaking the characteristic features of a miracle narrative: after the preliminary statement with the Gentile woman's request in 24a, 25f., there follows in 27b, 28 the debate that proves the woman's faith, then in 29 the granting of the request, and in 30 the confirmation of the cure. Stoevesandt, *op. cit.*, pp. 14ff., says with good reason that we must not regard the woman's ready wit as the reason for granting the request, for that is a modern idea. On the other hand, we must not try to expound the figure of speech in detail, and to force any profound interpretation into the diminutive form κυνάριον, as, e.g., in Bosch, *Heidenmission*, pp. 99f., with the suggestion that the reference here is not to the despised street dogs but to household dogs that are on no account allowed to starve and are not regarded as unclean; this would indicate a softening of the refusal: 'the Gentiles too belong in God's household in the end, even if they take second place'; and thus it is maintained that 27a must belong to the original text and signifies nothing except what is said in Matt. 15.24. This, however, completely mistakes the original point, which is that even on a clear refusal the woman does not abandon her hope, but finds one last support, so that on the ground of such trust Jesus gives her his help. The suggestion, as in Spitta, *Jesus und die Heidenmission*, pp. 81f., that the woman's being a Gentile played no part at all in the refusal, is certainly wide of the mark; Otto Michel, in the article κύων, ThWb III, pp. 1100–4, there pp. 1103f., who explains much as Bosch does, thinks it uncertain whether Jesus' figure of speech refers to the contrast between Jews and Gentiles; but there should really be no doubt about this. Only Mark 7.27b must not be understood exactly in the sense of Matt. 15.24; it is the supposed boundaries of which Jesus is speaking, and which he is then quite prepared to cross.

[3] In its Q form, which is best preserved in Matt. 8.5–10, 13, the narrative is

It may, of course, be asked whether these miraculous acts of help are necessarily connected with a real access of salvation to these Gentiles. An answer must take into account Jesus' eschatological proclamation, according to which the Kingdom of God has already come near, and is indeed already dawning in Jesus' message and mighty acts. We have to take Luke 11.20 par. as the point of departure for judging the connection between Jesus' message and his miracles. It there becomes clear how inextricably these are related to each other, and how they are meant to be understood in the light of the present coming of salvation.[1] Besides, the expulsion of demons, where Jesus' God-given authority confronts the hostile powers of this world, leads far beyond every particularist horizon. In working for the salvation of all Israel Jesus works for the salvation of the whole world. And as one has good grounds for speaking of an 'eschatology that is in process of realization',[2] this means that with Jesus' miracles the new day is already dawning for the Gentiles, too, and that the moment of their coming and worshipping has already been brought within reach.

---

marked by the thought of Jesus' ἐξουσία, and of healing merely through the word; cf. Heinz Eduard Tödt, *The Son of Man in the Synoptic Tradition*, ET 1965, p. 257. The Lucan version, on the contrary, has in the introduction 7.2–5 described the centurion as a God-fearing man, and emphasized in 6f. that he remains at a respectful distance (thereby continuing the line of thought from Matt. 8.8 and par.). In both cases the decisive thought is of πίστις, faith, that is to say of that trust that Jesus had not found in Israel (Matt. 8.10 par.). The Johannine version clearly contains secondary features: on the one hand it is no longer certain that the man is a Gentile—he is an official in the imperial service; and on the other hand the request is rebuffed here, too, by Jesus, thus completing a formal assimilation to Mark 7.24ff., although Jesus' answer is motivated quite differently, and is moreover typically Johannine; cf. Rudolf Bultmann, *Das Evangelium des Johannes* (KrExKomm NT 11), 1962[17], pp. 151ff.; Eduard Schweizer, 'Die Heilung des Königlichen: Joh 4.46–54', *EvTh* 11 (1951/2), pp. 64–75. On the different versions of the narrative cf. further Ernst Haenchen, 'Johanneische Probleme', *ZThK* 56 (1959), pp. 19–54, there pp. 23ff. The variations υἱός (John), παῖς (Matthew), and δοῦλος (Luke) may be explained by an original ᶜebed. On the question whether in some circumstances Matt. 8.7 must also be understood as a piece of parrying on Jesus' part, cf. Julius Schniewind, *Das Evangelium nach Matthäus* (NTD 2), 1950[4], p. 109.

[1] Liechtenhan, *Die urchristliche Mission*, p. 33, rightly says that—according to Jesus—no strict dividing line must be drawn between proclamation and healing: 'in both contexts we find people drawn into the sphere of God's rule, and gifts of the last days being offered, and the Gentiles are not excluded from them either.'
[2] Cf. Joachim Jeremias, *The Parables of Jesus*, ET, rev. ed., 1963, p. 230 (referring to Ernst Haenchen, modifying C. H. Dodd's thesis on Jesus' 'realized eschatology'); strangely enough the same writer, in *Jesus' Promise*, pp. 74f., takes this into account here not with regard to Jesus' own activities but only for the period after Easter.

In the important passage Matt. 8.11f. par. Luke 13.28f., whose authenticity can hardly be disputed, and which in Matthew was subsequently joined on to the narrative of the Gentile centurion, the old idea of the nations' pilgrimage is related to the concept, which is characteristic of Jesus, of the transcendent Kingdom of God.[1] With the reference to the coming of the 'many' in the last days, however, the relationship must above all be brought back to what is already beginning to take place in Jesus' own work.[2] Matt. 8.11 par. stands very close to some words of threatened doom that must also be considered in this connection.[3] In conjunction with the denunciation of the towns that will not accept Jesus' message, we read in Matt. 10.(14), 15 that it will be more tolerable for Sodom and Gomorrah on the day of judgment; and in the lamentation over Chorazin and Bethsaida in Matt. 11.21f. par. it is said that Tyre and Sidon would have repented in sackcloth and ashes if Jesus' mighty works had been done there, and that therefore in the days to come it would be more tolerable for them than for these Galilean towns.[4] Thus the places that have been condemned as godless according to Old Testament judgment will fare better than the townships of Israel that have experienced Jesus' words and works, but have rejected him. Such an antithetic reference to the Old Testament is intelligible only in the mouth of Jesus himself. Matt. 8.11f. par., too, is, as the version in Luke shows particularly clearly, primarily a message of threatened doom

---

[1] The Semitic nature of the language in the *logion* of Matt. 8.11f. par. Luke 13.28f. is clear; Jeremias, *Jesus' Promise*, pp. 55f. Matthew's word order may well be the earlier, because in Luke the transposition is explained by the composition of 13.22ff. Probably, too, Matthew usually keeps the oldest form of words, only Luke is to be preferred in 13.28 *fin* to Matt. 8.12a. The statement in Matt. 8.12b could be a later addition. Bultmann, *Synoptic Tradition*, p. 116, points out rightly that this threat contains no reference whatsoever to the person of Jesus; and this seems to me to be greatly in favour of its authenticity, at any rate, even Bultmann expresses the opinion on p. 128 that 'no firm conclusion' is possible on its authenticity or otherwise. Von Harnack, too, *Mission und Ausbreitung* I, p. 44, holds the opinion that in Matt. 8.11f. we have a saying 'that has the Gentile world in view, but whose prophetic manner arouses no suspicion of its authenticity'.

[2] The passage will be understood in its intention and actuality only if we bear in mind that it is not to be taken as referring purely to the future, but that the present and future aspects are inextricably bound up together.

[3] Cf. Liechtenhan, *op. cit.*, p. 35, on Matt. 8.11f.: 'Today we no longer quite realize how radical the words must have sounded which spoke of from all the four winds, who sit at table with Abraham, Isaac, and Jacob, while the sons of the kingdom stand outside.'

[4] Matt. 11.23f., the lamentation over Capernaum, is a later imitation of 21f., using ideas from 10.15.

directed to Israelites. But in this passage the Old Testament promise for the Gentiles is at the same time taken up; no part is played here by Jerusalem and the temple as the goal to be reached, but rather the idea of the nations' pilgrimage is strictly related to the *basileia* proclaimed by Jesus and is illustrated by the picture of the eschatological common meal with the fathers of the promise.[1]

Of course, one looks to the future for an acceptance of Gentiles who come from every quarter of the globe. Curse and blessing, however, are decided only through Jesus himself, through the trust that is put here and now in his powerful words and works.[2] If Matthew inserted the *logion* 8.11f. into the narrative of the Gentile centurion and his faith, that is only logical. For where Gentiles put their trust unconditionally in Jesus they accept the offer that Israel rejects, and therefore Jesus' acceptance of such Gentiles is simply a matter of course. To that extent there also belongs here the parable of the great banquet, transmitted in Luke 14.16–24 in a form that is not quite original but close to the original.[3] It concerns participation in the final salvation, from which the people for whom it was in the first place provided

---

[1] In contrast to the conventional expectation of the (imminent) end in this world, as presented by Deutero-Isaiah, for example, among others, we are dealing here with an expectation that has grown from a basically apocalyptic conception, however much it may differ from apocalyptic in its structure and in its hope of salvation for the present as well as for the future. As far as I can see, there seems to be no direct parallel to Matt. 8.11f. Of course, salvation is often described under the image of a common meal, especially in apocalyptic, but the idea of the pilgrimage of the nations is never joined in this way to the meal in the βασιλεία τῶν οὐρανῶν. One will therefore have to ask whether there is not here the Old Testament thought of the nations' pilgrimage adapted in a way characteristic of Jesus. For, as already mentioned, apocalyptic was anything but universalist, and as a rule counted on nothing else but the annihilation of the pagan nations. On Matt. 8.11f. one can, of course, point to the late Old Testament text Isa. 25.6–8; but this section of tradition, which comes from the beginnings of apocalyptic, deals with the transformation of Zion in the last days, not with a new age which is conceived as totally belonging to another world. For the Jewish comparative material see Jeremias, *Jesus' Promise*, pp. 60ff.; *id.*, *The Eucharistic Words of Jesus*, ET, 1955, pp. 154ff. (IV 2c; in rev. ed., 1965, V 3c). He, however, does not separate the occurrence within this-worldly eschatology from the apocalyptic conception.

[2] Cf. Only Luke 12.8f. (parr.); on this Tödt, *Son of Man*, p. 54; my book *Christologische Hoheitstitel*, pp. 30f., 33ff.

[3] Matt. 22.1–10 is still more thoroughly recast and Christologically revised. But in the Lucan text, too, it is certainly not only v. 20 that is subsequently inserted, as is assumed by Eta Linnemann, 'Überlegungen zur Parabel vom großen Abendmahl', *ZNW* 51 (1960), pp. 246–55; *id.*, *Gleichnisse Jesu, Einführung und Auslegung*, 1961, pp. 94ff.; apart from this her suggestions on the interpretation of details deserve consideration. The Lucan text, in which the servants are sent out again in 14.21–23, is certainly determined by the Church's missionary experience; cf. Jeremias, *Parables*, p. 64; Günther Bornkamm, *Jesus of Nazareth*, ET 1960, pp. 18f.

exclude themselves but to which others are then brought from the streets and highways. It is true that there is no express allusion here to the Gentiles, but in every case the conventional boundaries are broken down, and the later Church has with good reason related the text to the mission.[1] The case is similar with the words about the Ninevites and the queen of the south in Matt. 12.41f. par.: for those Gentiles who listened gladly even to Jonah and Solomon salvation can be expected, but not for 'this generation'. The words 'behold, something greater than Jonah (Solomon) is here' may, if they are authentic, have originally referred not directly to Jesus' person, as is suggested by the present connection with what is said about the sign of Jonah, but primarily to the new reality inaugurated by Jesus;[2] but again the reference is appropriate, for the final decision comes about through his authority and person. Thus the words of threatened doom that point to the possible pardoning of the Gentiles in the last days, and particularly Matt. 8.11f. par. with its theme of the Gentiles' table-fellowship with the patriarchs, show that Jesus understood his work among Israel from a universalist point of view, and as initiating a complete annulment of the particularist *Heilsgeschichte* in view of the *eschaton*.

The result thus far obtained is supported and supplemented by two further texts of the synoptic tradition. According to Mark 11.15–17, Jesus cleanses the temple. As his interference does not extend to the whole of the temple precincts, and in particular not to the sanctuary itself, there is no question of reforming the worship or of preparing the sanctuary itself for the *eschaton*.[3] The incident takes place in the forecourt of the Gentiles, and must be regarded as being a parabolic action: in the merely temporary holy place token space is created for the eschatological influx of the Gentiles;[4]

---

[1] Only indirectly can one draw lines of communication through Matt. 8.11f. and the parable in Luke 14.16–24 to the Lord's Supper, that is to say, to the eschatological prospect of it in Mark 14.25; the thought of blood poured out for many is not in the authentic version of the words at the Lord's Supper, and so the Lord's Supper must not be described as 'the moment when the mission to the Gentiles was born', despite Liechtenhan, *op. cit.*, p. 40; and similarly Bosch, *Heidenmission*, pp. 175ff.

[2] Cf. Bultmann, *Synoptic Tradition*, pp. 112f. There, incidentally, it is held that in itself the passage gives no cause to be regarded as having been coined by the Church, but that the parallelism with Matt. 11.21–24 leaves it open to suspicion, and that it may well originate from early Christian polemic. I cannot concur with this judgment, as I do not think the authenticity of Matt. 11.21f. is open to dispute.

[3] For this exposition, fraught with innumerable difficulties, cf., e.g., Gottlob Schrenk, art. ἱερός, etc., *ThWb* III, pp. 221–84, there p. 243.

[4] For important contributions to an adequate explanation of the narrative about

for according to Jesus' own promise the earthly temple will cease
to exist when God's Kingdom is finally manifested, and will give
place to the eschatological new creation. It is vital to observe the
correlation between Jesus' procedure in the temple and his words
about the destruction and restoration of the temple.[1] Only thus
does it become clear that what he is demonstrating about the

---

the cleansing of the temple we are indebted to Ernst Lohmeyer, 'Die Reinigung des
Tempels', *ThBl* 20 (1941), cols. 257–64; *id.*, *Kultus und Evangelium*, 1942, pp. 44ff.,
pointing out that Jesus' action in the court of the Gentiles must be understood par-
ticularly in relation to the Gentile nations. It is 'only indirectly a problem of the
Jewish temple, but directly the problem of the "Gentile nations" ' (*Kultus*, p. 48).
He is followed in this by Stoevesandt, *Jesus und die Heidenmission*, pp. 89ff.; R. H.
Lightfoot, *The Gospel Message of St Mark*, 1950, pp. 60ff. Similarly, but with some
reservation, Jeremias, *Jesus' Promise*, pp. 65f.

[1] The saying about the temple appears in Mark 13.2 parr.; Mark 14.58; Mark
15.29b par. Matt. 27.40a; Matt. 26.61, a parallel passage differing from Mark 14.58;
the variant from D W it Cypr. to Mark 13.2; further in Acts 6.14 and John 2.19
(juxtaposition of the texts in Bultmann, *Synoptic Tradition*, p. 120). If we compare
these seven forms, which vary markedly in detail, we can still recognize in some
degree, on the strength of the numerous common features, what the original saying
must have contained. In any case it is probable that the saying, contrary to Acts
6.14 and the short form in Mark 13.2 (which is to be preferred on the basis of textual
criticism) was formerly twofold—that is, it also contained a statement about the
restoration of the temple. The decisive and persistent ideas are: in the first sentence
καταλύω, ὁ ναὸς οὗτος, and in the last sentence οἰκοδομέω and the statement of
time 'after three days' (meaning a short eschatological period; cf. Bultmann,
Johannes, pp. 88f. n. 7). Although the passage is greatly abbreviated in Mark 13.2, the
passive voice has been kept as an original element; this form of expression was often
used in the Judaism of that time to describe God's actions. The transferring to Jesus
himself of the action mentioned in Mark 14.58; 15.29b par.; Acts 6.14 and Matt.
26.61, and also the Christological recasting in John 2.19, are secondary. Other later
elements are contrasting χειροποίητος/ἀχειροποίητος in Mark 14.58 (likewise
the ἄνευ χειρῶν in Mark 13.2 D W it Cypr.), the δύναμαι in Matt. 26.61, and the
replacement of οἰκοδομέω by ἀνίστημι in Mark 13.2 D W it Cypr., and by ἐγείρω
in John 2.19. For an analysis cf. the careful research by Richard Adolf Hoffmann,
'Das Wort Jesu von der Zerstörung und dem Wiederaufbau des Tempels' in *Neutestamentliche Studien für G. Heinrici* (Unters.z.NT 6), 1914, pp. 130–9. His thesis that
Jesus expected the destruction by the Roman world power, and the restoration by
the eschatological events following directly afterwards, is nevertheless erroneous.
Philipp Vielhauer has appositely set out, in *Oikodome, das Bild vom Bau in der christlichen Literatur vom NT bis Clemens Alexandrinus* (Diss. Heidelberg), 1939, pp. 62ff.,
that the frequently quoted and variously interpreted passage must have originally
referred to the eschatological destruction and rebuilding after a very short space of
time. For a reconstruction of the oldest wording cf. Ernst Lohmeyer, *Das Evangelium
des Markus* (KrExKomm NT I/2), 1959[15], pp. 326f. Marcel Simon, 'Retour du
Christ et reconstruction du Temple dans la pensée chrétienne primitive' in *Aux
sources de la tradition chrétienne* (Mélanges M. Goguel), 1950, pp. 247–57, prefers to
trace the presence or absence of the hope of restoring the temple to Jewish Christian
and Gentile Christian lines of thought respectively; but this is not practicable. For
the history of tradition Yves Congar, *Le mystère du Temple* (Lectio Divina 22), 1958,
pp. 158ff., is of little use.

earthly sanctuary that still exists is in truth related to the eschatological new creation; but at the same time it becomes clear that we have to deal here with a universal renewal, in which the Gentiles for whom a place in the Jerusalem temple was reserved, but refused by the Jews, likewise worship the true God and participate in the salvation of the last days.[1] Thus Jesus' authoritative action in the temple fits in completely with his message and his other actions.[2]

The tradition about the eschatological judgment of all the nations, in Matt. 25.31–46, is very closely connected with this narrative. This speech about the last judgment is pervaded with imagery, and contains, in the form in which we now have it, Christological elements imposed on it by the Church; but in its basic wording it goes back to Jesus, even if we cannot now say exactly what the original text was. On the day of judgment the view extends over the whole world, the Son of man himself declares his solidarity with the poorest people from all the nations, bases his judgment solely on deeds of mercy, and shows that even those who are not of the chosen people may quite unsuspectingly have done God's will in the right way.[3] Thus, in just as unprecedented a way as in Matt. 8.11ff. par., Jesus denied that Israel would have any priority for final salvation, and proclaimed the coming Kingdom of God as the reality of salvation that would comprehend all mankind.

The picture that we have been able to get from these texts about

[1] Joachim Jeremias, *Jesus als Weltvollender* (BFchrTh 33/4), 1930, pp. 35ff., has already pointed out the conjunction of the cleansing of the temple and the renewing of the world, and in connection with the saying about the temple has also emphasized its symbolic character (pp. 43f.), but in *Jesus' Promise*, pp. 65f., he has not taken this over unchanged. Sundkler, *RHPhR* 16 (1936), pp. 491ff., has shown in particular that the cleansing of the earthly sanctuary, which is at the 'centre' of the world, ushers in the cosmic *renovatio* and the manifestation of the heavenly temple; but, like Lohmeyer, *Kultus und Evangelium*, pp. 48f., he does not enter into a detailed study of the words about the temple, and he therefore incorrectly relates to the earthly temple the nations' eschatological act of worship for which Jesus had prepared.
[2] It is quite probable that Mark 11.17 with Isa. 56.7 in its present form has been added by the Church as interpretation, but it has hit on Jesus' purpose; for an analysis cf. Bultmann, *Synoptic Tradition*, p. 36. On the transformation of the part of the tradition in John 2.13–22 cf. Haenchen, *ZThK* 56 (1959), pp. 34ff., especially pp. 42ff. (the analysis there of the synoptic texts is less fruitful).
[3] Bornkamm, *Jesus of Nazareth*, p. 142; id., 'End-expectation and Church in Matthew' in Günther Bornkamm, Gerhard Barth, and Heinz Joachim Held, *Tradition and Interpretation in Matthew*, ET 1963, pp. 15–51, there pp. 23f.; my book *Christologische Hoheitstitel*, pp. 186ff.; but also Jeremias, *Parables*, pp. 206ff.

Jesus' attitude to the Gentiles has gained clear outlines.[1] The promises for all nations and the narratives of the acceptance of individual Gentiles must not be torn apart. Jesus, indeed, performed his own works on Israel, and did not in any way carry on a 'mission to the Gentiles'; but his activity extended to Samaria and far into Gentile territory; Gentiles came to him and showed an unconditional trust such as he had not met in Israel.[2] The gospel that was in many cases rejected by Israel was turned into words threatening doom against God's own people, and became a direct promise for the Gentiles, of whose acceptance by God in the last days the Old Testament was already aware. Thus Jesus' message and works in Israel became a witness among the Gentiles, and still more: as the eschatological event already began to be realized, salvation came within the direct reach of the Gentiles. No actual commission or order was given about a mission to the Gentiles, nor can Mark 13.10 be regarded as authentic,[3] yet Jesus, by proclaiming to Israel the Kingdom of God, preached the claim and the salvation of God for everyone to hear, and even the Gentiles heard the news.

When we see this attitude of Jesus to the Gentiles it clarifies for us the remarkably varied development of the mission in the early Church, with the primary concentration on Israel, then the

[1] How far any further parables may be drawn in is difficult to say; one would think first of the parable of the grain of mustard seed in Mark 4.30–32, and of the parable of the fishermen's net in Matt. 13.47–50. In the first case·one should not necessarily regard the ending as a secondary addition, even though the Old Testament quotation in the full wording might possibly be a later assimilation. In the second case there is no direct reference to the Gentiles, but on the other hand it is not permissible, in view of Jesus' attitude, to exclude the Gentiles completely from ἐκ παντὸς γένους (otherwise in Jeremias, *Parables*, p. 225). Mark 12.1–9 parr. is a product of primitive Christianity and must here be left aside; as the 'others' to whom the vineyard is given we must think first of the new people of God, but then these include the Gentiles too.

[2] That the Gentiles come to Jesus is a fact that rests on reliable historical tradition. The interpretation in which the New Testament reflects it is very varied: whereas Jesus, as was shown, regarded their coming as the beginning of the eschatological event, Mark has tried to interpret it Christologically—it is the fascination of the figure of Jesus that attracts the Gentiles. Matthew and Luke have explained the coming of the Gentiles from the point of view of Old Testament prophecy. In this connection Matt. 2.1–12 is also interesting; the story about the Magi on which it is based (for an analysis cf. *Christologische Hoheitstitel*, pp. 277f.) makes these Gentiles be led by the stars—i.e. by the works of the divine creation—to their Saviour.

[3] Similarly Mark 13.10 cannot be regarded as genuine in the sense suggested by Jeremias, *Jesus' Promise*, pp. 22f., according to which the message of God's victory in the last days is proclaimed to all nations as in Rev. 14.6f.; for it is precisely such purely future meaning that no longer had any place in Jesus' preaching.

particularist narrowing, but also on the other hand its openness to the Gentiles and the inauguration of a real mission to the nations. How that came about in detail must be examined more closely in the following pages.

To conclude this chapter there is one more question to be cleared up: Did Jesus during his lifetime actually commission his disciples to go out? On the basis of the commissioning words in Mark 6.7–11 par. Luke 9.1–5, as well as Luke 10.1–12 and Matt. 9.37f.; 10.5–16, there can be no doubt about it, however much the wording may have been influenced by later missionary experience.[1] Even as early as the story of the call in Mark 1.16f. the 'Follow me' is supplemented by the graphic idea of fishers of men; and in this connection we must not think first of later missionary work, but of the disciples' obviously being put at once into Jesus' own service of proclamation and mighty works.[2] The call to pray to God for workers for the harvest (Matt. 9.37f.) because the number of workers is too small must be understood in all its boldness. For according to the conventional view, the harvest workers are the angels who are sent out at the eschatological completion of things; but for Jesus it is already harvest-time, because God's Kingdom is at hand.[3] And according to the various texts concerned, he does not merely send his disciples out to spread the news of what they have seen and heard, but he makes them take part in the same full authority by which he himself works.

---

[1] On these texts see the Excursus, pp. 41ff. It is difficult to say to whom these commissioning words were addressed. Mark is already familiar with the concept of the twelve 'apostles' (3.14f.; 6.7ff., and especially 6.30); similarly Matt. 10. On the basis of the Marcan and Q tradition Luke tells of two commissionings, making the first (9.1ff.) refer to the Twelve in conformity with the Marcan material, and the second (10.1ff.) to seventy(-two) disciples. It cannot now be said for certain what was originally in Q, for Matthew probably took over from Mark the connection of the commissioning words with the Twelve, while on the other hand the seventy(-two) are of uncertain origin and meaning; Luke may well have been thinking here of the seventy nations of Gen. 10.

[2] Cf. G. Bornkamm, *Jesus*, pp. 148f.

[3] Cf. Schniewind, *Matthäus*, pp. 125f., on this passage. In my opinion it is erroneous to think of this as a product of the Church (so Bultmann, *Synoptic Tradition*, p. 98), for harvest and harvesting are New Testament images relating to the eschatological end, in contrast indeed to missionary service; cf. Mark 13.10, 27 par. Matt. 13.37ff. (v. 39, συντέλεια αἰῶνος, 'the close of the age'). It is true that ἐργάτης ('labourer') also occurs elsewhere; but the idea of a harvest worker is confined to this context. The direct application of the eschatological expectation to the present time is characteristic of Jesus' own attitude. Only John 4.35–38 brings in sayings related to this; and there it may be that the thought of Matt. 9.37f. is taken up and carried further; cf. ch. VI below, p.159.

They are not merely his messengers; they are his fellow workers. It is obvious that the activity of the disciples, like that of their master, is concentrated on Israel; but a general limitation, as expressed in Matt. 10.5b, 6, 23, can scarcely go back to Jesus. For what is laid upon them is the same message directed to the eschatological salvation of the whole world; and they, too, have to proclaim to men the Kingdom of God that has drawn near.[1]

EXCURSUS: ANALYSIS OF JESUS' WORDS OF COMMISSION

In the Synoptic Gospels Jesus' sending of the messengers has been handed down in four forms: Mark (3.14f.) 6.7–13; Luke 9.1–6; Luke 10.1–12 and Matt. 9.37f.; 10.5–16. The expansion in Mark 6.7–13 and in Luke 9.1–6 is clear; in Luke 10.13–16 there follow laments over the unrepentant towns of Galilee; these laments appear as the conclusion, but they are really an independent unit of tradition; in Matt. 9.36–11.1 we have a big arrangement of speeches, which has included in 10.1–4 the selection and list of names of the Twelve (par. Mark 3.13–19; Luke 6.13–16), in 10.17–25 certain sayings about persecution (partly par. with Mark 13.9–13; Luke 21.12–19), and in 10.26–41 some dicta about discipleship (Q). In Mark 6.12f. par. Luke 9.6 an editorial account of the carrying out of the mission is added to the sending forth and in Mark 6.30 par. Luke 9.10, as well as in Luke 10.17–20, there is an account of the messengers' return. These additions can be disregarded in what follows here.

If we carry out an analysis of the real traditions of the commissioning of the disciples, we ascertain first that according to historical tradition the four commissioning discourses can be traced back to only two more or less independent forms, namely to Mark 6.7–11 and the Q form in Luke 10.2–12, while Luke 9.1–5 is a direct parallel to Mark 6.7–13, and Matt. 9.37f.; 10.5–16 is a combination of the Mark and Q traditions. It is the observations on Matt. 10 and on Mark 6.7–11 par. Luke 9.1–5 that allow

[1] One must entirely agree with v. Harnack, *Mission und Ausbreitung* I, pp. 41f., in regarding Jesus' sending out of the disciples as 'the ground and basis' of all later missionary work, and in understanding the Gentile mission as a universal extension of that command; only here we have to differentiate still more precisely with regard to the early Church, and to try to find out what were the presuppositions of Jesus' work.

us to regard the form of Luke 10.1–12 as essentially an assimilation of the Q tradition.

From this we can make a number of inferences for the contents of the various commissioning discourses. The Marcan form, after an introductory account of the commissioning and the assignment of full authority (Mark 6.7 par. Luke 9.1)—supplemented editorially in Luke by a rather more precisely drawn up commission (9.2)—gives directions about the messengers' equipment (Mark 6.8 par. Luke 9.3). After this there come directions about behaviour in houses, about 'staying' till the journey is continued (Mark 6.10 par. Luke 9.4), and further an instruction about behaviour towards a 'place' that does not receive the message (Mark 6.11 par. Luke 9.5, in this parallel passage generalized into ὅσοι ἄν = whosoever). In many respects the Q form proves to be the earlier: here the request for labourers for the harvest stands at the beginning as an introduction (Luke 10.2); then follows the remark about sending out as sheep among wolves (3), and afterwards, as in Mark, a threefold instruction about equipment, behaviour in houses, and behaviour in towns (4–11). Apart from what is said, with some variation in detail, about equipment (4, enlarged by the admonition to salute no one on the road), it becomes much plainer here what is intended by the instructions about behaviour in houses and towns (5–7, 8–11). For entering the houses is originally accompanied by saying words of peace, which may on occasion return to the messenger (5, 6a, 6b); it is only in a supplementary way that board and lodging is discussed (with reference to the principle that the labourer is worthy of his hire) and going round from one house to another forbidden (7); this problem is also mentioned secondarily in the next verse (8b). Parallel to what is said about behaviour in houses there stands the instruction about procedure in towns, where a distinction is likewise drawn between acceptance (8a, 9) and rejection (10f.). Here the commission is clearly stated: it is a matter of proclaiming that the Kingdom of God has drawn near, and this is to be explicitly testified to men, even if the message is rejected, though in that case the messengers are to shake the dust from their feet; if the message is accepted, they are also to heal the sick. From this text it is clear how much the Marcan version has been pared down; there we read only of the messengers' remaining in a particular house, or alternatively of shaking off the dust in the case of rejection. The Matthean form proves to be entirely secondary. The request for labourers for the harvest (9.37f.) is connected with the calling of the Twelve (10.1–4). On their being sent out they are first ordered to go only to the lost sheep of Israel (5f.); then follows the commission to proclaim that the Kingdom of God has drawn near, and to perform mighty works (7f.). In the same sequence of *topoi* as in Mark and Q there comes the passage about the kind of equipment (9f.), then follow the directions about behaviour in houses and towns (11–14), which is here co-ordinated in such a way that when the messengers enter a township they are to find out who is 'worthy' that they should take up their quarters in his house and speak words of peace to him; but if in spite of all that the house is not 'worthy', their peace will return to them (11–13). As in Mark, the following instruction in which the rule about behaviour in towns is generalized (ὃς ἄν, 'any one') and moreover is extended to houses, concerns only rejection and shaking off the dust (14). The commission to heal the sick and proclaim the Kingdom of God does not appear in this passage, but v. 7 anticipates this in editorial form. From Q there follows the statement about what will happen on the day of judgment (v. 15 par. Luke 10.12), and in conclusion the words about being sent as sheep among wolves, extended to include the admonition to be wise as serpents and harmless as doves (v. 16; cf. Luke 10.3).

On comparing the various forms we can see that there is a common basic pattern, which is already enlarged in Q by an introductory request for labourers for the harvest, and by the concluding reference to what will happen on the day of judgment (Luke 10.2, 12 par.). To the basic form there belong, first the sending out, then the ruling about equipment, further the instruction about behaviour in houses, and finally that about behaviour in towns. In spite of all the divergences in detail and the perceptible paring down, this structure is kept throughout; its original slant can still be recognized, for it becomes quite clear from the Q form that the various instructions culminate in the proclamation of God's Kingdom and in mighty works. Surprisingly, the part that we can grasp with the least certainty is the first passage of the pattern, for neither in the form reported in Mark 6.7 (par. Luke 9.1; Matt. 10.1), nor in the expansion of Luke 9.2, nor in

the editorial version of the commission in Matt. 10.7f. do we come
to the original wording. We shall even have to ask whether this
part is not a secondary growth, obtained from the basic form of
the instructions about behaviour in towns (Luke 10.8, 11), especially as it tends to dwindle away. For according to Luke 10.9, 11
it embraces the commissions to proclaim and to 'heal'. This
setting side by side of preaching and miracle-working is in all the
commissioning discourses, as is shown in Mark 6.7; Luke 9.1f.;
Matt. 10.7f., and is therefore certainly an original element. Only
we have to consider whether the θεραπεύειν of Luke 10.9, which
approximates, perhaps not by accident, to the editorial ἰᾶσθαι in
Luke 9.2, is not already a weaker expression, while the extremely
characteristic idea of the ἐξουσία τῶν πνευμάτων τῶν ἀκαθάρτων of
Matt. 6.7, which has been kept in Luke 9.1 and Matt. 10.1, 8 as
well, may belong to the original material; in Matt. 10.8, however,
a whole series of miraculous deeds is put side by side according
to the picture of the story of Jesus. It follows from ἤγγικεν (ἐφ᾿ ὑμᾶς)
ἡ βασιλεία τοῦ θεοῦ (τῶν οὐρανῶν) of Luke 10.9, 11; Matt. 10.7
(Luke 9.2 in a weaker version) that the disciples who are sent
out are to repeat the same message that Jesus has delivered. In
Mark, however, this no longer comes out clearly; in the introductory passage in Mark 6.7 the sending out and the authority
over unclean spirits are mentioned; but in reporting the carrying
out of the mission Mark 6.12f. merely says ἐκήρυξαν ἵνα μετανοῶσιν,
which in any case takes up another characteristic element of Jesus'
preaching (and of John the Baptist's preaching: Mark 1.4, 15b),
namely the idea of conversion, but the other way round: the
preaching of God's Kingdom turns out no longer to have been of
dominating importance for the Marcan church. In 6.13 there
follows the mention of the driving out of demons, and then a
statement, which can be understood only in the light of the
Church's later situation, about anointing sick people with oil (cf.
James 5.14). Whether the commission to proclamation and mighty
works came first or not, we can state that it comes in—though at
times not explicitly—wherever the mission is dealt with. The
statement about sending the disciples out as sheep among wolves,
which was put at the beginning in the Q form, but then moved to
the end in Matthew, was certainly not at the beginning originally,
but on the other hand it may indicate that an authoritative com-

missioning belonged here or was supplied relatively early. The introductory passages with πορεύεσθε, etc., and even more with ἀποστέλλω, have obviously been put together later for this context.

Before the question of authenticity can be raised, the detailed instructions must be examined rather more closely. The provisions about equipment vary appreciably as to what is and is not allowed. In all four discourses it is forbidden to carry a knapsack (πήρα) or to take money or a purse; as far as they are mentioned, the taking of food for the journey (ἄρτος, Mark 6.8 par. Luke 9.3) and the putting on or possession of two under-garments are also forbidden (Mark 6.8 par. Luke 9.3; Matt. 10.10). Variations are found on the following points: whereas Mark allows the use of a staff and the wearing of sandals, both are forbidden in Luke and Matthew (cf. Mark 6.8f. with Luke 9.3; Matt. 10.10, and with Luke 10.4; Matt. 10.10); to this there is added in Luke only the order to salute no one on the road (Luke 10.4b). Permission to use a staff and to wear sandals is obviously a concession that seemed permissible because it did not ensure the means of subsistence. For the object of all these stipulations is that the disciple is completely without means in his service and venture, and remains dependent on other people for everything down to the last detail. If we want to understand the rule about behaviour in houses in its oldest form, we have to go back to the Q form in Luke 10.5f. But this instruction about greeting does not at first imply anything special in view of the Jewish custom of that time. Its peculiarity becomes clearer only through the context, as far as in v. 4b all greeting on the road is forbidden. Behind εἰρήνη there stands the Old Testament šālōm, which denotes salvation in the comprehensive sense; moreover, the peace greeting is understood as an effective utterance, and therefore in certain cases the saving power that goes to people can return to the messenger. But now on the lips of Jesus' messengers such a peace greeting is subsumed under the proclamation of God's Kingdom, whence it receives meaning and strength. With that, however, there also appears the meaning of the instruction about the behaviour in towns, as well as the intended climax: if the greeting is forbidden on the road and allowed only in houses as a word that brings salvation, then in each case a whole town is to be confronted with acts done under full authority and with the message of the Kingdom of God. The disciples' real commission is therefore related to their public activity. The direction as to behaviour in houses was early re-fashioned by the addition in Luke 10.7, and still more by the forms in Mark and Matthew. It was only with this that there emerged as a typical problem of missionary practice the question of board and lodging, a problem that was not within sight in the original form of the words about going into houses.

As to authenticity, we shall most probably have to ascribe the pattern to the early Church. How far the instruction about going straight on without greeting on the roads and about greeting in houses is authentic is difficult to say. On the other hand, the insistence that the disciples should go out with no equipment is radical in its nature and parallel to the words about following Jesus, which likewise demand the renunciation of private pro-perty; and thus it is entirely compatible with Jesus' attitude. Above all, however, we must regard as authentic the commission to act like Jesus himself in proclaiming that God's Kingdom had drawn near and in doing mighty works (though in some cases the action was to involve a curse); and so it is in Luke 10.8–11 that we are nearest to Jesus' intentions.

III

THE MISSION IN EARLY CHRISTIANITY

WE have only an insufficient picture of the beginnings of the very early Christian mission. The accounts are extremely fragmentary, having to be recovered from later writings by critical analysis and then arranged with reference to historical tradition. The presentation by Acts is an attempt, undertaken about the end of the first century AD, to turn the available material into a connected account, complete in itself; and it was predominantly influenced by the ideals of the post-Pauline period and by Luke's theology. It is necessary to go back to its traditions and to evaluate as well other material contained in the writing of the synoptists and Paul. Nevertheless it is not possible to understand more than the main trend of the mission and the basic lines of its history in the earliest period.

1. THE MISSIONARY WORK OF PETER AND THE VERY EARLY CHURCH

Peter, who even in Jesus' lifetime had a pre-eminent position among the disciples, was the first witness of the resurrection.[1] The appearance of the risen Lord meant that the shattered community was restored again, and it meant further that the Kingdom of God, which, as Jesus proclaimed, had drawn near, was realized still more intensively, for indeed the event of Easter was for the earliest Christians merely an anticipation of the events of the End. From this it followed that Jesus' message must continue to be proclaimed, and that the commission that he had entrusted to his disciples, far from being cancelled, was confirmed. The resurrec-

---

[1] I Cor. 15.5; Luke 24.34. Of literature we must particularly mention: Oscar Cullmann, *Peter; Disciple—Apostle—Martyr*, 1962², pp. 25ff.; *idem*, art. Πέτρος,, *ThWb* VI, pp. 99–112; Gerhard Schulze-Kadelbach, 'Die Stellung des Petrus in der Urchristenheit', *ThLZ* 81 (1956), cols. 1–14, especially cols. 4ff.; Erich Fascher, 'Petrus' in *Sokrates und Christus* (Beiträge zur Religionsgeschichte), 1959, pp. 175–223, especially 182ff.

tion appearance to Peter may have taken place in Galilee;[1] other appearances followed, but we cannot now say where they took place.[2] The fact that the first Church was constituted by the disciples' gathering together in Jerusalem is no doubt connected with the eschatological expectation and the special position of the holy city; as the cleansing of the temple was a sign for worshipping in the eschatological sanctuary, so the earthly Jerusalem became the eschatological place of the future new heavenly city of God.[3] It was in Jerusalem that the miracle of Pentecost took place, and extremely successful missionary activity by the first Christians began at once.[4] Peter, who in accordance with the early Christian view did not yet distinguish between sending and gathering, had a twofold task—he was the leader of the Church and he was the most influential missionary.[5] His position as leader of the Church is reflected particularly in two pieces of New Testament tradition, John 21.15ff. and Matt 16.18f., and again in a modified way in Acts 1–12. The missionary function is less strongly emphasized in our New Testament writings, but it can be inferred with certainty from several texts.[6] The traditions used by Luke in Acts 2–5 show Peter proclaiming the gospel among the Jews of Jerusalem;[7] we see from Acts 8.5–25, where two parallel accounts of the subduing of Simon Magus have been joined together editorially, that Peter as well as Philip worked in Samaria;[8] Acts 9.32ff.

[1] This is indicated particularly by the tradition of John 21.1ff., and indirectly also by Luke 5.1ff.

[2] This is shown by I Cor. 15.5ff.

[3] Cf. Dieter Georgi, *Die Geschichte der Kollekte des Paulus für Jerusalem* (academic thesis, Heidelberg, 1962, typescript), pp. 24ff.; Georg Fohrer and Eduard Lohse, art. Σιών-᾿Ιερουσαλήμ,, *ThWb* VII, pp. 291–338, especially pp. 311ff., 323ff., 332ff.

[4] The fact that the disciples continued their pre-Easter commission and made 'The kingdom of heaven is at hand' the starting-point of their preaching is shown above all by Q (Matt. 10.7 par. Luke 10.9); cf. Tödt, *Son of Man*, pp. 246ff.

[5] In Cullmann, *Peter*, pp. 34ff., 57ff., these two functions are much too sharply distinguished and separated, at least for the initial period; and I also consider the statement on p. 41, that Peter recognized later that his *charisma* was less in leading the Church than in the mission, to be out of place.

[6] It is in my opinion unjustified to deny Peter's missionary activity altogether (in opposition to Cullmann), as has recently been done by Ernst Haenchen, 'Petrus-Probleme', *NTSt* 7 (1960/61), pp. 187–97. Peter's missionary activity is also very properly acknowledged by Schulze-Kadelbach, *ThLZ* 81 (1956), cols. 10f.

[7] For the beginnings of the mission among the Jews cf. Leonhard Goppelt, *Christentum und Judentum im ersten und zweiten Jahrhundert. Ein Aufriss der Urgeschichte der Kirche* (BFchrTh II/55), 1955, pp. 72ff., though the mission's whole development is here forced into a very rigid pattern in relation to the *Heilsgeschichte*.

[8] Acts 8.5–25 contains several component parts: in 5–8 Philip's work in the town of Samaria; 9–13, continuing the narrative, tells how the Samaritans who have

(36ff.); 10.1ff. tell of Peter's missionary activity in western Palestine, especially in Caesarea.[1] When Paul, according to Gal. 1.18, specially visited Peter in Jerusalem, it may well have been in connection with the latter's missionary activity, and according to Gal. 2.8 Peter was, in fact, the representative of the Jewish Christian mission.[2] Later on Peter left Jerusalem and looked after the

---

hitherto followed Simon Magus are won over by Philip's preaching and baptized, and how Simon himself, overcome by the great miracle, accepts baptism; in 14–17 there follows the intervention of Peter and John, in 18–24 the account of Peter's rebuke administered to Simon Magus, and in 25 an editorial conclusion. In its present form everything has certainly been worked in together by Luke, but only 14–17 and 25 must be regarded as editorial in the strict sense. It is therefore a mistake for Cullmann, *Peter*, p. 36, to consider the legitimizing of the Samaria mission by Peter and John in 14ff. as historical; there is here a twofold line of Luke's thought: first he wants to combine the two narratives about Simon Magus, and therefore has to bring Peter in, and secondly he wants to show the apostle's predominant position in the Church's first period. This latter is appositely emphasized by Ernst Haenchen, *Die Apostelgeschichte* (KrExKomm III), 1962[13], pp. 256f., but I cannot agree with his analysis of 8.5–25 on p. 258, according to which 18ff. originally belonged to 9–11 and related that Simon wanted to buy Philip's miraculous power from him. Of course, the exposition of the second Simon Magus narrative in 18ff. is overlaid editorially because of its attachment to 14–17, and may at first have been a matter of buying not so much the ability to communicate the Spirit as the extraordinary miraculous power. But the two narratives about Simon have quite a different purport: 9–13 is a passage complete in itself, and the original reference of 18–24 to Peter cannot well be disputed. In 18–24 we must not overlook the fact that the story, at any rate from 21ff. onwards, has a strongly semitizing flavour. Otto Bauernfeind, *Die Apostelgeschichte* (ThHdKomm V), 1939, pp. 124f., was the first to take account of the existence side by side of these two stories of Simon from the point of view of the traditio-historical presupposition of this fact.

[1] Haenchen, *NTSt* 7 (1960/1) denies that these texts are evidence of missionary activity by Peter; he thinks that Acts 9.32ff. relates what Peter did in churches already existing, and that 10.1ff. is concerned with a quite unusual occurrence (though he takes a somewhat different line in *Apostelgeschichte*, p. 306). It is true that Acts 9.36ff. assumes the existence of a Christian community in Joppa, but that is by no means beyond doubt as regards 9.32ff., and 10.1ff. is meant to be understood, in the form taken over by Luke (on this see pp. 51ff. below), in the sense of a fundamental decision. If we disregard the Lucan construction of a tour of inspection, these texts that are brought into connection with Peter's work speak clearly enough.

[2] Other considerations on Gal. 1.18 may be found in Haenchen, *NTSt* 7 (1960/1), pp. 187ff. Gal. 2.8 may be the most decisive evidence for Peter's missionary activity, as in Gal. 2.1–10 the circumstances of the period after the Council at Jerusalem are also taken into account; cf. p. 80 below. Nor must we exclude I Cor. 9.5. If besides Peter several 'brothers of the Lord' are spoken of there, it shows that some of Jesus' own relatives were active in the early Church, as is also suggested by the special mention of Jesus' brothers in Mark 6.3, and the attribution of the Letter of Jude to 'Jude . . . brother of James'. James, of course, occupied an exceptional position and hardly left Jerusalem. When in I Cor. 9.5 Peter is distinguished from 'the other apostles', it may be that this indicates a special position; but moving from place to place—which means missionary activity—is assumed for them all. Further conclusions should not be drawn from this text, despite Günter Klein in his essay, to be discussed in detail later, on Gal. 2.6–9, *ZThK* 57 (1960), pp. 293ff. On this see p. 80 below.

mission outside Palestine, though of this we have only meagre and isolated scraps of information: according to Gal. 2.11ff., he stayed in Antioch; it is uncertain whether he was in Greece and Corinth;[1] he may at least have worked in Asia Minor, and finally he was in Rome.[2]

What were the main features of his missionary activity? From the indications that we can get from the tradition we can infer the following:

(*a*) As already suggested, the continued preaching of Jesus' message was based on the fact of his resurrection as an anticipation of the events of the End, and on the consequent confirmation of Jesus' message and of his commission to the disciples. But to this was added the essential driving force and dynamic element of the bestowal of the Spirit, which was likewise understood as a phenomenon of the last days.[3] The Kingdom of God, which Jesus had announced, thrust still further and more powerfully into the reality of the present, awoke in the whole of the primitive Church a white-hot expectation of its imminence, and now had to be made known afresh to men. Thus the gathering of the eschatological people of God, which had already been begun by Jesus, was taking place, and the disciples understood themselves to be the *ecclesia*, built on Peter as on the rock.[4]

---

[1] It has been suggested that the Cephas faction in I Cor. 1.12 (3.22) originated from the personal work of Peter in Corinth: thus Eduard Meyer, *Ursprung und Anfänge des Christentums* III, 1923, p. 441; Hans Lietzmann, 'Zwei Notizen zu Paulus: 2. Die Reisen des Petrus' (1930) in *Kleine Schriften* II, 1958, pp. 287–91; *id., An die Korinther I/II* (HbNT 9), 1949[4], pp. 6f., 167. But this is not very likely; Paul would have expressed this more clearly. In I Cor. 3.5ff. only Apollos is assumed to have worked in Corinth. On this cf. Maurice Goguel, 'L'apôtre Pierre a-t-il joué un rôle personnel dans les crises de Grèce et de Galatie?', *RHPhR* 14 (1934), pp. 461–500; Cullmann, *Peter*, pp. 55ff. At any rate, it is not out of the question that at that time Peter was working not in far-off Palestine but in regions nearer at hand.

[2] The indirect evidence of I Peter 1.1 suggests Asia Minor, and can be taken quite seriously. On the much-discussed stay of Peter in Rome cf. Cullmann, *Peter*, pp. 72ff.; Erich Dinkler, 'Die Petrus-Rom-Frage', *ThR NF* 25 (1959), pp. 189–230, 289–335; 27 (1961), pp. 33–64.

[3] On the connection between the working of the Spirit and the mission cf. Oscar Cullmann, 'Eschatology and Missions in the New Testament' in *The Background of the New Testament and its Eschatology* (in honour of C. H. Dodd), 1956, pp. 409–21, there pp. 412ff.

[4] The problem of Matt. 16.18ff. cannot be discussed here in detail. The connection between Peter as the authoritative apostle, the 'rock', and the idea of the *ecclesia*, and therefore of the *qāhāl*-idea of the Old Testament, is important. As in the teaching of Jesus, the idea of the people of God is thus held fast. It must not be said, as e.g., in Liechtenhan, *Mission*, pp. 47f., that the earliest Church took up the idea of the holy remnant; such a view is rightly contested by Goppelt, *Christentum und Judentum*, p. 74.

(*b*) In all this the priority of Israel was beyond question. Just as Jesus' own works were related to God's people as a whole, so Peter, too, worked first in Palestine, evidently including Samaria, and then principally among the Jews in the Diaspora.

(*c*) As Jesus received Gentiles because the Kingdom of God had drawn near, so Peter accepted non-Jews on the ground of their faith.

(*d*) Peter had not been afraid of mixing socially with Gentiles, and did not demand their circumcision, but up to the time of the dispute at Antioch the problem may not have been basically settled; perhaps, in view of the end that was expected soon, he did not think this necessary.

(*e*) With all the early Church, Peter from the beginning baptized all believers; this is clear from the ending (which is certainly traditional) of the Pentecost story, and also from the Cornelius narrative. Baptism was connected from the beginning not only with the bestowal of the Spirit but also and pre-eminently with the authority for the present forgiveness of sins—an authority given to Jesus' messengers with the commission in Matt. 18.18, and which according to Matt. 16.18 belonged especially to Peter's office.[1] Thereby Jesus' own work was continued probably in the most consistent way. However scanty the material, we may take it that the proclamation that God's Kingdom was at hand was directly continued here, that the new event that had taken place at Easter came to fruition, and that this was expressed particularly in baptism. The earliest Church therefore maintained the claim to the whole of God's people, but at the same time observed and followed out the line already drawn by Jesus' own acceptance of individual Gentiles and by his words in Matt. 8.11f. par.

What has been said can be quite well recognized in detail by the part of the tradition forming the basis of Acts 10.1ff. Luke

---

(We cannot here go into the specialized literature on Matt. 16.18f.) The view of the Church's once-and-for-all foundation also appears in a modified form in Rev. 21.14; Eph. 2.20; it is related in the former passage to the twelve apostles, and in the latter to the apostles and the early Christian prophets.

[1] The forgiveness of sins, according to Jewish theology the exclusive privilege of God, was claimed by Jesus, as is shown by Mark 2.5 par. Luke 7.48, and it was perhaps already included in the disciples' commission; in any case it was claimed by the Church after Easter. Early Christian baptism—in contrast to John's baptism, which set the seal on God's forgiveness in the last days—expressed the present forgiveness of sins, as already mediated by the eschatological gift of the Spirit.

undoubtedly made Acts 10.1–11.18 a central part of his picture of the early Church, and so we also have considerable editorial reshaping. But the main components of the original narrative can still be distinguished.[1] We can eliminate as Lucan the speech by Peter in 10.34–43, and with it also the vindication in Jerusalem, 11.1–18. One can see as the basis of ch. 10 the course of an old narrative[2] that tells of the God-fearing Gentile Cornelius and a vision that he was given, then of the Spirit's command to Peter to follow the centurion's messengers, and lastly of the bestowal of the Spirit on the Gentiles and of their baptism. With the introductory vision, the Spirit's command in v. 20, and the bestowal of the Spirit on the Gentiles, everything is concentrated on God's own activity; Peter is only an instrument and completes the reception, which God has willed, into the Church. Now, however, the narrative is combined with the report of a second vision, Peter's vision in 9–16, which obviously competes with the Spirit's instruction in 20. The supposition that it was only Luke who fitted this vision into the narrative[3] is unlikely, and the idea that it was Luke who invented 9–16 for this context is quite wide of the mark.[4] This, too, is certainly a fragment of tradition, complete and significant in itself, even if the original framework of the narrative has been lost through being introduced into the Cornelius story. There is expressed here in a way that is very much more a matter of principle than in the incident of 10.1ff. the thought that according to God's own will both Jews and Gentiles are participators in salvation and members of the Christian Church; for the vision has nothing to do with the regulations about food, and certainly nothing at all with the events in Antioch.[5] As the account of this vision was obviously already combined in pre-Lucan tradition with the Cornelius narrative,[6] the latter was already assigned the character of a fundamental event of universal validity,

---

[1] For a fundamental discussion still see Martin Dibelius, 'The Conversion of Cornelius' in *Studies in the Acts of the Apostles*, ET 1956, pp. 109–22; this analysis remains valid in spite of Haenchen's objection, *Apostelgeschichte*, pp. 301ff.

[2] Acts 10.1–8, 17b–26, 29b–33 . . . 44, 46–48a; on this in detail see Dibelius, *op. cit.*

[3] Thus Dibelius, *op. cit.*, pp. 110f., 117f.

[4] Against Haenchen, *Apostelgeschichte*, pp. 306ff.

[5] In this we must agree with Haenchen, *Apostelgeschichte*, pp. 306f., against Dibelius, *op. cit.*, pp. 110f.

[6] In that case 10.17a and the addition in 19, possibly, too, 27–29 and the introduction of the witnesses in 23b, 45, would belong with 9–16 to this part of tradition.

and it could therefore be further developed by Luke in the sense of a programmatic narrative. It cannot well be disputed that we have here an old tradition, for such a presentation would hardly have been possible after the discussions in Antioch.[1] Moreover, Gal. 2.11a, 12 confirms the view that Peter had no scruples about uncircumcised Gentile Christians, for the procedure of James's emissaries would have no motive if the people in question had been proselytes.[2]

Of course, in this view of the mission Peter was not an isolated individual but a representative of the earliest Church, or at least of a group characteristic of the earliest Church.[3] That it originated in Palestine is shown by the very old text Matt. 16.18f., and also by the importance that was attributed in this circle to Isa. 53 with its message of universal atonement, as can be seen especially in the passage about ransom in Mark 10.45 par. and in the *paradosis* of the Last Supper in Mark 14.22-24.[4] There also belongs to this early Palestinian layer of the tradition the saying in Matt. 23.15 (originally in Aramaic) where proselytizing is sharply pilloried in the course of an argument with the scribes and Pharisees.[5] It must, however, be said that Palestinian Christianity largely committed itself later on to a different course, which was then under the direction of James. Peter's final departure from Jerusalem may have been caused by external difficulties,[6] but more vigorous efforts by the legalists may also have contributed to it. Thus, in fact, we are confronted today with the (at first sight) curious state of affairs that the Petrine traditions have been preserved for us by Hellenistic Jewish Christianity. Matthew's special source and Luke's material for Acts 1-5; 10; 12 do not indeed go back directly to Jerusalem and Palestine, but to churches which existed outside Palestine and had taken over and preserved this concept.

[1] Haenchen, *Apostelgeschichte*, p. 306, proposes to fit the occurrence, which is still recognizable behind the Lucan narrative, into the period after Peter's departure from Jerusalem; and in his opinion that would not be till after the Apostles' Conference (cf. *NTSt* 7 [1960/1], pp. 191ff.). Similarly Liechtenhan, *Mission*, pp. 53f. But all historical probability is against this. Not only the Cornelius narrative but also the vision belong to a substantially earlier period.
[2] This view is supported by the wording (ἔθνη, οἱ ἐκ περιτομῆς).
[3] We must free ourselves of the idea that there was a uniform early Christian mission even with regard to the situations in Jerusalem and Palestine.
[4] Cf. *Christologische Hoheitstitel*, pp. 57ff.
[5] Cf. Jeremias, *Jesus' Promise*, pp. 17f., on the very archaic elements in this *logion*; these, however, do not prove its authenticity.
[6] Acts 12.17b is connected with the persecution by Herod Agrippa I about AD 44.

Peter certainly did not become a missionary to the Gentiles in the true sense.[1] But it is hardly likely that he ever approved unreservedly of the one-sided attitude of the strict Jewish Christians, and on that account Paul speaks quite appreciatively of him even after the Antioch affair.

2. THE PARTICULARIST JEWISH CHRISTIANITY OF PALESTINE

The Apostles' Conference was not the first occasion on which there were differences and controversies. It is probable that Peter's freer attitude quite soon collided with other currents. Matthew's special source, which, to judge by 16.18f., aimed at conserving Petrine traditions, made room for a particularist tendency[2] alongside the development of a Christian scriptural learning and firmer ties with the law—though without raising a demand for circumcision; and Acts 11.1ff. still reflects the fact that Peter's actions did not pass without opposition among the Jerusalem Christians.[3]

How is this explained? Quite apart from linguistic pointers,[4] we can see from the point of view that is taken in Matt. 10.5b, 6 and 10.23 and from the horizon indicated there, that these texts can be traced to Palestinian tradition. Not only the Gentiles but the Samaritans, too, are excluded from the Church's missionary activity; the proclamation of the gospel is concentrated exclusively on Israel. This limitation, based on the expectation of an early end (10.23), according to which there is not even enough time left for going through all the towns of Israel before the Son of man comes,[5] shows that this view is very old, and might well stand at

[1] Gal. 2.8 is again relevant.

[2] How Matthew, who is himself in some measure close to the basic attitude of this special source, regards the missionary task is shown below in ch. V. For the origin of these Matthean sources, cf. Bornkamm, 'End-expectation' in Bornkamm, Barth, and Held, pp. 50(f.) n. 5.

[3] That is true even if the whole of Acts 11.1–18 is regarded as editorial. But we have to ask whether vv. 1–3 do not preserve a very old tradition whose original continuation has been overlaid.

[4] On this cf. Jeremias, *Jesus' Promise*, pp. 19ff.

[5] Heinz Schürmann, 'Zur Traditions- und Redaktionsgeschichte von Matt. 10.23', *BZ* NF 3 (1959), pp. 82–88, seeks to show an original connection with the Q tradition of Matt. 10.19f. par. Luke 12. (8–10), 11f., which may possibly have some relation to Mark 13.9–11 (Mark 13.10 = correction of Matt. 10.23). He thinks it is a question of an authentic persecution *logion* and a word of comfort, which was not made to refer to the missionary situation till later. But in this examination Matt. 10.23 is completely isolated from Matt. 10.5f. and 15.24; and besides, many unknown

the beginning.¹ The instruction given in 5b, 6 disclaims any such motivation, but on the contrary with the words 'go rather to the lost sheep of the house of Israel' it provides a fundamental reason based on the special position of God's people of the Old Testament:² Israel, which has become unfaithful, is to be recalled to God before the last day dawns. This same thought is also behind the Matthean wording of the narrative of the Gentile woman who asks for her daughter to be cured. It is hardly a matter of chance that instead of a Syrophoenician Gentile woman we have here a Canaanite woman living as a stranger in the land of Israel (*gēr* and *gēr tōšāb* respectively).³ In particular we now find Jesus asserting (Matt. 15.24) that he is sent only to the lost sheep of the house of Israel,⁴ which in that case also means that the acceptance of one 'stranger' is already to be regarded as an exception. In this understanding of the matter the Gentiles remain outside the missionary field; according to 10.23 not even the Diaspora comes within view.⁵

---

quantities are used, so that the result is by no means convincing. Moreover, the verb τελεῖν makes sense only if one is thinking of a charge or commission. Other attempted solutions, in my opinion equally unconvincing, are Dom Jacques Dupont, ' "Vous n'aurez pas achevé les villes d'Israël avant que le fils de l'homme ne vienne" (Matt. X, 23)', *NovTest* 2 (1958), pp. 228–44; Ernst Bammel, 'Matthäus 10.23', *StTh* 15 (1961), pp. 79–92. Cf. also Werner Georg Kümmel, *Promise and Fulfilment*, ET (SBT 23), 1957, pp. 61ff., 64ff.

¹ The idea of the coming Son of man also points to this.
² There is some difference of opinion on the meaning of 'the lost sheep of the house of Israel', which also occurs in Matt. 15.24. Liechtenhan, *Mission* p. 33, presupposing its authenticity, assumes that it relates to those who belong to Israel by right but are excluded; οἴκου Ἰσραήλ would then be a partitive genitive. The genitive is understood in the same way grammatically if it is related to the Israelite community's remaining part that has actually let itself be called and gathered by Jesus. But there is also the possibility that we may have to do here, not with a partitive but with an explicative genitive, so that the whole house of Israel appears as a lost flock to which Jesus is sent; cf. Jeremias, *Jesus' Promise*, p. 26 n. 3. In any case this latter meaning should be preferred, for the claim to all Israel is a characteristic element of the proclamation, at least in the early period; this also results from the confrontation with the Gentiles (and Samaritans), Matt. 10.5b, 6; 15.24. On the Old Testament parallels cf. Schniewind, *Matthäus*, pp. 128, 184; Jeremias, *loc. cit.* That the idea of a remainder was actually taken up later is shown by Rom. 9.27–29; 11.2–5. See below, pp. 106f., 108f.
³ This change was probably already adopted by Matthew from his special source. Matt. 15.21 is an editorial introduction determined by the Marcan pattern. Verse 22 also shows traces of editorial revision ('from that region'; 'Son of David'). On the differences between Mark 7.24ff. and Matt. 15.21ff. cf. also p. 32 n. 1 above.
⁴ On the connection between Matt. 10.5f. and 15.24 cf. Wolfgang Trilling, *Das wahre Israel. Studien zur Theologie des Matthäusevangeliums* (Erfurter Theologische Studien 7), 1959, pp. 78ff.
⁵ There is much dispute as to the authenticity of these words; besides the authors

It is only from the eschatological hope that this attitude can be explained. To a great extent these Jewish Christians with their particularist attitude hardly differed from the previously discussed Jewish Christian group round Peter. Here, too, no doubt, the proclamation that the Kingdom of God had come near was continued and the missionary command taken seriously, and the expectation that the end was near shows that the idea of an eschatology in process of realization had been taken over, too. But side by side with this there are various peculiarities. Already the claim to all Israel has acquired a somewhat different meaning, for it is no longer a question of all those who have ever belonged to God's people, but of all Israel represented by the Jewish people who still hold to the temple; the Samaritans, on the other hand, are avoided.[1] The attitude towards Gentiles has changed more sharply. This may well be especially connected with the fact that elements of apocalyptic thought which Jesus took up, keeping them, however, within the framework of a decidedly non-apocalyptic way of thought and preaching, regained the ground that they had lost, and led to an increasing acceptance and use of the

mentioned on p. 29 n. 1 above, we may also refer to Bultmann, *Synoptic Tradition*, p. 155, and Erich Klostermann, *Das Matthäusevangelium* (HbNT 4), 1938³, pp. 86, 89, 135, for their unauthenticity, and to Schniewind, *Matthäus*, pp. 128, 130f., 184, Gustav Stählin, 'Die Endschau Jesu und die Mission', *EMZ* 7 (1950), pp. 97-105, 134-47, especially pp. 98ff. and Bosch, *Heidenmission*, pp. 76ff., for their authenticity. But both the undoubtedly authentic tradition about Jesus and also certain pointers in these sayings suggest weighty objections to their authenticity. The development of Mark 7.24-30 (without the addition in 7.27a) into the Matthean form of 15.21-28, and also Jesus' openness to the Gentiles' faith and their coming to him, compared with the consistently particularist attitude of Matt. 10.5b, 6, 23; 15.24, raise most formidable doubts; it does not make good sense for Jesus to single out Samaritans in particular and even enter Samaritan territory, and to forbid his messengers to do so. On the other hand Bultmann, *loc. cit.*, has pointed out that 15.24 looks back in a comprehensive sense to Jesus' mission as a whole; Jeremias, *Jesus' Promise*, pp. 26f., is—as far as I see—right in his objection to this extent, that the passive construction as a way of describing God's action does point back to a very old origin; but that changes nothing in the basic structure of the *logion*. Matt. 10.23 speaks of a διώκειν of the disciples; it is true that the authentic sayings about following Christ also deal with the disciples' having to accept affliction, but where the idea of persecution explicitly emerges, it is on the whole a later growth. Finally, there is also the reason that has already been mentioned several times, that it is through Jesus' attitude, which did indeed centre on Israel but was not on principle confined to it, that the whole subsequent development in the various movements of the very early Church are best explained—not least the particularist attitude of this group of Palestinian Jewish Christians.

[1] This may have been based on the fact that Jesus himself was rebuffed by the Samaritans; and perhaps there were also difficulties in the mission undertaken at one time or another by the early Church.

apocalyptic tradition and point of view.[1] Though there really is salvation for the nations, and not simply condemnation, as in the Jewish apocalyptic writings, and though it is not far off but right at the door, nevertheless the eschatological events are again arranged with the help of a temporal pattern and fitted into a Now and a Then.[2] The promise for the Gentiles expressed in our Lord's words in Matt. 8.11 par. was detached from its contemporary application, and again understood, as in Judaism, to refer solely to the future, and thus used as a fundamental theological decision about the missionary task. The accomplishment of this in the last days is, according to old tradition, the task of God himself; the result is that the mission remains confined to Israel, and any such work among the Gentiles is rejected.[3]

We have an interesting piece of evidence of this expectation in the New Testament, and are not reduced to arguing *a posteriori*. The Book of Revelation, which comes from Asia Minor at the end of the first century, has preserved in a not inconsiderable measure traditional material of early Palestinian Christianity. In Rev. 14.6f. we have the theme of the eschatological proclamation of the 'eternal gospel' in the last days, through the mouth of an angel, to all the nations of the earth, calling on them, in view of the judgment that is now beginning, to fear and worship the God who made heaven and earth.[4] It also appears from Jesus' words about

---

[1] Cf. Ernst Käsemann, 'Die Anfänge christlicher Theologie', *ZThK* 57 (1960), pp. 162–85; *id.*, 'Zum Thema der urchristlichen Apokalyptik', *ZThK* 59 (1962), pp. 257–84.

[2] We meet this line of thought, considerably reinforced, in the basic layer of Mark 13. Cf. pp. 69f. below.

[3] Cf. the material in Jeremias, *Jesus' Promise*, pp. 55ff. It is difficult to decide whether a mission among the Jews of the Diaspora was included: οἶκος Ἰσραήλ denotes the whole body of those who belong to a common ancestor, and that would include the Diaspora; on the other hand, πόλεις Ἰσραήλ can, of course, mean only the towns in their own country. But this restriction to the towns of Israel in Matt. 10.23 depends on the expectation of an imminent end; and so no decision can be reached. But it would not be out of the question that in the idea of the future national pilgrimage of the Gentiles there may also have been the thought that the nations may bring back the scattered people of Israel, as is expressed in Isa. 60.4; 66.20.

[4] On Rev. 14.6f. cf. Jeremias, *Jesus' Promise*, pp. 22f. The exposition that we read again and again in the commentaries, that it is a question here, not of 'the gospel' but of 'a gospel'—any message from God—is in my opinion quite erroneous. For if it is a question of a εὐαγγέλιον αἰώνιον, a gospel that remains for ever valid, then it simply cannot be described, with regard to its content, as anything other than the one gospel. Moreover, it is not a question of a frequently occurring and watered-down idea used in Revelation, but of one that is uniquely emphasized, still more so because the verb εὐαγγελίζειν stands directly beside it. The verb is also used in only two passages from Revelation in weighty contexts: in 10.7, which speaks of the

the last judgment in Matt. 25.31–46 that judgment will be passed
on the nations; but it will be a merciful judgment, and at the
tribunal the Gentiles' eyes are to be opened to perceive their true
Lord. Far from forgetting this tradition, the early Church combined it most closely with its own Christology, and related it to
the return of him who will appear at the last in unfettered power
and deal with all nations. But according to the view of particularist Jewish Christianity this eschatological hope and promise
for the nations meant that a mission to the Gentiles was not included but excluded.[1]

From this view of the mission the logical conclusion was drawn
when, in view of the various 'exceptions' granted to non-Jews,
circumcision and the unrestricted acceptance of the Old Testament
law was demanded. The difficulties involved in the propagation
of such a principle gave occasion, after no long time, for the
Apostles' Conference. In this way the early Christian mission
approached very closely to the Pharisaic outlook on proselytizing.
And now, as in later Judaism, there came the attempt to incor-
porate fully in God's people, newly gathered but coming from the
old covenant, at least the Gentile Christians who had been gained
outside Palestine. As can be seen from Gal. 2 and Acts 15, the
Judaizing movement that was now setting in did not proceed
from the Jerusalem church leaders of that time.[2] There must have
been circles which, although they were lively and active, had, at
any rate as yet, no authoritative standing, but played a not insignificant part in the Apostles' Conference.[3] The fact that the
Lord's brother James was one of the 'pillars' may have ensured

---

fulfilling of the 'mystery of God, as he announced to his servants the prophets
(εὐηγγέλισεν)', and just here in 14.6f., where the proclamation of the gospel to all
nations by the mouth of an angel is reported. Cullmann, 'Eschatology and Missions',
op. cit., pp. 415f., also connects the first rider from Rev. 6.1–8 with the proclamation
of the gospel in the world. But even if we do not regard the first rider as the bringer
of a plague, there is in any case no justification for giving him any special connection
with the task of proclaiming the gospel; cf. further Günther Bornkamm, 'Die
Komposition der apokalyptischen Visionen' in *Studien zu Antike und Urchristentum*,
pp. 204–22, there pp. 219f.

[1] The whole presentation that Jeremias has given in his book *Jesus' Promise to the
Nations* is largely applicable to this particularist Jewish Christianity, but cannot be
claimed at all for Jesus himself.
[2] We see this in Gal. 2.4f., 6ff., where the παρείσακτοι ψευδάδελφοι [sic] are
confronted with the 'pillars', and in Acts 15 from vv. 1f., 4, 7a, 24. For an analysis
and the separate problems of Acts 15 and Gal. 2.1–10 cf. pp. 77ff below.
[3] Gal. 2.3–5; Acts 15.7a.

for them a certain influence in the negotiations. And according to all that we know from post-New Testament traditions, it is not unlikely that James, together with the Jerusalem presbytery,[1] which was created on the Jewish model and later even put forward claims like those of the Sanhedrin, aligned himself with this movement, submitting in fact, as 'the Just', most strictly to the law, and so entering into the later Jewish Christian tradition.[2]

3. HELLENIST JEWISH CHRISTIANITY

Before we can discuss the decision of the Apostles' Conference, we must deal with another group which grew very quickly and soon became very influential in the early Church, namely the so-called 'Hellenists'. Diaspora Jews in Jerusalem had already been won over quite early for the gospel. The first real persecution of the Christians and the martyrdom of Stephen were connected mainly with the activities of these Hellenists, and so it was they first and foremost who were hit by the expulsion.[3] The Hellenists who were expelled from Jerusalem instituted a most intensive missionary activity at once outside Jewish territory proper:[4] Philip, who with Stephen was their most important representative, worked in Samaria; in the Gaza district he converted the Ethiopian chamberlain, and then he worked as a missionary, probably mainly in western Palestine with Caesarea as his centre.[5] The church in Damascus, too, about whose origin we hear no details, may be connected with the Hellenists.[6] Then in trustworthy accounts Acts names in particular Phoenicia, Cyprus, and Antioch in Syria, the latter soon becoming the centre of extensive missionary work, especially as a systematic mission to the Gentiles was undertaken there early.[7] We know but few names from this period; we have the lists in Acts 6.5 and 13.1, but we know nothing

---

[1] On this cf. Günther Bornkamm, art. πρέσβυς, πρεσβύτερος, *ThWb* VI, pp. 662f.

[2] Hegesippus in Eusebius *HE* II, 23.3ff.; cf. also Clement of Alexandria in Eusebius *HE* II, 1.3ff.

[3] Acts 6.1ff.; 6.8ff. with 7.54ff. On 8.1 cf. Haenchen, *Apostelgeschichte*, pp. 248f.

[4] On this cf. Marcel Simon, *St Stephen and the Hellenists in the Primitive Church*, 1958, pp. 1ff., 20ff.

[5] Acts 8.5ff., 26ff.; 21.8f., anticipated by Luke editorially in 8.40.

[6] This may be supported by the fact that Paul, when he was working at first from Damascus, had no contact at all with Jerusalem.

[7] Acts 11.19ff.; 13.1ff. The change to the Gentile mission is reported in Acts 11.20, where the variant Ἕλληνες is certainly to be preferred.

about most of the people named there. Apart from Philip, Acts tells us in rather more detail only about Barnabas, but his labours are appreciably reinterpreted. A native of Cyprus, he was at first a respected member of the early Jerusalem church; later, however, he was hardly a delegate of Palestinian Christianity to the church at Antioch, but rather one of the most influential representatives of that church itself.[1] It was also he who brought Paul into the missionary work of the Antioch church.[2] Hellenist Jewish Christianity spread out independently in the most dissimilar regions;[3] we need only to remind ourselves of the founding of the churches in Alexandria and Rome—again we have no knowledge at all of the details.[4] With all the common ground of its basic outlook, therefore, it was probably not an entirely uniform affair. Before Paul began to carry out his own missionary work, he worked as a missionary more or less independently from various centres of Hellenist Jewish Christianity, first from Damascus in Arabia, in Nabataean territory, then from his native town Tarsus in Cilicia, till he reached what was probably more systematically organized missionary work in Antioch.[5] Antioch was in the first place the base for missionary activity in Syria; it was probably not till after the Apostles' Conference that a missionary journey was undertaken into southern Asia Minor (Pamphylia, Pisidia, and Lycaonia).[6]

[1] Acts 4.36f. In face of this, 9.27 is historically very improbable, as is 11.22f. On this cf. Haenchen, *Apostelgeschichte*, pp. 280ff., 314ff. On the other hand, there are very pertinent references to Barnabas in 11.30 and 12.25 as a delegate from the Antioch church to Jerusalem; he also appears in 13.1 as a representative of that church; in fact, he is first in Luke's list here of the Antioch 'prophets and teachers'. We know nothing of the other men in 13.1; the John Mark mentioned several times later hardly achieved any importance on his own account, but, being Barnabas's nephew, accompanied him as his colleague, at least during the early period in which we are here interested.

[2] Acts 11.25f.

[3] On the external and internal conditions for the spreading of Christianity in the Roman empire cf. von Harnack, *Mission und Ausbreitung* I, pp. 23ff.

[4] Apart from the reference in Acts 6.9 to the synagogues of North African Diaspora Jews, the first mention of Alexandria is connected with the name of Apollos, whose name appears in Acts 18.24ff.; 19.1, as well as in I Cor. 1.12; 3.4ff., 22; 4.6, and 16.12, and who it appears was already a Christian, or at least close to Christianity, before he met Aquila and Priscilla. We are also in the dark about the beginnings of the church in Rome; it is quite possible, though not certain, that Aquila and Priscilla were already Christians when they went from Rome to Corinth; in Acts 18.2 they are described as Jews; cf. Haenchen, *Apostelgeschichte*, pp. 474f., and also p. 96 n. 4 below.

[5] Gal. 1.17; 1.21; Acts 11.25.

[6] There arises here the problem of Paul's Jerusalem journey, with which we shall

If we try to determine the predominating view of the mission in these Hellenist Jewish Christian churches, without going back to the Pauline letters which did not originate till later, we have to rely primarily on the material of the Antioch tradition in Acts,[1] the risen Lord's command to missionize in Mark 16.15–18; Matt. 28.18–20, and the little apocalypse of Mark 13, broadened by v. 10; there is also the extended form of Mark 7.24–30, the fragment of tradition underlying John 4.1ff., and the spiritualized form of Jesus' words about the temple in Mark 14.58.

We can see in the material of the Antioch tradition in Acts a relatively homogeneous picture which need not necessarily be regarded as specifically Lucan.[2] Comparing it with the other material in Acts, one is struck by the strong and persistent emphasis on the prophetic and charismatic element.[3] Add to this the explicitly cool attitude of Acts 6.13f. to the temple and to the unlimited validity of the law, in sharp contrast to the attitude of all

---

deal later, but there is also the question of the value of Acts 13f. as a source. I consider it erroneous to regard the two chapters merely as a 'model journey' composed by Luke, despite Hans Conzelmann, 'Geschichte, Geschichtsbild und Geschichtsdarstellung bis Lukas', *ThLZ* 85 (1960), cols. 241–50, there cols. 246f.; *id.*, *Die Apostelgeschichte* (HbNT 7), 1963, pp. 72ff.; likewise Georgi, *Kollekte*, p. 34 n. 1. My reasons will be found in the discussion of Acts 13f. below.

[1] We cannot here investigate in detail the difficult question how far one may speak in the literary sense of an Antioch 'source'. In my opinion, however, it is beyond question that Acts 6.1–6, 8–15; 7.54–8.2; 8.4–13, 26–39; 11.19–30; 12.25; ch. 13f.; 15.1–33 (with sundry Lucan additions) are presented from the point of view of the missionary work of the Hellenists who were driven out of Jerusalem, especially of the Antioch church regarded as a missionary centre; they show a chronological as well as an objective continuity. We may refer here to Joachim Jeremias, 'Untersuchungen zum Quellenproblem der Apostelgeschichte', *ZNW* 36 (1937), pp. 205–20, there pp. 214ff.; Rudolf Bultmann, 'Zur Frage nach den Quellen der Apostelgeschichte' in *New Testament Essays: Studies in Memory of T. W. Manson*, 1959, pp. 68–80, especially pp. 77f.; Jacques Dupont, *Les sources du Livre des Actes*, 1960, pp. 61ff.; and also Haenchen, *Apostelgeschichte*, pp. 75ff.

[2] We may merely refer to the characteristic εὐαγγελίζεσθαι, here repeated, used with a statement of the content of the message (8.12f., 35; 11.20; 14.15; this occurs elsewhere in Acts only in 5.42; 17.18); on the other hand, the absolute use of εὐαγγελίζεσθαι, is also of εὐαγγελίζεσθαι τὸν λόγον and εὐαγγελίζεσθαι τὰς πόλεις and so on, may well be Lucan. The use of *kyrios* shows, at least in Acts 11.20f.; 13.10f., 12; 14.3, singularities that may originate from the traditional material, as far as it is the preaching to the Gentiles that is specially meant here; in these passages the miraculous power is specially thought of. Even if Luke does not fundamentally distinguish this from the preaching among the Jews with its allusions to the Old Testament (but see p. 62 n. 3), yet it is significant that all reference—of which Luke is so fond—to the doctrine of the creation and the eschatological judgment, as well as the view of events in relation to the scheme of salvation, is absent.

[3] Acts 6.3, 5, 8; 8.6f., 13; 11.24, 27f.; 13.1f., 6–12; 14.3, 8ff.

Jewish Christianity of Palestinian origin.[1] But what is still more important is the missionary proclamation: according to 8.12 it is εὐαγγελίζεσθαι περὶ τῆς βασιλείας τοῦ θεοῦ καὶ τοῦ ὀνόματος Ἰησοῦ Χριστοῦ ('preaching the good news about the kingdom of God and the name of Jesus Christ'). How εὐαγγελίζεσθαι τὸν Ἰησοῦν ('preaching the good news of Jesus', 8.35) is actually carried out in relation to people who are Jews by descent, or who are familiar with the Old Testament, is shown by the narrative in 8.26–39.[2] The holy Scripture is made to focus on Jesus Christ.[3] But the

[1] That this is alleged by 'false witnesses' is an actual matter of fact, because it serves the accusation against Stephen; but it does not mean that it is untrue in substance. The same is true of Mark 14.57f. The influence of the Sanhedrin on the martyrdom of Stephen is obvious; cf. Johann Bihler, 'Der Stephanusbericht (Apostelgeschichte 6.8–15 und 7.54–8.2)', BZ NF 3 (1959), pp. 252–70. On the negative attitude of these Hellenists towards the temple, cf. also O. Cullmann, 'L'opposition contre le Temple de Jérusalem. Motif commun de la théologie johannique et du monde ambiant', NTSt 5 (1958/9), pp. 157–73, there pp. 167ff., but I do not think that the connecting lines he draws on pp. 159ff. between the Hellenists and Qumran are convincing. On the other hand, M. Simon, St Stephen, pp. 78ff., rightly points to the outlook of Diaspora Judaism, but in my opinion brings the figure of Stephen too exclusively into the foreground, and connects the Hellenists' outlook too quickly with the later Pseudo-Clementines. Walter Grundmann, 'Das Problem des hellenistischen Christentums innerhalb der Jerusalemer Urgemeinde', ZNW 38 (1939), 45–73, especially pp. 54ff., particularly emphasizes the part played by non-Jews and proselytes among the Hellenists, and therefore already sees in Jerusalem the beginning of the dispute with a 'Hellenist' Christianity of Gentile origin; but Hellenist Jewish Christianity is a phenomenon sui generis, to be understood in any case from its Jewish past.

[2] The question of the religious status of the chamberlain in Acts 8.26–39 is difficult to answer. Within the Lucan design of a sequence in the scheme of salvation he can only be a man belonging to Judaism, though, like the Samaritans, not of the same status. The Antioch tradition, taken up by Luke, obviously also sees him as a proselyte, as the winning over of the Gentiles (the God-fearer is still a Gentile) does not begin till 11.20ff. But what about the individual narrative? The proskynesis (8.27) that was performed in the temple, and also the possession of the prophetic scroll, suggest that he was a proselyte. But against this there is the fact that according to Jewish law no castrated person could be received. We must not say that the eschatological promise in Isa. 56.3–7 is already being fulfilled, for it would indeed have already been fulfilled when this Gentile went over to Judaism. It would rather be possible to suppose that 'eunuch' here is simply a title of honour, and is intended to signify the man's high position in the queen's court. Cf. Haenchen, Apostelgeschichte, pp. 259ff. Liechtenhan, Mission, pp. 52f. with n. 10, sees the real point of the ancient narrative in the fact that although the eunuch wished to serve the true God he could not even become a full member of the saved community of Israel, but only a 'God-fearer;' but that now through the Christian message and baptism he was given salvation without reserve.

[3] The thought here, however, is not primarily of previous prophecy that is now being fulfilled, but of the Old Testament itself as the evidence in which the history of Jesus is to be read. Just as in the speech attributed to Stephen, which originates from another tradition but also belongs to Hellenist Jewish Christianity, the Mosaic history is directly applied typologically to Christ (on this cf. Christologische Hoheitstitel, pp. 382ff.), so here the prophetic witness itself is already regarded as a message of Christ.

preaching is addressed not only to those who belong or come close to Judaism, but also to Gentiles.[1] So, as we already see in 11.20, there follows a εὐαγγελίζεσθαι τὸν κύριον Ἰησοῦν ('preaching the Lord Jesus') there; the narratives of the victory over the magician Bar-Jesus of Paphos in Cyprus (13.6–12) and of the mission in Lystra (14.8ff.) reveal what is meant—the heavenly *Kyrios* exercises direct power in the world by word and deed, and thus men turn from idols and are converted to the living God (14.15a),[2] and have πίστις τοῦ σωθῆναι ('faith to be made well', 14.9) in the sense of trusting in the superior power of the 'Lord Jesus';[3] for the missionaries achieve 'signs and wonders' in his name (14.3) and break the power of demons, so that even the proconsul at Paphos comes to have faith, being 'astonished at the teaching of the Lord' (13.12). For the Hellenist Jewish Christians it is now beyond question that Christ's message is for Jews and Gentiles.[4]

The missionary work carried out by Hellenist Jewish Christianity among Gentiles is sustained by a quite definite Christological concept. We can see this clearly by considering Matt. 28.18–20. The actual command to missionize among the Gentiles may be old—there is no need whatever to doubt, in view of the importance of prophecy in the whole of early Christianity, that it was a matter of genuine revelation and commissioning by the Lord[5]—but it is quite certain that the item of tradition at the end of Matthew's Gospel does not in its present form belong to the

---

[1] Baptism is mentioned only in Acts 8.12f., 36–38. It is not explicitly reported in 11.19ff. and ch. 13f. This indicates that baptism was also an established custom with the Hellenists. We can see, moreover, from Mark 16.15–18; Matt. 28.18–20, and the later New Testament traditions, how far baptism has its roots in Hellenist Jewish Christianity and later Gentile Christianity.

[2] Cf. I Thess. 1.9. Acts 14.15b–17 should be regarded as a Lucan enlargement; on this cf. Ulrich Wilckens, *Die Missionsreden der Apostelgeschichte* (WMANT 5), 1961, pp. 86ff.

[3] To understand the title *kyrios* in Hellenist Jewish Christianity cf. *Christologische Hoheitstitel*, pp. 112ff.

[4] Barnabas and Paul address themselves to Jews in Acts 13.14ff., to Jews and (God-fearing) Gentiles in 14.1ff., and to ordinary Gentiles in 14.8ff. It need not be disputed that the juxtaposition of the victory over the magician in Paphos, the sermon to Jews in Pisidian Antioch, and to Jews and God-fearing Gentiles in Iconium, as well as the missionizing to the Gentiles in Lystra, to which is joined a brief note on the activity in Derbe, has the character of a 'pattern'; but, as has been shown, this account of a missionary journey is not specifically Lucan in its main features, and there is no reason to deny that historically reliable accounts have been recorded.

[5] Spitta's thesis, in *Jesus und die Heidenmission*, pp. 61ff., that the risen Lord's missionary command has been constructed from an account of an occasion on which the disciples were sent out during the earthly ministry, is untenable.

earliest tradition.[1] Quite apart from the triadic formula of the command to baptize and the editorial interventions, the text, in view of the nature of its construction and the Christological outlook on which it is based, can only be regarded as being part of a later layer of the tradition. For on the one hand we have here a tripartite text with the assertion of authority in v. 18, the actual missionary command in 19, 20a, and the promise of help in 20b—three parts that must originally have been independent of each other;[2] and on the other hand the whole utterance is dominated by the theme of exaltation, which already represents a recasting of ancient eschatological expectation.[3]

Otto Michel has well demonstrated that in this text composition and Christology react on each other, as there is a certain enthronement pattern in the background of the text.[4] But before this is discussed we must take account of another and parallel text, in whose composition we can discern an older stage—namely Mark 16.15–18. Even if this item of tradition from the later Marcan addition may be somewhat assimilated to Marcan ways of expression as regards details,[5] it is on the whole an independent and comparatively ancient witness.[6] The commission is given to 'go into all the world and preach the gospel to the whole creation',[7] and this is supplemented in v. 16 by the reference to belief as a condition of salvation, and also to baptism which is to be performed. Then in 17f. there follows the promise of 'signs' performed in Jesus' name,[8] which accompany the preaching. The missionary command itself (15f.) is therefore connected with the

[1] This is indirectly admitted by Ernst Lohmeyer, ' "Mir ist gegeben alle Gewalt!" Eine Exegese von Matt. 28.16–20' in *In Memoriam Ernst Lohmeyer*, 1951, pp. 22–49 (though on pp. 43ff. he defends the view that the command was quite an old one), when he ascribes the text to primitive Galilean Christianity, which he thinks also proclaimed the gospel in the Decapolis and Syria. The thesis of a second early church in Galilee, however, is an untenable construction.

[2] Thus, too, Otto Michel, 'Der Abschluß des Matthäusevangeliums', *EvTh* 10 (1950/1), pp. 16–26, there pp. 19f.

[3] The exaltation concept grew out of messianology, but it shows a very close connection with the Hellenist Jewish Christian view of Jesus as *Kyrios*. On this cf. *Christologische Hoheitstitel*, pp. 112ff.; 126ff.

[4] Michel, *EvTh* 10 (1950/1), pp. 22f.; so, too, Jeremias, *Jesus' Promise*, pp. 38f.

[5] This would be possible with εἰς τὸν κόσμον ἅπαντα; cf. Mark 14.9, from which the duplication of ὁ κόσμος ἅπας and πᾶσα ἡ κτίσις would then be explained.

[6] Michel, *EvTh* 10 (1950/1), p. 21, rightly declines to see in Mark 16.15–18 merely an imitation of Matt. 28.18–20, as is frequently done in commentaries.

[7] The terms of Mark 16.15 are discussed in more detail in connection with Mark 13.10; cf. pp. 70ff. below.

[8] Cf. the report of the mission's accomplishment in Mark 16.20.

idea of help—a connection that meets us again in Matt. 28.19, 20a
and 20b, although the idea is grasped differently there.[1] It is noteworthy that πορευθέντες (εἰς) appears in Mark 16.15 as well as in
Matt. 28.19.[2] Thus in Mark 16.15–18 we again come on a text
which both gives the commission to a universal mission among
all the nations of the earth and at the same time strongly emphasizes the charismatic element—the mighty deeds of the one who
commissions being in mind here.

But now back to Matt. 28.18ff. What distinguishes this text
compared with Mark 16.15ff. is the more sharply marked Christology. The concept of Jesus' exaltation, which becomes settled in
Hellenist Jewish Christianity, is expressed here with the help of
the enthronement pattern.[3] The ceremonial rite of ascending the
throne is taken over in various parts of early Christian tradition,
and is expressed most completely in Phil. 2.9–11, where the enthronement, the actual exaltation, is followed by the proclamation
bestowing the name; this is followed, finally, by the acclamation
of the powers, implying the thought of the exercise of sovereignty.
However, we must not rush to bring Matt. 28.18ff. one-sidedly
into connection with this pattern.[4] Certainly, missionary command
and promise of help have already been joined together before, as
in Mark 16.15ff.; for Matt. 28.20b, taken by itself, shows no more
direct connection than 19, 20a with the enthronement pattern.
The joining of 18 and 19f. is a somewhat different matter. This
word of authority, indeed, as Matt. 11.27 par. shows, is also
according to its origin not determined by the enthronement rite.
And in view of the close relation between Matt. 11.27a and Matt.
28.18, it would not be out of the question for Jesus' commission
for the making known of his message through the disciples now
to take the place of the idea of the revelation of the knowledge of

[1] Michel's conclusion, *EvTh* 10 (1950/1), p. 20, is also important: 'In contra-
distinction to Matt. 28.19, therefore, the ὄνομα is understood here not liturgically
but charismatically, and this is extremely important for the character of the two
compositions.'
[2] On πορευθέντες κηρύξατε cf. Matt. 10.7; 11.4 par.; Luke 13.32, but also Matt.
10.(5b), 6.
[3] In Mark 16.15–18 with v. 19 joined on to the missionary command, the thought
of the exaltation is added.
[4] Trilling, *Das wahre Israel*, pp. 32ff., clearly felt that the enthronement pattern
must not be uncritically accepted (any more than the characterization as a church
rule, as was formerly suggested); but he then looks for an Old Testament model in
divine speech; this, however, leads one quite astray in this passage.

God through 'the Son'.[1] But in 28.18ff. things are rather different, because here the thought of granting complete authority to Jesus is brought into connection with the lordship over heaven and earth—that is, with the idea of exaltation. This suggests following the enthronement pattern. But it must be seen that the three basic elements of Matt. 28.18ff. are primarily of different origin and that they had already exercised a more or less mutual attraction; it is only thus that the modification of the enthronement pattern becomes intelligible. For the words about authority in 18b are not a direct saying about the act of enthronement, but one of revelation which makes known the exaltation that has been accomplished. The theme of the proclamation is taken up in 19, 20a in the sense, not that the ascension of the throne is now being made known to the powers, but that the risen Lord is sending his earthly messengers to all nations. Finally, v. 20b expresses the theme of the exercise of sovereignty when it speaks of the Lord's presence and support to the end of the world.

With this pattern Old Testament concepts are taken up. In this case the primary reference is not to Dan. 7.14;[2] although the enthronement theme is there, too, it is just in that unbroken form according to which the bestowal of sovereignty coincides with the service of all the nations and the final exercise of sovereignty. Besides, the concept of exaltation does not hang together causally with the early Christian expectation of the Son of man's return, but is rather derived from royal messianology, in which particularly Ps. 109.1 LXX (= Ps. 110.1) played a part.[3] There, in fact,

---

[1] On Matt. 11.27 and 28.18 cf. *Christologische Hoheitstitel*, pp. 321ff., 331f. Matt. 11.28–30 likewise brings a kind of 'help theme', first of all the thought of present help, but this is addressed to all men as a Saviour's call: 'Come to me, all who . . .', etc., corresponding to the 'all' in 27a.

[2] As against Michel, *EvTh* 10 (1950/1), p. 22; Lohmeyer, ' "Mir ist gegeben alle Gewalt" ', pp. 33ff.; Trilling, *op. cit.*, pp. 6f.

[3] There are only two pieces of evidence for connecting the words about exaltation with the Son of man concept: Luke 22.69 is clearly editorial, as the parallel texts show; certainly it might be that in Acts 7.56 a slightly older tradition appears; as the view of Jesus as the future Messiah was already joined with the concept of the Son of man, as Mark 14.61f. shows, it might not be impossible that in the recasting of messianology to the exaltation concept this combination, too, was taken over; indeed, the remarkable nature of the declarations in Acts 7.56 is explained precisely by the combination of the theme of the Son of man concept with messianology. But even if Acts 7.56 were to be pre-Lucan, there is no reason to connect the Son of man concept with Matt. 28.18–20, too, as there are no indications there of any such connection. In any case the ἐξουσία idea has its specifically Christian previous history, as Matt. 11.27 shows, and it has no direct connection with Dan. 7.14.

we find both the *Kyrios* title that emerges in Phil. 2.9–11 and the enthronement theme which occurs repeatedly and which contains as a promise—that is, holds out the prospect of—the final lordship over the world powers. This is taken by Hellenist Jewish Christianity to mean that the heavenly lordship of Christ, which has already begun, has yet to be followed by the realization of the royal power in the last days.[1] The Old Testament theme of the subjection of the nations is now replaced by the thought of the gospel to the Gentiles in the last days; but it is not now, as in Rev. 14.6f., through the mouth of an angel from heaven, but through the disciples and gospel witnesses from the time of Jesus' exaltation till the συντέλεια τοῦ αἰῶνος, ('close of the age'). Baptism is here a sign of the present activity of the exalted one, who even now bestows salvation on those who accept the gospel.

So much may be said about the item of tradition that was taken up by Matthew. To understand the details of 19, 20a we must have regard to editorial intervention, or at least to the influence of later views. That is quite clear as regards the triadic baptismal formula, which may well have been used in the second half of the first century,[2] but not in the Christianity of the pre-Pauline period.[3] But even μαθητεύσατε is specifically Matthean to such an extent[4] that one must ask whether there was not originally here, in conjunction with πορευθέντες, a term of proclamation. There is equally clear evidence of Matthean thought, or perhaps of the views of his church, which was rather more strictly tied to the law and to Jesus' interpretation of it, in 20a: 'teaching them to observe all that I have commanded you'.[5] It is true that in spite of these later

---

[1] Cf. in details *Christologische Hoheitstitel*, pp. 112ff., 126ff., 189ff.

[2] Already in Paul: II Cor. 13.13.

[3] The variant that occurs at times in Eusebius has not the evidential value of an independent ancient text, and need not be considered here, despite Lohmeyer, *op. cit.*, pp. 28ff., and Ernst Lohmeyer and Werner Schmauch, *Das Evangelium des Matthäus* (KrExKommNT Sonderbd.), 1958[2], pp. 412ff. For a detailed discussion of the problem cf. F. C. Conybeare, 'The Eusebian Form of the Text Matt. 28.19', *ZNW* 2 (1901), pp. 275–88; Eduard Riggenbach, *Der trinitarische Taufbefehl Matt. 28.19 nach seiner ursprünglichen Textgestalt und seiner Authentie untersucht* (BFchrTh 7.1), 1903.

[4] On this cf. Otto Michel, 'Menschensohn und Völkerwelt', *EMZ* 2 (1941), pp. 257–67, there pp. 263f. The connections with the Son of man concept, made still more firmly in this essay than in *EvTh* 10 (1950/1), need modifying.

[5] Cf. Gerhard Barth, 'Matthew's Understanding of the Law', in Bornkamm, Barth, and Held, pp. 131ff., though this starts from Dan. 7.14. It is also to be noted that in spite of the enthronement pattern and the theme of the ἐξουσία over heaven and earth, the κύριος title is not taken up here by Matthew, but from v. 20a Jesus is seen as the διδάσκαλος, this being in relation to the μαθηταί (pointed out by Günther Bornkamm).

elements the original structure of the item of tradition is preserved and allows us an essential *a posteriori* inference about the missionary views of early Hellenist Jewish Christianity. We thus see that the command to missionize is not there related to the sending by the earthly Jesus, but is traced to the exalted Jesus. But the mission to the Gentiles is not now regarded as an additional instruction, as in the case of Peter, but the commission is directed to all nations as a matter of course. Jesus is indeed already installed as ruler over the whole world. Therefore the eschatological aspect has fundamentally changed. For if the Palestinian Jewish Christians looked steadily towards the end and to the coming of the Gentiles that was then to take place, the exaltation concept brings out the conviction that an essential step towards the final completion has already been taken, and that therefore the bringing in of the Gentiles can now begin. But how could such a mandate that concerned all nations come about? In Jesus' commission it was a matter of the eschatological call to the gathering of God's people; the sending was concentrated on Israel, but at the same time it necessarily reached out further. Particularist Jewish Christianity had then designed an apocalyptic division into two periods, and, according to old Jewish tradition, it had reserved the second and last step for God himself. Hellenist Jewish Christianity, on the other hand, took seriously the universal aspect of Jesus' commission, which Peter, too, had not disputed, and therefore did not rely, even in the first place, on Jesus' earthly commission, but understood the missionary command as a commission of the exalted Lord, the ruler of worlds. Here we have the first fundamental motivation of the Gentile mission, obtained in reliance on and modification of the oldest expectation of primitive Christianity. Even Peter might indeed have regarded the Gentile mission as quite possible, but more or less as a special case, determined by special divine guidance. With Matt. 28.18–20, however, a starting-point was provided that allowed a systematic mission to the Gentiles.

If we look at these contexts, we can understand that what is said in Mark 13.10 about the Gentile mission is quite natural. Certainly we have here very special lines of thought, and the mission among the nations is fitted into a different complex of ideas, so that the context must be examined rather more closely.

The eschatological discourse in Mark is based, as is generally acknowledged, on old traditional material. But how its origin can be more precisely explained is a matter of controversy.[1] Neither the thesis that it is a question of a Jewish model, an 'apocalyptic broadsheet',[2] nor the assumption that the evangelist constructed the discourse himself out of several collections of sayings,[3] is convincing, for the relatively complete total picture cannot be so explained. Without prejudice to older tradition of one kind or another, in Mark 13 we meet first of all with what is already firmly stamped as a Christian apocalypse, which must come from early Palestinian Christianity.[4] The orientation towards the final end, the knowledge of the 'beginning of the sufferings' already arriving, and the need to endure in the eschatological affliction, determine the association of ideas.[5] The Church has its existence in the period immediately preceding the *eschaton*; the interval between Jesus' death and his return contains no independent function, nor is the exaltation concept to be seen. At the same time the apocalyptic fondness for dividing into periods is quite recognizable, just as the ideas on this theme bear the stamp of Jewish post-biblical tradition. We must, of course, separate Mark 13.32, 33–36, for 28–31 expresses the certainty that the end is near, though this is appreciably weakened by what is said about essential ignorance of the future and by the relevant exhortations. The

[1] Cf. the survey of the history of research in G. R. Beasley-Murray, *Jesus and the Future. An Examination of the Criticism of the Eschatological Discourse Mark 13 with Special Reference to the Little Apocalypse Theory*, 1954, pp. 1–112.
[2] So especially Gustav Hölscher, 'Der Ursprung der Apokalypse Mrk 13', *ThBl* 12 (1933), cols. 193–202; similarly Bultmann, *Synoptic Tradition*, p. 122; Erich Klostermann, *Das Markusevangelium* (HbNT 3), 1950[4], pp. 131f.; Friedrich Hauck, *Das Evangelium des Markus* (ThHdKomm II), 1931, pp. 135f. (with reservations); Johannes Sundwall, *Die Zusammensetzung des Markusevangeliums* (Acta Academica Aboensis, Humaniora IX: 2), 1934, pp. 76ff.; Marxsen, *Evangelist Markus*, pp. 180ff.; presupposing a 'broadsheet' of Christian origin, W. L. Knox, *The Sources of the Synoptic Gospels* I, 1953, pp. 103ff.; Martin Albertz, *Die Botschaft des Neuen Testaments* I/1, 1947, pp. 180f.
[3] In different ways Lohmeyer, *Markus*, pp. 285f.; Vincent Taylor, *The Gospel according to St Mark*, 1952, pp. 498f., 636ff.; Werner Georg Kümmel, *Promise and Fulfilment. The Eschatological Message of Jesus*, ET (SBT 23), 1957, pp. 95ff.; Erich Grässer, *Das Problem der Parusieverzögerung in den synoptischen Evangelien und in der Apostelgeschichte* (BZNW 22), 1957, pp. 153ff.
[4] This has been seen most clearly by Eduard Meyer, *Ursprung und Anfänge des Christentums* I, 1921, pp. 125ff., especially p. 129; but he did not separate the secondary elements, although he felt that some uncertainty with regard to the coming of the parousia already crept in at the end of the discourse.
[5] The following might belong to the oldest form of this Christian apocalypse: Mark 13.5–8 (without v. 7 fin.), 9, 11–13, 14–23, 24–27, 28–31.

parenetic conclusion is obviously an editorial appendage, although the evangelist reaches back to church tradition; 32 was perhaps added earlier. In 1-4 Mark has put his own introduction in front of the eschatological prophecy, and by means of the disciples' question in 4 as well as the statement at the end of 7, 'but the end is not yet', he has drawn a clearer distinction between the first and second periods by understanding the time of the ἀρχὴ ὠδίνων ('beginning of the sufferings') as a period with 'only' historical events and tribulations, preceding the eschatological events proper (5ff.), and the second period as one of θλῖψις ('tribulation') of cosmic range (14ff.).[1] An important preliminary stage for this distinction already existed, as the idea of a Gentile mission that should necessarily precede the end had already been fitted into the pre-Marcan tradition.[2]

Mark 13.10 was for a long time regarded as an editorial insertion,[3] but this view has rightly been subject to revision. Any claim that it originally belonged to the eschatological discourse cannot, indeed, be defended,[4] as the break in continuity is too

[1] It must not be overlooked that the endings of v. 7 and v. 8 have different aims, for whereas 8 fin. seeks to make a close connection directly between the events of 5-9 and 11-13 and those of 14-27, 7 fin. marks a clear caesura.

[2] On the disciples' question in v. 4, and on the Marcan understanding of the discourse, see pp. 115ff. below.

[3] Thus again recently Taylor, *Mark*, pp. 507f.; Marxsen, *Evangelist Markus*, pp. 119f.; Günther Harder, 'Das eschatologische Geschichtsbild der sog. kleinen Apokalypse Markus 13', *Theol Viat* 4 (1952), pp. 71-107, there pp. 78f.; Hans Conzelmann, 'Geschichte und Eschaton nach Mc 13, *ZNW* 50 (1959), pp. 210-21, there pp. 218f.

[4] Beasley-Murray, *Jesus and the Future*, pp. 194ff.; *id.*, *A Commentary on Mark Thirteen*, 1957, pp. 40ff., where the eschatological discourse is regarded on the whole as authentic tradition about Jesus; similarly Bosch, *Heidenmission*, pp. 153ff.; he thinks it is a collection of Jesus' eschatological sayings (pp. 149ff.); in dealing with the objections to the authenticity of Mark 13.10 he goes into the divergence from other sayings, but then simply decides that it belongs to the 'dialectic of the faith of primitive Christianity that it takes one saying seriously without neglecting or weakening the other' (pp. 144ff., the quotation p. 147); Matt. 10.23b he thinks is also an authentic saying of Jesus, 'which, analogously to the words about the mission to the Gentiles in Mark 13.10 par., also expects a mission to the Jews during the whole of the intervening time' (p. 157); the terms of Mark 13.10 are discussed on pp. 155ff., but not in connection with the question of authenticity; more than forty pages are devoted to Mark 13.10, but this yields no really useful or at any rate methodically convincing result. C. E. B. Cranfield, *The Gospel According to Saint Mark* (Cambridge Greek Testament Commentary), 1959, pp. 387ff., 398ff., who assumes the 'substantial' authenticity of the collection of sayings in Mark 13, at the same time treats v. 10 as an individual saying of Jesus that was inserted afterwards. Julius Schniewind, *Das Evangelium des Markus* (NTD 1), 1949⁵, pp. 165f., 169, is very much more cautious.

obvious for that.[1] Nor is Kilpatrick[2] convincing when he tries to achieve an unbroken line of thought by different arrangement and punctuation.[3] Jeremias' view, that it is a question of a formerly isolated saying that exists in its more original form in Matt. 24.14 and has to be related to the eschatological message of God's victory through the mouth of an angel, also fails to meet the case.[4] To come to an adequate understanding of Mark 13.10 as regards the history of its tradition we must examine the various elements that were certainly produced for this context. The phrase πάντα τὰ ἔθνη we have also met in Matt. 28.19; it is very close to πᾶσα ἡ κτίσις in Mark 16.15 and Col. 1.23, and to ὅλος (ἅπας) ὁ κόσμος in Mark 14.9 and 16.15 and Rom. 1.8, formulas that have more frequently been used in view of the world-wide mission. In the case of πάντα τὰ ἔθνη it becomes clear from its repeated use in Old Testament quotations—Mark 11.17; Acts 15.17; Rom. 15.11; Rev. 15.4—that the phrase had been coined long before, and was taken over by early Christianity.[5] In the same way, κηρύσσειν and τὸ εὐαγγέλιον are current terms in early Christian preaching and mission, even if the absolute τὸ εὐαγγέλιον is later than the verb (εὐαγγελίζεσθαι = *bissar*), which was already used in Palestinian tradition. As τὸ εὐαγγέλιον is primarily a *nomen actionis*, which, like the verbs εὐαγγελίζεσθαι and κηρύσσειν, shows the content of the

---

[1] Jeremias, *Jesus' Promise*, pp. 22f. n. 6.

[2] G. D. Kilpatrick, 'The Gentile Mission in Mark and Mark 13.9–11' in *Studies in the Gospels* (*Essays in Memory of R. H. Lightfoot*), 1957, pp. 145–58. Referring to considerations by Burkitt and Turner, he connects καὶ εἰς πάντα τὰ ἔθνη with εἰς μαρτύριον αὐτοῖς in v. 9, and he allows to κηρύσσειν εἰς only the meaning 'preach in', not 'preach to'. The rest of 10 is taken as closely connected with 11, πρῶτον being related, not to the end, but to the bringing to trial. The effect of this would be that it cannot be a matter of a proclamation to the Gentiles, but of a world-wide mission among Jews, but so that the μαρτύριον, especially through the disciples' sufferings, takes place before the eyes of the Gentiles, too: 'The Gospel is to be preached outside Palestine and the signs of times are to be read by Gentiles as well as Jews, but that is as far as Mark goes' (p. 157). That is also how he understands Mark 14.9.

[3] Cf. Austin Farrer, 'An Examination of Mark XIII 10', *JThSt* NS 7 (1956), pp. 75–77; he points out especially that Matt. 24.14 already speaks for the usual interpretation of Mark 13.10, and moreover that κηρύσσειν εἰς is given significance by the fact that πάντα τὰ ἔθνη, is 'a large collective expression': 'The Gospel may be delivered "into the bosom of" so great a body' (p. 78); to this there is a reply from G. D. Kilpatrick, 'Mark XIII 9–11', *JThSt* NS 9 (1958), pp. 81–86, esp. pp. 83ff. Cf. further Beasley-Murray, *Commentary*, pp. 42ff.; Jeremias, *Jesus' Promise*, p. 23 n. 5.

[4] Jeremias, *Jesus' Promise*, pp. 22f. He interprets Matt. 24.14 according to Rev. 14.6f., regarding the πρῶτον of Mark 13.10 as secondary. Similarly he relates Mark 14.9 to God's latter-day message of victory to all nations.

[5] Cf. especially Luke 24.47; Acts 14.16; Rom. 1.5; 16.26; II Tim. 4.17; but also Matt. 25.32.

proclamation in the very act of proclaiming,[1] the connection of κηρύσσειν with τὸ εὐαγγέλιον was not of necessity suggested,[2] though this must have happened fairly early, as can be seen from I Thess. 2.9 and Gal. 2.2.[3] In any case, κηρύσσειν and τὸ εὐαγγέλιον are ideas that have already been suggested to Mark, even if he gives both of them a special interest.[4] This has certainly been disputed as to τὸ εὐαγγέλιον; Mark, it is said, 'was the first to bring the noun εὐαγγέλιον into the synoptic tradition'.[5] But that is certainly not so; passages like Mark 8.35 and 10.29 show no specifically Marcan character, and are much better explained if the duplication ἕνεκεν ἐμοῦ καὶ (ἕνεκεν) τοῦ εὐαγγελίου—that is, the saying about following in relation both to the person of Jesus and to the gospel preached in the period after Easter—has already been given previously; likewise there is no Marcan formation in the wording of 1.14 which summarizes Jesus' preaching and speaks of εὐαγγέλιον τοῦ θεοῦ, nor is this certain even in the later expansion καὶ πιστεύετε ἐν τῷ εὐαγγελίῳ in 1.15. Mark's distinguishing feature, as is shown especially in 1.1,[6] is that he makes the idea of 'gospel' a guiding thought for his comprehensive presentation of Jesus' work and so for the whole tradition about Jesus.[7] Thus there is no reason to regard as editorial the saying about preaching the gospel to all nations in Mark 13.10, where this identification of the gospel idea with the tradition about Jesus cannot be clearly seen. That is strongly supported by the use of πρῶτον and δεῖ. With Mark there is no consistent or even approximately uniform use of δεῖ. He adopts the word where it is presented by the tradition, and so we find that its use is quite varied. Of the six passages, moreover, two must be eliminated because of a special meaning;[8] of the other four, Mark 8.31 is characterized by the idea of testimony from the

[1] Cf. Gerhard Friedrich, art. εὐαγγελίζομαι, *ThWb* II, pp. 705ff., 718ff.; Marxsen, *Evangelist Markus*, p. 91; Einar Molland, *Das paulinische Euangelion. Das Wort und die Sache*, 1934, pp. 31ff., 38ff.

[2] Cf. Gerhard Friedrich, art. κηρύσσω, *ThWb* III, 701ff., especially pp. 709ff.; Molland, *op. cit.*, pp. 41ff.

[3] Besides several passages in the synoptists cf. Col. 1.23.

[4] There is a clearly pre-Marcan use of κηρύσσειν in Mark 1.4, 7; 3.14; 6.12.

[5] Marxsen, *Evangelist Markus*, p. 83.

[6] But Mark 1.1 reads explicitly τὸ εὐαγγέλιον Ἰησοῦ Χριστοῦ; but it may be asked whether the υἱοῦ θεοῦ, which is not ill-attested, is original.

[7] Cf. Marxsen, *Evangelist Markus*, pp. 83ff., especially pp. 90ff.; Günther Bornkamm, art. 'Evangelien synoptische', *RGG³* II, cols. 760f.

[8] In Mark 13.14 δεῖ denotes what is unfitting, and in 14.31 it characterizes a situation of painful pressure.

Scriptures, and 13.7 by the idea of a necessary stage in the plan of salvation;[1] Mark 9.11 and 13.10 are close to each other in that in both cases we read πρῶτον δεῖ, but with very different purport. Mark 9.11 speaks of another necessary stage, conditioned by the promise to which the Scripture testifies. In 13.10, on the contrary, no Old Testament prophecy is claimed,[2] and therefore an eschatological-apocalyptic meaning of the δεῖ can no more be disputed here than in 13.7.[3] The πρῶτον of 13.10 is very instructive, too, for while it serves in 9.11 (12) to indicate a sequence of events and to point out the actuality of what follows, it expresses in 13.10 a fact that is holding up the event to follow, namely the end.[4] This gives the intervening time between Easter and the parousia a positive mark, whereas in the apocalypse that forms its basis it was characterized only negatively by the theme of endurance. It must be added that with a mark of that kind the intervening period acquires its own independent importance for the Church,[5] but

---

[1] For distinguishing the various usages of δεῖ in the New Testament cf. especially Erich Fascher, 'Theologische Beobachtungen zu δεῖ' in *Neutestamentliche Studien für R. Bultmann* (BZNW 21), 1957², pp. 228–54. The fact that in Jewish and Christian thought there can be no ἀνάγκη-concept as there is in Greek follows simply from the idea of God. Nevertheless the δεῖ could be adopted in various ways. Behind all the various usages is the thought of God's sovereignty and of his previously proclaimed will for man's salvation. On the use of δεῖ in connection with scriptural evidence cf. Tödt, *Son of Man*, pp. 167f., 188ff. In John the idea is developed soteriologically.

[2] This is done first in Luke; cf. pp. 130f. below.

[3] A rather different view in Tödt, *op. cit.*, pp. 189f. Mark 13.7 shows, in fact, that the δεῖ is adopted not because of a scriptural saying but together with it. The passage in Dan. 2.28, written in the future in the Aramaic text, is reproduced in the LXX and Theodotion with δεῖ, and this combines well with the idea of the divine historical plan and the accomplishment of salvation in the last days—an idea that dominates the apocalyptic concept. Cf. Martin Noth in 'Das Geschichtsverständnis der alttestamentlichen Apokalyptik' in *Gesammelte Studien zum AT* (ThBüch 6), 1960², pp. 248–73; Dietrich Rößler, *Gesetz und Geschichte. Untersuchungen zur Theologie der jüdischen Apokalyptik und der pharisäischen Orthodoxie* (WMANT 3), 1960, pp. 55ff. On the πρῶτον of Mark 7.27a cf. the next paragraph.

[4] From this the question could arise whether the κατέχον idea of II Thess. 2 is not to be related to the mission; on this cf. pp. 142f. below. But what must be rejected for that passage might not have been without influence here: the Church that inserted Mark 13.10 would then have radically historicized the idea, and thus the decisive component of God's right to decree would be adopted like the idea of repentance and conversion, important in late Judaism in connection with that of delay. On this complex of questions cf. August Strobel, *Untersuchungen zum eschatologischen Verzögerungsproblem auf Grund der spätjüdisch-urchristlichen Geschichte von Habakuk 2.2ff.* (Suppl. to *NovTest* II), 1961, though this does not go into Mark 13.10.

[5] Of course, πρῶτον is to be understood here not in the sense of 'above all' but with a temporal meaning—cf. Beasley-Murray, *Commentary*, p. 41. In no circumstances is πρῶτον secondary, as it is only through it that the temporal presuppositions for inserting the missionary idea were created; *pace* Jeremias, *Jesus' Promise*, p. 23 n. 1. Kümmel, *Promise and Fulfilment*, p. 84, rightly says that πρῶτον here has the

that characteristically the exaltation concept is not adopted in this connection. The saying is thought of apocalyptically to such a degree—it is just this strictly apocalyptic kind of argumentation in Mark 13.10 that makes it impossible to attribute it to the evangelist—that we may indeed ask whether it would not, from the point of view of historical tradition, be better placed before 16.15–18 and Matt. 28.18–20.[1] But it may be that we have here two parallel stages of development. Whereas in the one case the task of the Gentile mission was defined fundamentally by Christology, in the other case a far-reaching modification of the apocalyptic tradition was undertaken, and the old idea of God's latter-day message to the Gentiles was taken up in a new form by reference to the fact of missionary preaching among all the nations.[2] In both cases it appears that the Gentile mission has become a matter of course and remains an inseparable element in the life of the Church till the return of Jesus Christ.[3]

One last question has still to be asked. In what relation did this Church that carried on the Gentile mission stand to the Jews and to missionary work among them? It cannot well be doubted that early Hellenist Christianity, which itself came out of Judaism, saw and acknowledged the mission to the Jews, too, as a matter of course. But for the whole of primitive Christianity this was, in fact, no problem, and for that reason the concentration on the question of the Gentile mission and its motivation is only too easy to understand. Among the texts that we have so far discussed it is

---

sense of 'first . . . until' (*erst noch*), and is therefore a precondition (cf. Hauck, *Mark*, p. 156; Grässer, *Parusieverzögerung*, p. 159), not, of course, understood to mean that the end of the world can be brought about by a mission; on this cf. Walter Freytag, 'Mission im Blick aufs Ende' in *Reden und Aufsätze* II (ThBüch. 13.2) 1961, pp. 186–98, especially pp. 187ff. Neither must the mission be described as a preliminary sign of the end, for in this passage it is simply a question of a task for the intervening time till the end comes, without prejudice to the mission's relation and alignment to final salvation.

[1] Thus E. Meyer, *Ursprung und Anfänge* I, pp. 15f., 300ff.; von Harnack, *Mission und Ausbreitung* I, pp. 39ff.; Klostermann, *Markus*, p. 232.

[2] Lohmeyer, *Markus*, pp. 272f., has not taken adequate account of this transformation.

[3] Conzelmann, *ZNW* 50 (1959), p. 219, expresses the matter well: 'Certainly Mark is lacking in systematic presentation in relation to the scheme of salvation. . . . The epoch of the mission is not yet described as such, and is not yet interpreted by an idea of the Church historically conceived'—but this is true primarily of the pre-Marcan stage of Mark 13; the evangelist himself tries to develop the idea somewhat further.

presupposed as a matter of course in Mark 13.9–13 that the testimony also concerns the Jews, and that the disciples will therefore
be handed over to councils and synagogues and brought before
princes and kings (v. 11),[1] and will be hated 'by all' for the sake
of the name of Jesus (v. 13). The mission among the Jews is also
mentioned in Acts 11.19f.; ch. 13f.; indeed, we can see here a
plain sequence of the activity among the Jews, among Jews and
God-fearers, and among the Gentiles (11.19f.; 13.14ff.; 14.1ff.;
14.8ff.), so that it can be assumed that the Jewish mission was even
given precedence. That is also shown in the enlarged form of the
narrative of the Syrophoenician woman, where we now read in
Mark 7.27a, ἄφες πρῶτον χορτασθῆναι τὰ τέκνα. The πρῶτον quite
clearly assumes a δεύτερον in this passage, and thus the precedence
of the 'children' is determined by the already established fact of
the Gentile mission. It is a different πρῶτον from that in Mark
13.10, for there it is a matter of 'first' or 'previously' before the
eschaton comes, but here on the contrary, as in Mark 9.11f., of a
co-ordination in the plan of salvation; in Mark 13.10 the πρῶτον
is related to the Gentile mission, but in 7.27a to the missionary
work among the Jews. This is a matter of recognizing the priority
of the choice of Israel—a priority that is taken into account in
the Church's mission, too. The phrase πρῶτον Ἰουδαίοις which
Paul uses so frequently has its root here, and was adopted but not
created by him. The fact that it could be understood in various
ways will be shown in later sections. Here we must point out
that not only Paul but other New Testament writers adopted this
principle, especially Matthew and Luke; in Acts it became so
much a formal pattern that Paul is not allowed to go to the
Gentiles till he has been rebuffed by the Jews.[2]

The tradition underlying John 4 is also to be fitted into the
context of the question as to the relation of Hellenist Jewish
Christianity to the Jews.[3] How much this narrative depends on
'Hellenist' thought is shown especially in the attitude to the forms

---

[1] On the courts named in this *logion* and its parallels cf. August Strobel, 'Zum
Verständnis von Röm. 13', *ZNW* 47 (1956), pp. 67–93, there pp. 72ff.

[2] Cf. Acts 13.46–48; 18.6; 28.25–28.

[3] To this belong John 4.5–9, 16–19, 20–26, 28–30, 40 (though 20–26 is certainly
revised); cf. Bultmann, *Johannes*, pp. 127f. Early Hellenist Jewish Christianity can
also be seen in the characterization of Jesus as 'prophet' in v. 19; this is equated in
v. 25 with 'the Christ' as a designation of the earthly Jesus; cf. *Christologische Hoheitstitel*, pp. 218ff., 362, 380ff.

of worship in the Jerusalem temple and the whole of Jewish worship of God; the closeness to Acts 6.11–14 is hardly accidental.[1] The period of the worship of God during which people did not really even know what they were doing is now over: the time of the eschatological worship of God, when there is no longer any need of a temple, but when the true worshippers worship the Father in spirit and truth, has come. But without prejudice to the present annulment of all the earlier contrasts in forms of worship, Israel's priority in the plan of salvation is preserved; it is expressly laid down that salvation comes from the Jews.[2] A similar attitude to the Jewish temple and form of worship is to be found in the Marcan story of the passion (14.58)—a somewhat later passage, but hardly likely to be editorial. In this new form of the temple saying the end of the Jews' earthly sanctuary is envisaged, and at the same time with the spiritualizing of the concluding sentence the new saved community and its true divine service are indicated.[3] Nothing emerges here expressly on the relation between Jews and Gentiles, but in the very renunciation of the Jewish cult the separating boundaries disappear.

Hellenist Jewish Christianity shows a relatively uniform conception of the mission.[4] The exalted Christ, as Lord over the

---

[1] In connection with John 4.19ff. there has lately been an inclination to point to Qumran parallels, and then to consider whether the tradition may have originated in Aramaic Jewish Christianity. It is, in fact, striking that in the Qumran texts the thought of the bestowal of the Spirit, and a related conception of truth, occur several times (e.g. 1 Q S III, 6f.; IV, 20f.). But we must not overlook the fact that there the concept of the presence of God's Spirit stands in a quite definite context, namely the contrast of the two spirits, through which the eschatological expectation, too, has quite a different imprint from the one in primitive Christianity. Further, we must not confuse the attitude to the temple and a partial tendency towards a 'spiritualizing' of cultic ideas (e.g. 1 QS IX, 3ff.) with the complete refusal, expressed in John 4.20f. and Acts 6.13f., of a ritual cult, for in Qumran a purified temple cult for the last days was probably expected. Lastly, the strictly particularist thought of the Qumran sect again meant that the problem of Jews and non-Jews played no part at all. For comparative material and on the relation to John 4 cf. Rudolf Schnackenburg, 'Die "Anbetung in Geist und Wahrheit" (Joh. 4.23) im Lichte von Qumran-Texten', *BZ NF* 3 (1959), pp. 88–94.

[2] Cf. especially John 4.20–24. Bultmann, *Johannes*, p. 39 n. 6, eliminates 4(22a), 22b as a gloss, but this is unnecessary; cf. Hermann Strathmann, *Das Evangelium nach Johannes* (NTD 4), 1959⁹, p. 88; C. K. Barrett, *The Gospel according to St John*, 1955, p. 198.

[3] On the temple saying cf. ch. II, p. 37 n. 1 and ch. 5, pp. 115ff. On the spiritualizing reinterpretation of Jewish cultic ideas in Hellenist Jewish Christianity cf. Wenschkewitz, *Spiritualisierung*, pp. 110ff.

[4] To this understanding of the missionary task there corresponds a fairly fixed type of missionary sermon, which we can see particularly in I Thess. 1.9f. and Heb. 5.11ff., and also with modifications in Acts 14.15–17; 17.(22ff.), 30f. On this cf. Wilckens, *Missionsreden*, pp. 8off.

whole world, has ordered the mission among all the nations, and the mission to the Gentiles is the characteristic feature of the time between Jesus' resurrection and his return. That does not mean that Israel's priority in the plan of salvation is cancelled; but the main emphasis falls, in fact, on the much-debated Gentile mission. The 'Christians' (Acts 11.26) coming from Judaism and from paganism feel themselves to be the new saved community who have become participators in the grace of God and who bow to the *Kyrios* Jesus.[1]

4. APOSTOLIC CONFERENCE AND DECREE

Thanks to the work of the Hellenist Jewish Christians, the sphere of the mission had been extended far beyond Palestine to include the territories of Phoenicia and Syria as far as Cyprus and Cilicia. Paul had acquired a solid reputation as a missionary— that may already have been the case when Barnabas called him to Antioch—but he had not yet begun his own great missionary work. He therefore appears, together with Barnabas, at the Apostles' Conference as a delegate from the Antioch church. As sources for the Conference we have Gal. 2.1–10 and Acts 15.1–33; the Pauline account should have preference, but Acts 15.1ff. is not without value, only we must notice that in the Antioch tradition adopted by Luke the Conference and the Decree were already combined (as is shown by the passage in vv. 23–29, which in its main features is not Lucan at all),[2] and that in particular the whole of the middle part, the account of the actual proceedings, has been completely transformed by Luke. Of course, Luke's hand can also be seen in many of the details elsewhere, but there is no reason to distrust the account in Acts 15.1f., 4a, 5, 7a . . . 12 . . . 20f., 22–33.

The Conference was occasioned by the exertions, mentioned above, of the Palestinian Jewish Christians, who took a strictly particularist attitude and who wanted to compel the Gentiles who

[1] Among Paul's opponents in II Corinthians we come across later representatives of a Hellenist Jewish Christianity, in whom the mission had to a great extent become assimilated to later Jewish propaganda and, in its conduct, to the miracle-workers of the time. On this cf. Georgi, *Gegner des Paulus*, pp. 31ff., 219ff.; also Günther Bornkamm, *Die Vorgeschichte des sogenannten Zweiten Korintherbriefes* (*SAH* phil.-hist.Kl 1961/2), 1961, pp. 10ff.

[2] I shall come back to this, pp. 84f.

were converted to Christianity to be circumcised and observe the law. The argument must have been kindled above all by the question of circumcision, and according to Acts 15.1f. the Jerusalem discussion was preceded, as is historically quite probable,[1] by a sharp argument between Paul and Barnabas with these Judaizers in Antioch.[2] The church thereupon decided to send the two principal representatives of the Antioch mission, together with a few others, to a conference at Jerusalem, and it may be supposed on the strength of the words 'I went up by revelation' (Gal. 2.2a) that it was a matter of a decision through the mouth of a prophet, as in Acts 13.1–2.[3] Among the companions whom Acts 15.1f. does not name in detail was the Gentile Christian Titus, whom Paul explicitly mentions in Gal. 2.1, 3f., and who was uncircumcised. The decision therefore came from Antioch, and not, as is sometimes asserted, through a decree of a superior ecclesiastical court in Jerusalem.[4] According to Gal. 2.2 the gospel as it is being preached to the Gentiles is to be laid before the leaders

[1] Cf. Johannes Weiß, *The History of Primitive Christianity*, ET 1937, I, pp. 263ff. παρεισῆλθον in Gal. 2.4 is also to be understood in this sense, and does not refer to anything that went on during the Jerusalem negotiations. Thus also Hans Lietzmann, *An die Galater* (HbNT 10), 1932³, p. 11; Heinrich Schlier, *Der Brief an die Galater* (KrExKomm VII), 1949¹⁰, p. 39; Albrecht Oepke, *Der Brief des Paulus an die Galater* (ThHdKomm IX), 1957², p. 47.

[2] At the Apostles' Conference, and therefore also in Gal. 2.1ff., the people concerned are in any case Judaizers in the real sense, however it may be with Paul's immediate opponents in Galatia. That they were unconverted Jews is quite out of the question, despite Walter Schmithals, 'Die Häretiker in Galatien', *ZNW* 47 (1956), pp. 25–67, there pp. 26ff.

[3] Thus with Georgi, *Kollekte*, pp. 10f. The assumption that it is a question of a personal revelation by dream as in Acts 16.9, or of ecstasy as in Acts 22.17 (II Cor. 12.1ff. can be eliminated), is less probable; Acts 16.6f. would come nearest. Cf. Lietzmann, *Galater*, p. 9; Schlier, *Galater*, p. 35; Oepke, *Galater*, p. 44.

[4] Here we must take issue in particular with Ethelbert Stauffer, 'Petrus und Jakobus in Jerusalem' in *Begegnung der Christen* (Festschrift O. Karrer), 1959, pp. 361–72, according to which the special position of Peter was founded in the *vocatio* before and after Easter which was at once developed by Jewish Old Testament legal tradition, so that we really have to do here with a function of church government. Paul, it is argued, gave up his initially autonomous position after three years, and in effect compromised with the central authorities of Jerusalem. James, the only one besides Peter to have a special revelation of the risen Lord as recorded in the official list, and a protagonist of the strict observance of the Torah, replaced Peter in the control of affairs; he had his first great success at the Apostles' Conference, for he succeeded in having the negotiations carried on in Jerusalem and the supreme authority thereby acknowledged. Paul's 'journey to Canossa'—i.e. to Jerusalem—was a capitulation on church law in spite of its success in church politics. In criticism cf. also Georgi, *Kollekte*. pp. 11f.—Günther Bornkamm rightly expresses (orally) the opinion that one should not speak of an apostles' 'Council' at all, because this implies the idea of a central church authority provided with full legal powers.

of Palestinian Jewish Christianity (who are on an equal footing),[1] so that, as is shown by the concluding words of v. 2 about running in vain, the unity of Christians is in no case broken.[2] For this passage must be understood to mean that there can be no Gentile church that is severed from Jewish Christianity. Paul, too, stands firmly by the precedence of Israel and of Christians who come from Judaism in the plan of salvation, but in this connection he will acknowledge no legal claims whatever. 'To the Jews first', which was never disputed even by Hellenist Jewish Christianity, may indeed have been the negotiating basis on which the Conference came together and came to an agreement. The Antioch delegation was received in Jerusalem by the whole Church and its leaders, but the Judaizers also took at least some part in the deliberations.[3] According to Gal. 2.3f., the discussion probably came to a head very soon on the practical question of circumcision, and so on Titus, whom Paul took with him, hardly by accident, as a representative of the Gentile Christianity[4] which was not bound to the Jewish Law. According to Acts 15.5 (7a), it was former Pharisees who tried to insist that all Christians should keep the Mosaic Law. For the further course of events and the result we have to go to Paul.[5] Of course, Paul condensed the account considerably, and he also took some account of how the situation

[1] The report of Barnabas and Paul about the work among the Gentiles is also mentioned in Acts 15.4 fin., 12; it is possible that 4 fin. is an editorial addition, while in 12 and 25 the fact that Barnabas's name comes first points to old tradition; in 12, moreover, the working of signs and wonders among the Gentiles is stressed as a decisive theme; this often occurs elsewhere in the Antioch traditions.

[2] Cf. Schlier, *Galater*, pp. 36f., who begins by interpreting Paul's words correctly, but then draws problematic conclusions about 'the principle of connexion with the tradition' and about the judgment of the church authorities, where, as it seems to him, the 'decisive authority' is represented by 'the earlier gospel and the earlier apostolate'. Georgi, *Kollekte*, pp. 13f., rightly points out that when Paul speaks of 'running', it is always in relation to the formation of churches and their growth. It is inadequate for Lietzmann, *Galater*, p. 10, to say that the success of the Pauline mission depended on whether it was acknowledged or rejected as non-Christian by the eyewitnesses of Jesus' life.

[3] Cf. Acts 15.4f.; Gal. 2.2; κατ' ἰδίαν δὲ τοῖς δοκοῦσιν ('privately before those who were of repute') points to discussions in the narrower circle.

[4] Gal. 2.3 can only be taken to mean that the demand for Titus's circumcision was actually made at the Apostles' Conference; cf. especially Oepke, *Galater*, p. 45: ἀλλ' οὐδὲ . . . ἠναγκάσθη περιτμηθῆναι is to be understood as 'resultative'. 'All the overt and veiled onsets of the opponents failed before the determination of Paul and the reasonableness of the δοκοῦντες' (*ibid.*).

[5] It is probably only Acts 15.22ff. that contains the accurate news that in confirmation of the agreement two delegates from the Jerusalem church travelled to Antioch with Barnabas and Paul.

had changed when he wrote to the Galatians; but on the other hand he is greatly concerned, as he already emphasizes in Gal. 1.20, to present an exact account of the Jerusalem proceedings.[1] The people 'of repute' or the 'pillars',[2] namely the group of three—

[1] The peculiar intermingling of exact report and taking into account of the new situation should be carefully noted in Gal. 2.1–10. Verse 1 is report; that also holds good for 2, but there is a shifting of stress in so far as Paul speaks in the first person singular, thereby also bringing into view his present independent work as a missionary among the Gentiles. Verse 3 is again a report, but 4 shows a clear connection between the situation then and now: he again has to do with 'false brethren . . . who slipped in; our freedom which we have' (present) 'in Christ Jesus' was assailed in both cases. Verse 5a reports on the outcome in Jerusalem, but this has its lasting consequences for the Galatian controversy, too, hence the final clause in 5b. In 6a, c the report on the Conference is taken further, but this is interrupted in 6b by a parenthetic remark relating to the present. In 7f. the view shifts perceptibly from the Jerusalem situation, in which the representatives of two churches stood face to face, to the situation that has come about in the meantime, where Paul and Peter stand face to face as representatives of missionary work among Gentiles and Jews respectively. The report is not resumed until 9, 10a, with an additional note by Paul in 10b. —Besides the above, a few more exegetical notes are necessary: 4 and 6 begin with sentences that end in anacoluthon; cf. Schlier, *Galater*, pp. 38ff.; in 5 οἷς οὐδέ is, of course, to be read: on this cf. especially Lietzmann, *Galater*, p. 11. We can best understand the difficult parenthesis in 6b in the sense that special precedence was accorded to the Jerusalem apostles because of their connection with Jesus, and this means that ποτέ must not be related to the time of the Jerusalem negotiations; cf. Schlier, *Galater*, pp. 42f.; Georgi, *Kollekte*, pp. 17f., against Oepke, *Galater*, p. 48. It may be also supposed that in 7f. the view changes to the existing situation, because Peter's name is mentioned; Paul does not mention him otherwise, but he is connected with Peter's work in the Hellenist sphere, as indeed in this passage the missionary activity of Peter and Paul is explicitly mentioned. Günter Klein, 'Galater 2.6–9 und die Geschichte der Jerusalemer Urgemeinde', *ZThK* 57 (1960), pp. 275–95, puts forward the thesis that on the contrary 7f. is a fully official document of the Jerusalem decisions—which explains why for once Paul uses the name 'Peter'—and reflects the real positions of the time of the Conference when Peter was still the most influential person, while on the other hand 6 and 9 would point to the shifting of power that has meanwhile taken place in favour of the 'pillars', in which case the parenthesis of 6b must very probably be related to the Conference, but that this parenthesis does not indicate precedence, but a continual absence of authority; but this view is untenable, for the mention of Paul and Barnabas together in 9 shows that this passage harks back to an earlier situation. Georgi also, *Kollekte*, p. 7 n. 2 and pp. 17f. (cf. also pp. 18ff.), is rightly against Klein. At the time of the Conference the leadership of the Jewish Christianity of Palestine was in the hands of a council of three, which was later followed by James as the sole leading authority. Whether it can be inferred from 9 that at the time of the Conference James already had precedence among the 'pillars' is not quite certain, because the sequence of names can be explained differently; cf. Haenchen, *NTSt* 7 (1960/1), p. 193. The much-discussed question whether Peter had already left Jerusalem at the time of the Conference cannot be answered on the basis of Acts, but because of the presence of the council of three it may be very unlikely, so that we may use Gal. 2.9 as an argument in this matter. This would certainly affect the dating of the Conference, for the Jerusalem deliberations would then have to be put into the period before Herod Agrippa's persecution *c*. AD 44. On primitive Christian chronology cf. the Excursus, pp. 86–94 below.

[2] It is not quite certain whether is δοκοῦντες a firmly established title, for in Gal. 2.6a, 9 Paul uses it in a periphrastic turn of speech. But most probably the δοκοῦντες will be identical with the στῦλοι. The designation στῦλοι has an ecclesiological and

Peter, James, and John—who were competent to speak for the
Jerusalem church, agreed with Barnabas and Paul, according to
Gal. 2.9, 10a, and abandoned the requirement that Gentile
Christians should observe the legal ordinances,[1] expressly con-
firmed by a handshake the community of Gentile and Jewish
Christians, and decided that thenceforward the Jewish Christians
of Palestine associated with Jerusalem should devote themselves to
missionizing among the Jews, while the Hellenist Jewish Christians, with Antioch as their centre, should undertake the mission
among the Gentiles; and they further agreed that on account of
Israel's priority in salvation a collection should be taken by the
Gentile Christians for the 'poor' in Jerusalem.[2] Of course, the
decision 'that we should go to the Gentiles and they to the circumcised' (Gal. 2.9) does not denote a division into two missionary
spheres,[3] nor does it mean that the one side has to devote itself
only to Gentiles and the other to Jews; it rather indicates the
main emphasis and purpose of the missionary activity;[4] in particular
it may well mean that the two groups are not to compete with
each other or interfere in each other's work. Thus the door was
barred to the Judaizers and opened wide to the Gentile mission.
The responsible people in Jerusalem, with Peter certainly among

---

an exchatological element, and is thus in close relation to Matt. 16.18 and Acts
21.14; this again confirms the strongly eschatological standpoint of the whole primitive Church. On this cf. Schlier, *Galater*, p. 45; C. K. Barrett, 'Paul and the "Pillar"
Apostles' in *Studia Paulina* (*in honorem Johannis de Zwaan*), 1953, pp. 1-19.

[1] On the question of freedom from the law cf. ch. IV, pp. 100ff.
[2] For details of this cf. Georgi, *Kollekte*, pp. 21ff.; but he stresses too one-sidedly
the Christians' position in Jerusalem as the eschatological suburb of salvation; this
will certainly have played a dominating part in that community's understanding of
itself, but was hardly acknowledged unreservedly by the Hellenist Jewish Christians
with their easily recognizable criticism of the temple and temple worship; on the
other hand, the theme of priority in the scheme of salvation carried weight here, too,
and must therefore be given greater consideration (cf. also the 'before me' in Gal.
1.17a). It is, of course, right that no sort of legal prerogative was involved in it;
above all it is rightly made clear that the collection has nothing at all to do with a
tax, as it was not paid regularly; it was a matter of gifts presented on one single
occasion by the Gentile Christian churches that had been converted to the faith
(as against Stauffer, *op. cit.*, p. 370, who asserts that James imposed, 'under the
guise of a collection for the poor, a church tax for the central church in Jerusalem').
[3] Thus again Stauffer, *op. cit.*, p. 370. Cullmann, *Peter*, pp. 48f., speaks of a
separation into two different 'missionary organizations' that were to be kept together only by the collection, the separation, however, not being feasible.
[4] On this cf. Haenchen, *Apostelgeschichte*, pp. 408f.; Georgi, *Kollekte*, pp. 18ff.,
who even contemplates regarding εἰς in the sense of 'for', 'in the interest of'; but
this is very improbable.

them, were convinced of the legitimacy, indeed the necessity, of the Gentile mission, and wanted to put no barriers in its way. This did not yet finally solve the problems; they promptly emerged again in another form.[1]

After the Antioch delegation had returned, the mission to the Gentiles could be continued. In all probability there now followed on the one hand a collection for Jerusalem,[2] and on the other hand the sending of Barnabas and Paul on a more extensive missionary journey to Cyprus and southern Asia Minor, as reported in Acts 13. It was not till after this that there occurred the dispute reported in Gal. 2.11ff., between Paul and Peter;[3] this led to further discord within the Antioch church, and to Paul's parting from Barnabas and beginning his own missionary work independently of Antioch.[4] Although the problem of circumcision had been settled by the

[1] Johannes Munck, *Paul and the Salvation of Mankind*, ET 1959, would deny that there was any opposition between the Jewish Christians and Paul in their view of the missionary task, arguing that that is a superseded construction of the Tübingen School (pp. 69ff.). Paul, he thinks, proceeds in principle from his recognition by the Jerusalem authorities (pp. 93ff., 231ff.); and we cannot speak of any diversity between the Hellenist and the Palestinian early Church (pp. 218ff.). According to him, Judaizing is in general a Gentile Christian heresy, which Luke erroneously connected with Jerusalem (pp. 87ff., 231ff.). The early Church followed Jesus' conception of the Law and his radical criticism of it (pp. 247ff.). In the Gentile mission it was only the question of the sequence in the scheme of salvation that was in dispute; while the early Church favoured the priority of the mission to the Jews, Paul wanted to reverse the order and missionize first among the Gentiles; and this view was explicitly approved at the Apostles' Conference (pp. 255ff., 275ff.).—In this investigation Baur's one-sided thesis is replaced by one at least equally one-sided, which by no means does justice to the complicated state of affairs, and moreover is too ready to throw overboard the Tübingen School's valid observations. Hellenist Jewish Christianity does not even come into sight, and the various efforts in Palestinian Jewish Christianity are also ignored.

[2] Acts 11.27–30 and 12.24f. may be news of the first taking of a collection; so Georgi, *op. cit.*, pp. 32ff. It is not even impossible that the actual occasion was a famine in Palestine and a prophetic command. If the Apostles' Conference was held as early as AD 44, it might be supposed that the collection belongs to the time of distress that came over Palestine between 47 and 49; on this cf. Joachim Jeremias, 'Sabbathjahr und neutestamentliche Chronologie', *ZNW* 27 (1928), pp. 98–103, though he puts the Conference in the year 48 and makes the journey with the collection coincide with the deliberations; cf. further Haenchen, *Apostelgeschichte*, pp. 55f.

[3] That would mean a much longer period between the Conference and the events related in Gal. 2.11ff. and Acts 15.36ff. than we can discern at first glance. In that case Paul's difference with Peter would probably fall into the end of the forties, especially as the further chronology of Paul's activities on European soil is fixed by the Gallio inscription and points to the early fifties.

[4] Behind the differences recorded in Acts 15.36–38 there, of course, lurks the much more far-reaching dispute of Gal. 2.11ff. According to 15.39, Barnabas goes with John Mark to his native Cyprus, but obviously remains in touch with Antioch. According to 15.40ff., Paul again goes to southern Asia Minor, but pushes on to Galatia and then to Europe.

conference at Jerusalem, the question how strict Jewish Christians and Gentile Christians could live together had not been cleared up. No trouble seems to have originated here for the Hellenist Jewish Christians, and Peter himself probably had no uneasy conscience about it;[1] but the Palestinian Jewish Christians with their legalistic outlook, now under the leadership of James, insisted that full community of life with uncircumcised Christians was not possible; although they had recognized the Gentile Christians as such and had given up the insistence that they should be circumcised, they felt obliged to draw a hard and fast line here. Peter respected this demand and ceased to sit at table with Gentiles. For his part he was probably concerned to keep the Church in unity, and therefore tried to show consideration to these strict legally-minded Jewish Christians. In this matter even Barnabas did not share the thorough-going attitude of Paul, who could appeal to the handshake in Jerusalem.[2] We do not know how things developed afterwards, and we can do no more than hazard a conjecture: probably it was a matter of a renewed agreement between the representatives of Palestinian Jewish Christianity and those of the Antioch church—Peter and Barnabas may have acted together as intermediaries—so that even community at table was restored, though on condition that a number of minimum requirements on cultic ordinances were observed by the Gentile Christians; for the so-called Apostolic Decree, which dealt with this matter, undoubtedly had a cultic sense originally.[3] If my historical judgment of the Decree is adequate,[4] a not unimportant readiness to compromise could be noticed on the part of the Palestinian Jewish Christians, and one may wonder whether

[1] That Peter met this problem of common meals in Antioch for the first time and at first simply accepted the arrangement that was usual there (thus Haenchen, *NTSt* 7 [1960/1], pp. 195f.) is highly improbable, for even at the conversion of Cornelius at Caesarea there was obviously no circumcision, but probably full community at table with Gentile Christians.

[2] Gal. 2.11–13.

[3] It has again been asserted lately by Stauffer, *op. cit.*, p. 370, that in Acts 15.20, 29 (21.25) it was originally a matter of three deadly moral sins, in accordance with the Western Text. But cf. Werner Georg Kümmel, 'Die älteste Form des Apostel-dekrets' in *Spiritus et Veritas* (Festschrift K. Kundsins), 1953, pp. 83–98; Haenchen, *Apostelgeschichte*, pp. 390f., 410ff.

[4] Thus already Carl Weizsäcker, *Das apostolische Zeitalter der christlichen Kirche*, 1902³, pp. 146ff., 158ff., 167ff., whom many exegetes have rightly followed. Lyder Brun, 'Apostelkoncil und Aposteldekret', in Lyder Brun and Anton Fridrichsen, *Paulus und die Urgemeinde*, 1921, pp. 1–52, tried without conclusive reasons to show the homogeneity of the Conference and the Decree.

it was not Peter who used his influence to press for full com-
munion among Christians after he had abandoned this for a time
for the sake of having the question cleared up.

From this point of view we can explain a number of details of
our tradition which are historically in dispute:

(*a*) Even in the pre-Lucan Antioch tradition the Apostles'
Conference and the decision about the Apostolic Decree were
taken together.[1] That is understandable because of the special
interest of the church there in these two decisions, and it shows
that the question of circumcising Gentile Christians and of
community of meals with them was regarded as an inseparable
unity.[2]

(*b*) If the Antioch tradition put the report contained in Acts
15.1–23 after the missionary journey to southern Asia Minor,
this may show that the problems could not in fact, be finally
cleared up till during this later period; in that case, of course,
Paul had to be brought into association with, or perhaps
claimed as a supporter of, a decision with which he himself
really had nothing more to do.

(*c*) That Paul does not know of the Apostolic Decree, or at
least does not regard it as binding, is indicated not only by his

---

[1]A separation of sources, as undertaken by, e.g., J. Weiß, *Primitive Christianity* I,
pp. 261ff., can no longer be made; he considers that Acts 15.1–4, 12 is the remainder
of a report on the Conference, and that Acts 15.5–11, 13–33 is the report of the
decision about the Decree, with a mention of Paul and Barnabas added in vv. 22 and
25.

[2] From this point of view the suggestion put forward by Rudolf Bultmann,
Theology of the New Testament I, ET 1952, p. 56 n. 1 (§8.2); *id.*, 'Zur Frage nach den
Quellen der Apostelgeschichte', *New Testament Essays*, pp. 71ff. (referring to Wilhelm
Bousset, 'Der Gebrauch des Kyriostitels als Kriterium für die Quellenscheidung in
der ersten Hälfte der Apostelgeschichte', *ZNW* 15 (1914), pp. 141–62, there pp.
156ff.), that Acts 15.1ff. may be a narrative of the deliberations in which the Apostolic
Decree was settled, with Paul, and perhaps Barnabas, too, being fitted in afterwards,
becomes intelligible. In fact, the piece of tradition leads up to the Decree, containing
in 15.23–29 what is intended to be an authoritative letter to the Christians in Antioch,
Syria, and Cilicia (v. 23); in this passage there is a backward glance at the Conference
(vv. 24–27), and then the two decisions are summarized (vv. 28f.). It is not impossible
that, as Bousset suggests (pp. 157f.), 25f. was inserted by Luke; but this proves
nothing for the thesis that Paul and Barnabas were not present at the event reported
in Acts 15. The real narrative in 15.1ff. and 30ff., as far as it has not been overlaid
editorially, deals exclusively with the first assembly, in which Paul also took part.
In any case the report in Acts 15.1ff. is independent of Gal. 2.1ff., despite Weizsäcker,
op. cit., pp. 175ff.

letters[1] but also by another thread of the tradition in Acts, where according to 21.25 Paul, on his arrival in Jerusalem, was told by James of the decision contained in the Apostolic Decree.[2]

(*d*) Lastly, the question of Paul's journeys to Jerusalem is also cleared up; it is generally acknowledged that the three journeys in Acts do not agree with the evidence in Gal. 1.18 and 2.1; but there is disagreement on the relation of the accounts to each other. Even if Gal. 1.18 and Acts 9.27ff. correspond in spite of all the difference in presentation,[3] Gal. 2.1ff. cannot be equated with Acts 11.29f. (12.25), nor can Acts 11.29f. be identified with Acts 15.1ff.[4] It could be shown that the chronological arrangement of Acts 15.1ff. is subordinated to a definite line of thought, and this later date is therefore quite excluded. The precise time of the Conference at Jerusalem was apparently quite ignored in the tradition that was available to Luke. On the other hand, it could already be pointed out that a collection was brought from Antioch to Jerusalem in the period between the Apostles' Conference and the Decree, and that according to Acts 11.29f. and 12.25 Barnabas and Paul took part in it; this second journey as related by Luke might actually represent a third journey of Paul to Jerusalem, a journey of which we hear nothing in his letters;[5] so that the journey referred to in Gal. 2.1ff. must be chronologically put between Acts 9.27ff. and 11.29f., or more exactly, between 11.25f. and 11.29f.[6]

It was not till Paul had been working for a longer period in Antioch that things became difficult there and that this produced the break with Paul and a decree supplementing that of the

[1] An allusion might possibly be found in the emphatic 'to me' of Gal. 2.6; thus Georgi, *op. cit.*, p. 17; cf. also Schlier, *Galater*, p. 42 n. 4; Oepke, *Galater*, p. 54.
[2] Against this, but unconvincingly, is Haenchen, *Apostelgeschichte*, p. 412.
[3] On this cf. Haenchen, *Apostelgeschichte*, pp. 280ff.
[4] On the attempted solutions cf. Haenchen, *Apostelgeschichte*, pp. 57f.; more detailed and easily grasped in the earlier edition of his commentary (1956), pp. 55ff.
[5] In Gal. 1f. Paul's sole concern is to present the facts up to the Conference's fundamental decision. His not mentioning a later journey with a collection is not contradicted by Gal. 1.20. Georg Strecker's thesis, 'Die sogenannte zweite Jerusalemreise des Paulus (Acts 11.27–30)', *ZNW* 53 (1962), pp. 67–77, that Acts 11.29f. and 12.25 is unhistorical, is in my opinion quite erroneous.
[6] Gaps and bias in the reporting of Acts are not to be overlooked, and errors are not to be disputed, but its historical value must not be underestimated. In view of today's very widespread criticism of Acts, this needs to be explicitly stressed, without thereby acknowledging its presentation and its detailed statements *in toto*.

Apostles' Conference. The decisions about the minimum conditions for Gentiles on cultic questions certainly played an important part in the mission districts from Palestine to within southern Asia Minor.[1] But the early Christian development quickly went beyond this.[2] For as the attempt was made to disregard Paul, so he at once went out on his great missionary work in northern and western Asia Minor, in Macedonia and Greece, beyond the older mission fields in the east, and in large measure determined by his work the further shape and history of the mission.

EXCURSUS: EARLY CHRISTIAN CHRONOLOGY

1. Luke 3.1f., with its sixfold synchronism, lays down the time of John the Baptist's coming, and at the same time it claims to give the date of Jesus' work.

(*a*) If it is calculated by the years of his government, the fourteenth year of the Emperor Tiberius would take us to AD 28/29; so, for instance, Eduard Meyer and Erich Klostermann.[3] On the other hand, if we include the co-regency under Augustus since AD 11/12, we should come to 26/27; thus Theodor Zahn; but as to this Gustav Hölscher rightly emphasizes that the co-regency of Tiberius, unlike that of Augustus himself, has never been included (cf. only Jos. *Ant.* XVIII, 32, with XVIII, 224).[4] But there also exists the possibility of calculating the fourteenth year of Tiberius according to the civil (Seleucid) year, which would take us to 27/28; thus Cichorius and Joachim Jeremias.[5] In any case we must notice that Luke 3.1f. is a subsequent reconstruction that goes back to the evangelist and offers no absolutely reliable

[1] That southern Asia Minor belonged to Antioch's sphere of influence may be inferred from the fact that according to Acts 13f. an Antioch delegation missionized in it.

[2] On the historical value of the Decree cf. Weizsäcker, *op. cit.*, pp. 179ff. That even with the Apostolic Decree the problems between Jewish and Gentile Christianity of that district were not completely solved can be seen in the increasing separation of legalistic Jewish Christian circles from the main Church, and also in the sometimes complete severance of Gentile Christians from Judaism; on this cf. von Harnack, *Mission und Ausbreitung* I, pp. 68ff., 73ff.

[3] Eduard Meyer, *Ursprung und Anfänge des Christentums* I, 1921, p. 46 n. 1; Erich Klostermann, *Das Lukasevangelium* (HbNT 5), 1929[2], pp. 50f.

[4] Theodor Zahn, *Das Evangelium des Lucas* (KommNT III), 1920[3, 4], pp. 175ff., esp. pp. 182ff.; Gustav Hölscher, *Die Hohenpriesterliste bei Josephus und die evangelische Chronologie* (*SAH* phil.-hist. Klasse 1939/40 Nr. 3), 1940, p. 27.

[5] C. Cichorius, 'Chronologisches zum Leben Jesu', *ZNW* 22 (1923), pp. 16ff.; Joachim Jeremias, art. 'Chronologie des Urchristentums', *RGG* I[2], col. 1535.

information, as is shown not least by the sixth item of the synchronism.

(*b*) Pontius Pilate was in office for ten years as Procurator of
Judea. For a more exact fixing of dates we are helped by the
information, on the one hand, that his predecessor Valerius Gratus,
who was in office for eleven years, was appointed under Tiberius
and was therefore in Palestine probably from AD 15 onwards (Jos.
Ant. XVIII, 33, 35b), and on the other hand that Pilate was
removed from office by Tiberius shortly before the latter's death
and arrived in Rome to find Tiberius already dead (Jos. *Ant.*
XVIII, 89); he must therefore have been recalled before March 37,
probably at the end of 36 or the beginning of 37. So we can say
with reasonable certainty that he became Procurator in the autumn
of 26, especially since his first official action was to put the army
into winter quarters; this led to the insurrection because of the
fact that the standards bore portraits of the emperor (Jos. *Ant.*
XVIII, 55–59; *Bell.* II, 169).[1] For Pilate we have to rely solely on
Jewish and Christian sources, as we have no Gentile traditions
apart from Tacitus' quite general note, *Ann.* XV, 44, that Christ
was executed under the Procurator Pontius Pilate.[2]

(*c*) Herod Antipas, one of the sons of Herod the Great, became
Tetrarch of Galilee and Perea after his father's death in 4 BC (Jos.
Ant. XVII, 317f.). His notorious marriage to Herodias is connected with a journey to Rome (*Ant.* XVIII, 110f.), which was
probably earlier than AD 26, as Tiberius then left the capital for
good;[3] the value of the account in Mark 6.17f. is certainly not
undisputed, as Josephus gives other motives for Antipas' procedure against the Baptist (*Ant.* XVIII, 116–19).[4] The date of
John's death in the fortress of Machaerus (*Ant.* XVIII, 119)
cannot be given more precisely. Antipas' rule came to an end
when in the year 39 he tried, at Herodias's instigation, to obtain
the kingship, and for so doing was deposed and banished by
Caligula (*Ant.* XVIII, 240ff., esp. 252).[5]

[1] On this cf. Hölscher, *op. cit.*, pp. 24f.
[2] On Pilate cf. Klostermann, *Markus*, p. 158 (excursus); Paul Winter, *On the
Trial of Jesus* (Studia Judaica 1), 1961, pp. 51ff.
[3] Cf. Hölscher, *op. cit.*, pp. 27f.; Jeremias, *RGG* 1², col. 1535.
[4] On this cf. Martin Dibelius, *Die urchristliche Überlieferung von Johannes dem Täufer*
(FRLANT 15), 1911, pp. 126f.; Hölscher, *op. cit.*, pp. 28ff.
[5] On Antipas in detail cf. Schürer, *Geschichte des jüdischen Volkes* I, 1901³, ⁴, pp.
431ff. (ET I, 2, 1890, pp. 17ff.).

(*d*) Philip is of no direct importance for the history of early
Christianity. He ruled from 4 BC to AD 34 as Tetrarch of Gaulonitis,
Trachonitis, Batanea, and Paneas (Jos. *Ant.* XVII, 189). From 34
onwards his territory was for some years governed directly from
Rome.[1]

(*e*) Lysanias, the Tetrarch of Abilene (Jos. *Ant.* XIX, 275) is
likewise of no importance in our context. No further details are
known about his life.[2]

(*f*) The statement in Luke 3.2a is difficult in more than one
respect. First, ἐπὶ ἀρχιερέως in the singular is followed by two
names; secondly, Annas as High Priest in office has nothing to do
with the time mentioned in v. 1, as he was deposed in AD 15 (Jos.
Ant. XVIII, 26, 34). His successors, Ishmael, Eleazar and Simon,
ruled for only short periods, about two and a half years altogether
(*Ant.* XVIII, 34f.). Then followed Caiaphas, whose accession to
office must have been between AD 17 and 19; he ruled till the feast
of the Passover in 37, and then he, too, was deposed (*Ant.* XVIII,
35a, 95).[3] Added to this is a fact from historical tradition: the
oldest synoptic material does not mention at all by name the High
Priest officiating in the time of Jesus (Mark); he was identified
later with Annas (John's source), and only at a further stage,
historically accurate, with Caiaphas (Matt. and John); in Luke
the two names are incorrectly co-ordinated.[4]

2. For the date of Jesus' death we have some guide in that in
any case the crucifixion took place on a Friday; whether that
Friday was the 14th or 15th Nisan is an open question because of
the divergence of the synoptic and Johannine statements. In spite
of uncertain factors, the astronomers' calculations tell us with some
ground for confidence that in the years 27, 30, and 33 Friday may
have been on either the 14th or 15th Nisan; for the 15th Nisan
(synoptic chronology) the year 31, too, would in some circumstances be a possibility.[5] Jeremias thinks that 33 is improbable,
and concentrates the debate on 30 and 31, entirely disregarding the

[1] Cf. Schürer, *op. cit.*, pp. 425ff. (ET, pp. 10ff.).
[2] Cf. Klostermann, *Lukas*, p. 51.
[3] On this cf. Hölscher, *op. cit.*, pp. 14ff.
[4] The first observations on this are already in Wellhausen *passim*, then in Hölscher,
op. cit., pp. 22ff.; now cf. particularly Winter, *op. cit.*, pp. 31ff.
[5] Cf. the thorough discussions by Jeremias, *Eucharistic Words*, pp. 10ff. (I, 2; rev.
ed., I, 3).

year 27. But this decision is not justified. Hölscher rightly points out that the crucifixion of Jesus in the year 27 would coincide with the riots in Pilate's first year of office (Jos. *Ant*. XVIII, 55–62; *Bell*. II, 169–77); and he also brings into the question the mention of the forty-six years in John 2.20, which, as the reconstruction of the temple can be shown to have begun in the year 20/19 BC, likewise brings us to AD 27.[1] The other pointers to Jesus' age, Luke 3.23 and John 8.57, are only quite general and allow no conclusion about the year of his death. Moreover, the date of his birth cannot be determined, for neither the statement that Jesus was born under Herod the Great (up to 4 BC) nor the reference to the star, which may possibly coincide with the Jupiter-Saturn conjunction in the year 7 BC, nor the tax levy which did not take place till AD 6, gives us any precise information on the date of Jesus' birth; the early Church tried in various ways to connect it with important events that occurred about that time.

3. The next important date for early Christian chronology is the death of Agrippa I.

(*a*) Agrippa was a grandson of Herod the Great, and a son of Aristobulus, who was born of the Hasmonean princess Mariamne and was executed by his own father in 7 BC. After an unsettled early life Agrippa became the favourite of the future Emperor Caligula in Rome. After being imprisoned under Tiberius, he was made king by Caligula immediately after the latter's accession to power in AD 37, and was given Philip's tetrarchy, which had been under Roman government since 34 (Jos. *Ant*. XVIII, 126, 143–204, 228–39). In the year 38 he came to Palestine, and in 39, after Herod Antipas had been exiled, he obtained Galilee and Perea in addition (*Ant*. XVIII, 252). He was also able to gain the favour of the Emperor Claudius, who in 41 bestowed on him Judea and Samaria, as well as Lysanias' tetrarchy, so that the whole of his grandfather's territory was now in his hands (*Ant*. XIX, 236ff., esp. 274f., 351). His death occurred at the time of the games *pro salute Caesaris*, which were also a celebration of the founding of Caesarea (*Ant*. XIX, 343–52; cf. Acts 12.20–23). These games had been held at the beginning of March at regular four-year intervals since 9 BC, and were the first since he had become ruler

---

[1] Cf. Hölscher, *op. cit*., pp. 26f.

of Caesarea. If we add to this the information that the king died after being in office for eight years—the seven years mentioned by Josephus in *Ant.* XIX, 351, must according to XIX, 343, be changed to eight—both take us to the year 44. After his death the territory was governed by a procurator (*Ant.* XIX, 360ff., esp. 363).[1]

(*b*) According to Acts 12, Agrippa's persecution of the Christians must have preceded his death by a short time, and was therefore probably early in 44. As the feast of the Passover did not take place that year till after Agrippa's death, we have to ask whether, in view of Acts 12.3(ff.), we must not go back a year. But it is more likely that Acts 12.3–17 should have been assimilated to Jesus' passion; moreover, the Passover typology as a time of deliverance may play a part in this story of Peter.[2] According to Acts 12.17 it is probable that Peter then left Jerusalem for the last time. According to Acts 12.2 James the son of Zebedee suffered martyrdom at that time; and there is a good deal to suggest that his brother John also lost his life at the same time; this may be supposed from the Papias tradition and the Syrian martyrology, as well as from Mark 10.38f.[3] The failure to mention him in Acts 12.2 may be connected with the tendency that perhaps already existed at the the end of the first century to identify John the son of Zebedee with John of Ephesus, and conversely it would be clear that John is not mentioned in Acts 15, in contrast to Gal. 2.1ff., because at the time when this item of tradition was given its final form—that is, when the Apostles' Conference and Decree

---

[1] On this cf. Eduard Schwartz, 'Zur Chronologie des Paulus' (1907) in *Gesammelte Schriften* V, 1963, pp. 124–69, there pp. 127f.; further Haenchen, *Apostelgeschichte*, p. 54 n. 4; also Schürer, *op. cit.*, pp. 562f. (ET, pp. 150ff.), and Kirsopp Lake, 'The Chronology of Acts' in *The Beginnings of Christianity*, part I, vol. V, 1933, pp. 445–74, esp. pp. 446ff. κατὰ πενταετηρίδα (Jos. *Ant.* XVI, 138) denotes the regular four-year interval, the festival being repeated in every fifth year; cf. Liddell and Scott, *A Greek-English Lexicon*, 1940⁹, p. 1360. It must also be remembered that Josephus dates according to imperial years, i.e. from the autumn onwards. The first games therefore are in the year 10/9 BC, and this in a four-year cycle takes us to AD 43/44. According to Eusebius, *De mart. Pal.* XI, 30, the 5th Dystros was the appointed day for the festival, and so the games celebrated under Agrippa must have taken place on 5 March 44 (so Schwartz, pp. 127f.).

[2] So on the one hand Schwartz, *op. cit.*, p. 128 n. 1; Haenchen, *Apostelgeschichte*, p. 54; on the other hand August Strobel, 'Passa-Symbolik und Passa-Wunder in Act. xii 3ff', *NTSt* 4 (1957/8), pp. 210–15.

[3] So Schwartz, *op. cit.*, p. 129, and in detail his 'Über den Tod der Söhne Zebedaei' (1904) in *Ges. Schriften* V, pp. 48–123; also the material in Erwin Preuschen, *Die Apostelgeschichte* (HbNT IV/1), 1912, pp. 75f.

were connected together and arranged as later—it was known that John the son of Zebedee was no longer alive.[1]

4. The Apostles' Conference must in that case be put before the persecution of the Christians under Agrippa, i.e. at the latest in the winter of AD 43/44. That is supported by the placing of the meeting (this has already been discussed) between Acts 11.25f. and 11.27ff.,[2] and by the address of the letter mentioned in 15.23. The thesis that the year of the Apostles' Conference is the same as that of Agrippa's death has already been put forward in various ways, but on the assumption—problematic in my opinion—that Acts 11.27ff., and especially 11.30 and 12.25, are identical with the journey to the Conference, though the reference to the famine and the bringing of a collection clearly point to a later time.[3]

5. From here we come to the question of the date of Paul's conversion. According to Gal. 1.18 and 2.1 there are three plus fourteen years between his conversion and the Conference, the initial years being included according to the ancient method of counting, so that we are to reckon with an actual span of time of about fifteen years. There is indeed the possibility of understanding the statements of time in Gal. 1.18 and 2.1 as parallel, i.e. as referring in both cases to the conversion, in which case there would be an interval of thirteen years altogether;[4] but the use of ἔπειτα as a connecting word and of the preposition διά in Gal. 2.1 makes this less probable.[5] Allowing for fifteen years in between, we should put the apostle's conversion in the year 29, or at the earliest 28 (if the other solution were adopted, it would be 30/31),

[1] Ed. Schwartz, 'Chronologie', pp. 129, 137. The linguistic form of Acts 12.2 also presents difficulties, as Schwartz stresses, p. 129 n. 1.

[2] See p. 85 above.

[3] Cf., e.g., Ed. Schwartz, *op. cit.*, pp. 131ff.; Julius Wellhausen, *Kritische Analyse der Apostelgeschichte* (Abh.d.Gesellsch.d.Wissenschaften zu Göttingen NF XV/2), 1914, p. 30; Preuschen, *Apostelgeschichte*, p. 96; W. Bousset, *ZNW* 15 (1914), pp. 156ff.; Eduard Meyer, *Ursprung und Anfänge* III, pp. 169ff.; Rudolf Bultmann in a review, *ZKG* NF 12 (1930), p. 91; Maurice Goguel, *The Birth of Christianity*, ET 1953, pp. 294ff.; Karl Heussi, *Die römische Petrustradition in kritischer Sicht*, 1955, pp 6off. (excursus on early Christian chronology). As a rule the date of the Conference is given as 48; thus Jeremias, *ZNW* 27 (1928), pp. 98ff.; Haenchen, *Apostelgeschichte*, p. 57; Georgi, *Kollekte*, p. 142; cf. also the survey of the various attempted solutions that is given in Paul Feine and Johannes Behm, *Einleitung in das Neue Testament*, 1956[11], pp. 125ff.

[4] So Ed. Schwartz, *op. cit.*, p. 137, and recently Haenchen, *Apostelgeschichte*, p. 58; Georgi, *Kollekte*, p. 5 n. 2.

[5] Cf. Oepke, *Galater*, pp. 43, 51f.; also Schlier, *Galater*, p. 34.

and this would quite fit in with the fixing of the year 27 as the date of Jesus' death. As to Paul's activities up to the Apostles' Conference we know nothing except what we are told in Gal. 1.17–24, and our knowledge of the ensuing time up to the journey with the collection and the sending of Barnabas and Paul into eastern Asia Minor is also very slight.

6. The next more or less fixed date is that of the famine mentioned in Acts 11.27f. It is at this time that the collection, decided on at the Apostles' Conference and prompted by the words of a prophet, was carried through for the first time. Paul Wendland, who treated Acts 11.27ff. and Acts 15 as duplicates, nevertheless considered whether the idea of bringing the collection had not been transferred here from a later journey to the earlier one; the solution proposed above may perhaps meet this difficulty better.[1] Although there was no world-wide famine under Claudius, there were a number of partial famines under his government. Palestine, too, was affected; this was under the Procurator Tiberius Alexander, who was in office from 46 to 48 (*Ant.* XX, 51–53, 101).[2] According to Joachim Jeremias the distress was increased by the sabbatical year 47/48, and only the harvest of 49 brought relief.[3] As the distress was first predicted by Agabus, the years to consider for Acts 11.27ff. and for the journey of Barnabas and Paul to Jerusalem are most probably 46/47—possibly 48.

7. The most certain date in the whole of early Christian chronology is that of Paul's stay in Corinth; the evidence is the Gallio inscription. Gallio was Proconsul in Achaia from May 51 to May 52 (possibly 52/53).[4] It follows that Paul must have stayed in Corinth from the winter of 49/50 to the summer of 51 (Acts 18.1–18). These dates agree with the information in Acts 18.2, where reference is made to a decree of Claudius that is to be put in the year 49.[5] The whole chronology of Paul's independent

---

[1] Paul Wendland, *Die urchristlichen Literaturformen* (HbNT I/3, 1912², ³), pp. 317f., and ch. II, pp. 82f., 85 above.
[2] Cf. Haenchen, *Apostelgeschichte*, p. 55(f.) n. 5.
[3] Joachim Jeremias, 'Sabbathjahr und neutestamentliche Chronologie', *ZNW* 27 (1928), p. 98.
[4] On this see particularly Adolf Deißmann, *Paul*, ET 1926², pp. 61ff.; Haenchen, *Apostelgeschichte*, pp. 58ff.
[5] Cf. Haenchen, *Apostelgeschichte*, p. 58.

missionary work can be obtained from his visit to Corinth. He set out from Antioch in the spring of 49, and travelled through Asia Minor (Galatia, be it noted) and Macedonia as far as Athens and Corinth. He returned to the East (Acts 18.18–22) in 51. The next journey to Asia Minor, particularly to Galatia (Gal. 4.13) and Ephesus, was in the spring and summer of 52. Paul stayed in Ephesus and the province of Asia from 52 till the spring of 55 (Acts 20.31; more exactly 19.8–10, 22: three months and two years and 'a while'). The departure from Ephesus, the activity in Macedonia, and the three months' stay in Corinth thus come in the year 55 (Acts 20.1–3). The journey to Jerusalem was begun in the spring of 56 (Acts 20.13ff.).[1]

8. One last difficult question, which is less important for our context, is the change of office of the Procurators Felix and Festus (Acts 24.27). Haenchen, after an exhaustive discussion, arrives at the year 55. But Georgi has shown that there are weighty objections to this date. For according to Jos. *Ant.* XX, 137ff., and *Bell.* II, 247ff., the events under Felix are narrated in conjunction with Nero's accession to power (54); otherwise they would be bound for the most part to have taken place already. Moreover, the intrigues between Jews and Syrians about Caesarea that set in with the Procurators' change of office, and the relevant imperial decree, were essential factors in preparation for the Jewish war; this, too, tells against too early a date. Further, Pallas was again freed after his fall in 55, and was not finally disposed of till 62; and finally διετία is linguistically more likely to refer to the duration of Paul's imprisonment than to Festus' period of office. We have no firm clues for determining the date of the change of office. Paul was probably held in custody from 56 to 58 and taken to Rome in 58.[2]

9. If we are to judge by I *Clem.* 4–6, the death of Paul and of Peter probably took place nearly simultaneously at Rome. We may go with some certainty into the beginning of the sixties; a connection with the Neronian persecution of the year 64 is pos-

---

[1] In this fixing of the dates of Pauline missionary activity since 49 I agree with Georgi, *Kollekte*, pp. 142ff.; he also arranges Paul's various letters in order of time. Otherwise in Haenchen, *Apostelgeschichte*, p. 64.
[2] Haenchen, *Apostelgeschichte*, pp. 60ff.; Georgi, *Kollekte*, pp. 144ff.

sible, but cannot be proved.[1] The Lord's brother James was stoned to death in the year 62, that is almost at the same time, under the High Priest Ananus II (Jos. *Ant.* XX, 200).

[1] Cf. most recently Cullmann, *Peter*, pp. 95ff.; Dinkler, *ThR* NF 25 (1959), pp. 207ff.

IV

PAUL'S CONCEPTION OF MISSION

PAUL carried out such a great work as a missionary, and developed in his letters such an individual view of the mission, that he cannot simply be fitted into the various missionary efforts of the primitive Church, but must be treated independently. It is, of course, beyond question that he built on the presuppositions of the primitive Church. He worked for years in the sphere of Hellenist Jewish Christianity, and for a considerable time he stood side by side with Barnabas in the missionary work of the Antioch church. Of course, he exercised an important influence there, and by his own personality and theological ideas helped to shape and define the work. But the period in which he built up independently of Antioch a missionary work of his own and conceived the idea of journeying across the whole world became of fundamental importance.[1] According to the evidence of Acts and of his own writings, Paul went on from the old Antioch mission-field in southern Asia Minor, founded churches in the region of Galatia,[2] and then at first left northern and western Asia Minor to get to

---

[1] Cf. v. Harnack, *Mission und Ausbreitung* I, pp. 79ff. Of course, there is no question here of a supposed 'missionary strategy' that has turned its back on Jerusalem and its face towards the Roman Empire—a 'strategy' against which Munck, *Paul*, pp. 282ff., falsely argues, trying instead to direct the Pauline mission on to Jerusalem. The correct view is taken by Gottlob Schrenk, 'Der Römerbrief als Missionsdokument' in *Studien zu Paulus* (AThANT 26), 1954, pp. 81–106: 'It is a matter of the total comprehension of the *oikoumenē*; he thinks universally—in nations' (p. 82). Hans Lietzmann, *An die Römer* (HbNT 8), 1933⁴, p. 121, had spoken already of the 'apocalyptic perspective' in which Paul surveys the whole world. Georg Eichholz 'Der oekumenische und missionarische Horizont der Kirche. Eine exegetische Studie zu Röm. 1.8–15', *EvTh* 21 (1961), pp. 15–27, esp. pp. 20ff., emphasizes the obedience of the witness 'who has a message that he owes to the world'. Cf. particularly Günther Bornkamm, 'Christus und die Welt in der urchristlichen Botschaft' in *Das Ende des Gesetzes*, 1958², pp. 157–72: the mission's course and aim are determined by the *Kyrios*, to whom the world belongs (p. 158). Of the older researches we may mention Paul Wernle, *Paulus als Heidenmissionar* (Samml. gemeinverst. Vortr. 14), 1899; Johannes Warneck, *Paulus im Lichte der heutigen Heidenmission*, 1914².

[2] It has been shown by Schlier, *Galater*, pp. 5f., Oepke, *Galater*, pp. 5ff., and others, that it is the region and not the province of Galatia that is meant, and that therefore the so-called North Galatian theory is to be preferred on all grounds. This follows in any case from the use of Γαλάται as the form of address in 3.1.

Macedonia and Greece.[1] He made Corinth an important mission centre, where he stayed a year and a half.[2] He must already then have formed the plan of pushing out further in a westerly direction;[3] but before that he turned his attention to the province of Asia, which was as yet largely or wholly untouched by the Christian message; and so his next mission centre became Ephesus.[4] Troublesome arguments with opponents and internal crises in the Church made it impossible, both in Asia Minor and in Macedonia and Greece, to finish the work in a short time.[5] It was not till after three years that Paul could regard the mission as finished,[6] and now at last it was a case of pushing on to Rome, and from there opening up new lands for the gospel.[7] In the whole eastern half of the empire, from Jerusalem to Illyricum, he had taken the gospel where as yet there were no churches, and he now saw before him the further great task of missionizing in the western half of the empire, above all in Spain.[8] A journey to

[1] There is no reason to doubt that Paul was conscious here of divine guidance; Acts 16.6–10 may contain a stylized but essentially correct account.

[2] Cf. Acts 18.11. Martin Dibelius and Werner Georg Kümmel, *Paul*, ET 1953, pp. 69ff., rightly point out that the usual conception of the Pauline missionary journeys is not accurate. Paul worked from various 'travel centres', going out first from Damascus, then from Tarsus and Antioch; Corinth and Ephesus later became the centres of his independent missionary work.

[3] Here the imperial capital, Rome, was an important goal in view, though only as a station on the route; cf. Rom. 1.10, 13; 15.22f.

[4] Paul's principle was to take the gospel where it had not been preached: Rom. 15.20f. The beginnings of the church at Ephesus probably go back to Aquila and Priscilla, as may be inferred from Acts 18.18f.; cf. Haenchen, *Apostelgeschichte*, pp. 483f. But we see from Acts 19.1ff. that followers of the Baptist's teaching had probably gathered there; they may have been close to the Christian message, but obviously favoured syncretism; how far, according to Acts 18.24ff., Apollos was associated with this is a difficult question. In any case Paul may have regarded this territory as a country where there had as yet been no mission. On this see Ernst Käsemann, 'The Disciples of John the Baptist in Ephesus', *Essays on New Testament Themes*, ET (SBT 41), 1964, pp. 136–48; Eduard Schweizer, 'Die Bekehrung des Apollos, Apg. 18.24–26', *EvTh* 15 (1955), pp. 247–54; Haenchen, *Apostelgeschichte*, pp. 489ff.

[5] On this cf. especially Günther Bornkamm, *Die Vorgeschichte des sogenannten Zweiten Korintherbriefs* (SAH phil.-hist. Kl. 1961/2), 1961; Georgi, *Kollekte*, pp. 43ff.

[6] Cf. Acts 19.8, 10; 20.31. It has already been mentioned (p. 16 above) that Paul missionized only in the central towns instead of over a whole region.

[7] Schrenk, 'Römerbrief', p. 82: Paul writes to the Romans at a point of time 'when he sees that focal points for the gospel's progress have been created everywhere in the East, enabling him to regard his commission there as completed'.

[8] Rom. 15.19, 23f. The question whether Paul himself was in Illyricum is of minor importance. He probably specifies this place as representing for him primarily the ancient boundary separating the eastern and western halves of the empire. But he very probably knew that the gospel had already reached this border territory, perhaps straight from his own mission field; cf. Adolf Schlatter, *Gottes Gerechtigkeit*, 1952[2], pp. 387f.

Jerusalem was to form the conclusion of his work in the East; but it became the end of all his missionary work. It was only as a prisoner, after the legal action had dragged on for a long time, that he was at last able to reach Rome, and it is evident that he was never able to leave that town again.[1] Thus his independent missionary activity is essentially confined to the period from the year 49 to about 56.[2]

Paul did not entertain a moment's doubt that the gospel must be preached in the whole world. In his letters this concern is expressed in a great variety of ways. His view of the mission is inseparable from his entire theological thought; it therefore leads us into almost all the problems of his theology, and it can be dealt with here only in a very abbreviated form.

From the moment of his conversion Paul knew that he was called to a mission among the Gentiles. Gal. 1.15f.: 'But when he who had set me apart before I was born, and had called me through his grace, was pleased to reveal his Son to me, in order that I

---

[1] For the history of the Pauline mission we have in the first place Paul's letters, especially the correspondence with the church at Corinth and Rom. 15. There is no disputing that I Cor. is a homogeneous document, with at the most a few small insertions (6.1-11, 12-20?); cf. Günther Bornkamm, 'Herrenmahl und Kirche bei Paulus' in *Studien zu Antike und Urchristentum*, 1963[2], pp. 138-76, there pp. 173ff.; id., *Vorgeschichte des 2. Kor.*, pp. 34f. n. 131. II Cor., on the contrary, is a collection of letters, whose component parts probably originated in the following sequence: the apology, II Cor. 2.14-7.4 (minus the non-Pauline later insertion 6.14-7.1); parts of the 'letter of tears', chs. 10-13; the letter of reconciliation, 1.1-2.13 and 7.5-8.24; and the collection letter, ch. 9. On this cf. in detail Bornkamm, *Vorgeschichte*, pp. 16ff.; a rather different account in Georgi, *Kollekte*, pp. 78ff., 83ff., who regards ch. 8 as a separate letter of recommendation standing in point of time between the letter of reconciliation and ch. 9.

Acts from 15.40 onwards presents an account, incomplete but fairly well rounded off, of Paul's work up to and including Corinth (15.40-18.17). The report of the long period from his first leaving Corinth to the end of his work in Ephesus (18.18-19.40) is very fragmentary. But here, too, characteristically abbreviated and stylized, the most important events are noted: the talk with the Baptist's disciples in Ephesus, 19.1-7; Paul's successful work in that town, 8-20; his plans for the journey, 21, and the difficulties that were put in his way, 23-40, here particularly concentrated on external difficulties that were actually present, for we may count with some certainty on an imprisonment in Ephesus; cf. Adolf Deißmann, 'Zur ephesinischen Gefangenschaft des Apostels Paulus' in *Anatolian Studies presented to Sir W. M. Ramsay*, 1923, pp. 121-7; Wilhelm Michaelis, *Die Gefangenschaft des Paulus in Ephesus und das Itinerar des Timotheus* (Neutest. Forsch. I/3), 1925; id., *Einleitung in das Neue Testament*, 1961[3], pp. 240ff.; finally Georgi, *Kollekte*, pp. 59f. In Acts 20.1-21.17 we have a quite reliable account of Paul's journey to Jerusalem, and then there follows in 21.18-28.31 the broadly developed, but in its main features objective, description of the legal action and the journey to Rome.

[2] On dates cf. Haenchen, *Apostelgeschichte*, pp. 58ff.; Georgi, *Kollekte*, pp. 142ff.; and Excursus, pp. 92f. above.

might preach him among the Gentiles . . .'[1] He therefore speaks in Rom. 1.5 of his special χάρις καὶ ἀποστολὴ εἰς ὑπακοὴν πίστεως ἐν πᾶσιν τοῖς ἔθνεσιν ('grace and apostleship to bring about the obedience of faith . . . among all the nations').[2] And this thought also plays a characteristically important part in his account of the Apostles' Conference: 'those who were of repute' see that he has been entrusted with 'the gospel to the uncircumcised', and acknowledge the *charis* that has been given to him; for as God qualified Peter 'for the mission to the circumcised', so he qualified Paul 'for the Gentiles'.[3] His concept of apostleship is characterized by the fact of his being simultaneously converted, entrusted with the gospel, and sent out to the Gentiles.[4] He is conscious that, however much equality there may be, his apostolic office is different from that of the people who were apostles before him. Not only had he been a persecutor of the Church; it was only through an extraordinary appearance of the risen Lord that he received this 'grace', so that his office is based solely on the activity of the exalted Lord; but in particular he is in a different position from the Jerusalem apostles, as he is commissioned to serve among the Gentiles.[5] He is 'under obligation both to Greeks and to barbarians, both to the wise and to the foolish' (Rom. 1.14). If the phrase 'Jews and Greeks' is to be understood as presupposing

[1] Besides Paul's own account of his conversion in Gal. 1.13–16a we have the threefold tradition of Acts. Acts 9.1–19 goes back to an older tradition; 22.1–21 and 26.2–23 are free Lucan versions of this, underlining the importance of the event for early Christian history. Acts 9.1ff. and Gal. 1.15f. aim at showing that the converted Paul is destined to be a missionary to the Gentiles (9.15); what 'the Lord' says here to Ananias is said by Ananias to Paul in 22.14, and is repeated by the Lord on the occasion of the vision in the temple in 22.21; in 26.16–18, as in Gal. 1.15f., the commission is directly connected with the appearance on the road to Damascus.

[2] On this use of χάρις cf. Rom. 15.15f.; I Cor. 3.10; Gal 2.9. The 'grace given to me' is his special office. The concept thus used stands near to χάρισμα, but must not be identified with it. It can hardly be without good reason that in all the passages Paul spoke of χάρις; in I Cor. 12.4ff., 28 the ἀποστολή is counted among the services of the Church—it is not, however, characterized as χάρισμα (similarly in Rom. 12.3ff.).

[3] Gal. 2.7–9a. The phrase εἰς τὰ ἔθνη is an abbreviated expression for εἰς ἀποστολὴν τῶν ἐθνῶν; Lietzmann, *Galater*, p. 13; Oepke, *Galater*, p. 50.

[4] Cf. particularly the context of Gal. 1.11–2.21.

[5] We cannot here go into the controversial problem of the concept of apostleship and its origin. Hans von Campenhausen, 'Der urchristliche Apostelbegriff', *StTh* 1 (1947 [Lund, 1948]), pp. 96–130, is still fundamental. A different view is found in Günter Klein, *Zwölf Apostel*, pp. 20ff.; Walter Schmithals, *Das kirchliche Apostelamt* (FRLANT 79), 1961, but I cannot assent at all to the derivation from *gnosis* and to a complete denial of the concept of apostleship for the primitive Church. Georgi, *Gegner des Paulus*, pp. 39ff., stresses the missionary commission one-sidedly, but in my opinion that is not the constitutive element of the concept of apostleship.

the special choice of Israel, the decisive contrast being between the Jew and the Greek as a Gentile, the phrase 'Greeks and barbarians', on the other hand, comes from the self-confidence of the Hellenist who prides himself on the advantage of Greek culture—a dividing line that for Paul has even less validity as regards the spreading of the gospel than has the position of Israel in the scheme of salvation.[1] The apostolic office means for him a commissioning for service from which he cannot by any means withdraw.[2] It is nothing less than an ἀνάγκη that lies on him and drives him to preach the gospel, enabling him as a free man to become a Jew to the Jews, but also a Gentile to the Gentiles. But this fate is the object of his love, and he stands as a slave of the gospel in the glorious freedom of God's children, and he is therefore able to bring to all those who are enslaved by the powers of this world the joyful message that makes us free.[3]

The world-wide aspect of Paul's missionary activity, and the determination that his apostolate should be to all Gentiles, is based on the gospel itself and its world-wide horizon. It is not simply a message to Israel, or the fulfilment of the particularist *Heilsgeschichte* of the Old Testament people of God; it is rather the light, the φωτισμός in the darkness of a world that has been usurped by 'the god of this world' (II Cor. 4.1ff.); the word of the cross is the divine wisdom as opposed to all worldly wisdom (I Cor. 1.18ff.). Therefore the powers of this world are overcome by the preaching and spreading of the gospel, and Paul is led as a missionary in a triumphal march through the countries, propagating the εὐωδία Χριστοῦ ('savour of Christ', II Cor. 2.14ff.).[4] For this reason, too, he can rejoice when as a prisoner he has the opportunity for an *apologia* (Phil. 1.12ff.), for it concerns God's lawsuit

[1] Cf. Eichholz, *EvTh* 21 (1961), pp. 25f., who points out that the contrast between Greeks and barbarians occurs to Paul here because with the projected journey to Spain he is thinking of leaving the sphere of Greek culture; so, too, the expression 'wise and foolish' should be understood accordingly.

[2] On the thought of indebtedness cf. Paul S. Minear, 'Gratitude and Mission in the Epistle to the Romans' in *Basileia (Festschrift W. Freytag)*, 1959, pp. 42–48. He denies that it is only an illustration from the law as to debt. 'To the extent that Paul was indebted to God for his call, to that very extent he was indebted to those Gentiles for whose sake God had called him' (p. 44).

[3] For an understanding of I Cor. 9.14ff. cf. Ernst Käsemann, 'Eine paulinische Variation des *"amor fati"*', *ZThK* 56 (1959), pp. 138–54, esp. pp. 152f.

[4] On θριαμβεύειν τινά, which may have more than one meaning, but which can here be intended only in the sense that God is triumphant, cf. most recently G. Bornkamm, *Vorgeschichte des 2. Kor.*, p. 30 n. 114.

with the whole world, and he can particularly answer for it at the court of imperial Rome itself. God lays claim to the world as his creation, by reconciling it to himself and so making it a new community of salvation (II Cor. 5.17ff.). Just as all men are under sin, and no flesh can of itself achieve righteousness—because all are descended from Adam, through whom sin came into the world, and all likewise sin and must sin—so in Christ the new Adam has appeared, through whose redemptive act all fallen creatures may again be saved (Rom. 5.12ff.).[1] For God made him to be sin who knew no sin, and through his death he reconciled the *kosmos* to himself (II Cor. 5.19, 21). With this act of reconciliation the new age has now already dawned. In and with the resurrection God has exalted Jesus as *Kyrios* and thus enthroned him as ruler over the whole world (Phil. 2.9ff.). The confession which the powers are already offering before his throne, and to which the Church in the midst of the present world testifies, is the motive power and the aim of the Gentile mission. The message must be preached in the whole world, so that men acknowledge their true Lord, join in the confession, and bow in thankful praise before him (Rom. 10.14–18; 15.7–13).[2] Where the confession κύριος Ἰησοῦς ('Jesus is Lord') is spoken, and belief in the risen Lord lives in the heart, men are not put to shame, but stand under the κύριος πάντων, who makes them all rich (Rom. 10.9–13). On these presuppositions the mission to the Gentiles can no longer be for Paul an exceptional phenomenon. From the concept of the exaltation he realized, as no one did before him, the all-embracing reality of the Christian message, and he understood that the gospel itself, with its universal claim, demands that the mission should be to all human beings, including the 'Greeks and barbarians'.

This understanding of the gospel enables us to see the meaning of Paul's wrestling about the law. Beside the one 'truth of the gospel'—a truth that must be maintained—there is in his report of the Apostles' Conference his weighty reference to the 'freedom which we have in Christ Jesus'. Freedom belongs just as much as

[1] For details now cf. Egon Brandenburger, *Adam und Christus. Exegetisch-religionsgeschichtliche Untersuchung zu Römer 5.12–21 (I Kor. 15)* (WMANT 7), 1962; also Rudolf Bultmann, 'Adam und Christus nach Röm. 5', *ZNW* 50 (1959), pp. 145–65.
[2] Cf. G. Bornkamm, 'Christus und die Welt' in *Das Ende die Gesetzes*, pp. 158, 166ff.; Eduard Schweizer, 'Jesus Christus, Herr über Kirche und Welt' in *Libertas Christiana* (Festschrift F. Delekat, BEvTh 26), 1957, pp. 175–87, esp. pp. 180ff.

universality to the gospel. Here, of course, it is not a matter of a freedom based on man's essential nature, as it was regarded in Greek and Hellenist thought, but of a freedom understood eschatologically, based on being free from all subjection to the powers of this age. It is a freedom to which Christ has set us free (Gal. 5.1), a freedom that can release us even from sin and death.[1] This freedom is the sign of those who belong to the heavenly Jerusalem, while the earthly Jerusalem with its children is still enslaved (Gal. 4.21–31). For even the law itself, if it is understood as the way of salvation, is servitude, and if it were imposed on the Gentiles it would simply lead from one slavery to another. It would destroy freedom again, because man would again have to depend on himself and his own achievements and strength. Where the letter of the law is imposed and its observance is demanded as an unconditional necessity, man is simply handed over again to sin and death and defrauded of his salvation. And therefore Paul has to pronounce on the Judaizers who brought about the Apostles' Conference the severe judgment that they are '*false* brethren'.[2] This uncompromising attitude in the Antioch dispute can be rightly judged only if this context is kept in mind. For Paul it is a clear Either/Or, which must not be blurred by any concessions whatever that would restore power to the law of the letter and so keep mankind under the power of sin and death. For the law cannot overcome sin and death, or lead to true righteousness and to life, but is destined to do nothing but drive men still more deeply into sin and to bring them to realize that as long as they depend on themselves they are lost (Rom. 3.20; 7.7ff.; Gal. 3.19ff.).[3] But where salvation has dawned, where Christ has appeared, there the end of the law has come (Rom. 10.4).[4] For the present context it is above all important that in his argument with the Judaizers

---

[1] On the concept of liberty cf. Heinrich Schlier, art. '*ἐλευθερία*', etc., *ThWb* II, pp. 484–500, esp. pp. 495ff.; Bultmann, *Theology*, §38 (I, pp. 330ff.); Günther Bornkamm, *Das urchristliche Verständnis der Freiheit* (Neckarauer Hefte 8), 1961, esp. pp. 10ff.

[2] We cannot here discuss Paul's later opponents of whom we learn something in Galatians, I and II Corinthians and Philippians, as this does not directly touch the understanding of the mission.

[3] Cf. Bultmann, *Theology*, §§27 and 39 (I, pp. 259ff., 340ff.); Günther Bornkamm, 'Sünde Gesetz und Tod. Exegetische Studie zu Röm. 7' in *Das Ende des Gesetzes*, pp. 51–69.

[4] It must be expressly emphasized that on the basis of the context of Rom. 10.1–4 the word *τέλος* cannot be used in the sense of 'aim' or 'fulfilment', but only in the sense of 'end'.

Paul naturally speaks again and again of the law that appears in the Old Testament, but that he is also concerned to show that no one is unaffected by God's law. For as God has given witness of himself to all mankind through the works of his creation, thus leaving no more excuse to the Gentiles than to the Jews (Rom. 1.18ff.; 3.1ff.),[1] so he has given his law both to the Gentiles and to the Jews—for the latter revealed in the Old Testament, and for the former written in their hearts—so as to call them to account for it and some day to judge them (Rom. 2.1ff., 14ff.).[2] Paul does not mean that men are simply exempt from all law; God's demand remains, and is to be complied with faithfully.[3] But salvation cannot and must not be based on the carrying out of the law; otherwise the gospel as a liberating message of salvation and God-given righteousness would be nullified (Gal. 5.2ff.).

---

[1] The ἔθνη concept in primitive Christianity was first clearly thought out and precisely defined by Paul. Early Christians, in the main, took over from Judaism the traditional concept, according to which the people outside Israel are only indirectly in contact with God's actions, and therefore—this was usual in the propaganda of Jews of the Diaspora, for instance—have, in fact, first of all to be led to the true God. Paul's idea is quite different: the Gentiles too, live directly on God's actions and revelation, and because of their guilt and deluded blindness they are brought, equally with the Jews, under God's judgment. In fact, the real situation of Jews and Gentiles becomes manifest only in the light of the gospel, and in just the same way all men are brought to a sense of their responsibility before God and convinced of their sin. On the concept 'Gentiles' in the Old and New Testaments cf. Johannes Blauw, *Goden en Mensen. Plaats en Betekenis van de Heidenen in de Heilige Schrift*, Groningen, 1950, esp. pp. 19ff., 109ff., 123f.; on Rom. 1.18–3.20 we may refer merely to Günther Bornkamm, 'Die Offenbarung des Zornes Gottes (Rom. 1–3)' in *Das Ende des Gesetzes* (*Ges. Aufs.* I), 1961³, pp. 9–33.

[2] On this cf. Günther Bornkamm, 'Gesetz und Natur. Röm. 2.14–16' in *Studien zu Antike und Urchristentum*, 1963², pp. 93–118, esp. pp. 98ff.; also pp. 111ff. on the function of conscience as confirmation of the law that is not withheld from the Gentiles.

[3] We cannot here go into the Pauline parenesis; we will merely point out that besides the understanding of the law as a self-chosen way of salvation in the sense of the ἰδία δικαιοσύνη (ἐκ νόμου), and of the function of the law for the ἐπίγνωσις ἁμαρτίας (that the law is holy and just and good, Rom. 7.12, is related primarily to this), Paul knows the law, too, as a witness of the promise *(γραφή)* and as an expression of God's will; but this must be taken over and comprehended from the point of view of the commandment of love; it does not contravene freedom, and can moreover really be fulfilled; cf. Gal. 5.13ff.; Rom. 13.8ff. For Paul, therefore, the idea of judgment according to 'works' remains unchanged (besides Rom. 2.6ff. cf. esp. II Cor. 5.10; Rom 14.10–12), and the radicalized parenesis on the judgment must not be regarded as an illogicality beside the doctrine of justification; thus Herbert Braun, *Gerichtsgedanke und Rechfertigungslehre bei Paulus* (Unters. z. NT 19), 1930, esp. pp. 92ff., 96ff. It is rightly stressed by G. Bornkamm, 'Sünde, Gesetz und Tod', pp. 68f., that that function of the law which drives the unredeemed soul more and more deeply and inescapably into sin has by no means gone once for all, but remains present as having been overcome, as remains the case with the *iustitia aliena* on which the Christians may live.

The righteousness that God grants and brings about can be grasped in faith alone. Its reality depends on one's being totally bound to the Lord, because it is only in trust and unconditional self-giving that it can be what it is, namely God's eschatological decision on man's salvation that has now been granted. As the concept of righteousness as it is understood in the Old Testament is one of relationship, so the New Testament concept, too, is to be understood solely as the saving presence of God in Christ, with the believer's existence bound to that presence alone. But this righteousness that is made known in the gospel is available not only to the Jews but in the same way to the Gentiles, too, as, in fact, the gospel with its news of the universal saving action in Christ is directed to the whole world (Rom. 3.27ff.).[1] For Paul this is shown nowhere more clearly than in Abraham, the 'father of many nations' (Rom. 4.17). For he trusted the divine 'promise' and was justified by faith long before he was circumcised (Rom. 4.1ff.). As circumcision merely sealed his faith, so the law, too, was not given till much later than the promise, and is nothing else than a custodian till Christ comes (Gal. 3.17ff.; Rom. 4.11).[2] For the Jewish tradition it is unheard of that promise and faith should be put first as a matter of principle,[3] but in the light of

[1] Cf. Ernst Käsemann, 'Gottesgerechtigkeit bei Paulus', *ZThK* 58 (1961), pp. 367–87; also Bultmann, *Theology*, §28 (I, pp. 270ff.).

[2] We need not take into account here the diversity of argumentation in Gal. 3 and Rom. 4. It is shown particularly in the different uses of the concept 'seed of Abraham'. Whereas in Gal. 3.16ff. this concept is interpreted in a consistently Christological way, and it is only on the basis of faith and baptism 'into Christ' that Christians, too, can be said to be 'the seed of Abraham' (3.26ff., 29), Rom. 4.13ff. speaks of the seed of Abraham much more directly in relation to believers. This is connected with the fact that in Gal. 3 the thought is more clearly linked with the *Heilsgeschichte*, whereas in Rom. 4 Paul is interested in presenting the believing Abraham as the prototype of the believer generally, who relies on the God 'who gives life to the dead and calls into existence the things that do not exist' (v. 17). The law is therefore looked at from a different angle in the two places; in Rom. 4 it is regarded as the way to salvation, but in Gal. 3 the function within the *Heilsgeschichte* is stressed, and there is also mention of the curse from which we must first be freed by Christ, through his taking it upon himself. The connection of Rom. 4 with the *Heilsgeschichte* has been too strongly emphasized by Ulrich Wilckens, 'Die Rechtfertigung Abrahams nach Römer 4' in *Studien zur Theologie der alttestamentlichen Überlieferungen* (Festschrift G.v.Rad), 1961, pp. 111–27; in Rom. 4 itself the peculiar fragmentariness which Paul sees in history is obvious, though the earthly and temporal element is not simply ignored.

[3] On Abraham in Judaism cf. Otto Schmitz, 'Abraham im Spätjudentum und Urchristentum' in *Festschrift A. Schlatter*, 1922, pp. 99–123; Martin Dibelius, *Der Brief des Jakobus* (KrExKomm XV), 1959¹⁰, pp. 157ff.; also Otto Kuß, *Der Römerbrief* (in parts since 1957), pp. 187ff.

the knowledge of Christ it is a necessary conclusion.[1] At the same time Paul was able to make clear from this point of view the universal horizon both of God's saving action and of the faith that justifies. For all particularist barriers have fallen here: as 'the father of the nations' Abraham is 'the father of all who believe', whether they come from circumcision or from uncircumcision.[2] Where God's grace is bestowed on man, there can indeed be only a faith like Abraham's; and because of this, not only must works be entirely put aside (Phil. 3.4ff.), but all precedence in the scheme of salvation ceases, too. The individual who stands before God and receives his justification is detached from all previous conditions relating to salvation; he has become a fellow participant in and a fellow heir of God's new world, and has been put into the community of the Church of Jesus Christ.

This point of view also gives the idea of election an essentially new aspect in Paul's writings. Not that the election of Israel is finished with; we are to come back to that at once; but this line is cut by a quite different one, which is concerned with the election of believers (Rom. 8.28–30). The sovereign freedom of the God who shows mercy (Rom. 9.14ff.) is stressed here, as well as God's action of justification (Rom. 9.30ff.). Election is election in view of Christ's which is independent of the special history of the election of Israel; it is nowhere else but in the believing acceptance of the Christ event that we are shown what election really is, and so in the end it can be spoken of only in conjunction with faith and not in theoretical discussion.[3] It is in this way that Paul

---

[1] On this cf. Christian Dietzfelbinger, *Paulus und das Alte Testament. Die Hermeneutik des Paulus, untersucht an seiner Deutung der Gestalt Abrahams* (ThEx NF 95), 1961, pp. 36ff.

[2] One should notice the very precise phrasing of Rom. 4.11f.

[3] On this cf. Erich Dinkler, 'Prädestination bei Paulus' in *Festschrift für Günther Dehn*, 1957, pp. 81–102. Alongside many weighty observations there are a few pieces of exposition that in my opinion need correcting: thus Paul cannot be said to contrast the election of the nation with that of the individual, as is asserted here; moreover, the Christological aim of the election idea should be much more strongly emphasized, as this theme cannot be adequately grasped from the point of view of anthropology (cf. pp. 97f.); further, it is insufficient to think of Israel's priority only in a temporal sense; and lastly it is very questionable whether the two lines of the election idea in Paul's writings can be so untied that in the end it is a question of the historical and eschatological conditions imposed on human existence. When Anders Nygren asserts in his *Commentary on Romans*, ET 1952, p. 369, that 'the concept of predestination is the most theocentric idea there is', what was for Paul simply the constitutive Christological element is mistakenly understood in a different way. According to Goppelt, *Christentum und Judentum*, p. 113, the chapters describe 'not a step-by-step

can understand in its presuppositions the Gentiles' participation in salvation.

As the idea of election clearly shows, Paul's range of ideas includes the history and destiny of the people of Israel, even as a quite decisive element. Unless one took into account the question of God's people of the Old Testament, any description of the apostle's view of the mission would be only fragmentary.[1] For Paul himself, as for previous missionary work, 'to the Jews first' is an incontestable principle.[2] But in what sense can we speak of Israel's priority? The election of Israel is not different from election in general, in that it is a decision in view of Christ; Israel has experienced a history of a special promise and of guidance to salvation revealed by God, and is marked out by this in the present as in the past (Rom. 3.1ff.; 9.1ff.). It follows that the gospel is first meant for that nation that was specially chosen. But by building on its own righteousness and disdaining God's righteousness, which is to be received in faith, Israel has rejected the salvation offered to it. Does that mean that its election has become invalid and its rejection inevitable? God's anger certainly falls on the Jews, who have rejected the Lord Jesus, persecute the Church and seek to prevent the gospel from being preached (I Thess. 2.15f.).[3] They are struck by spiritual blindness, and the glad

---

penetration into God's plans, but a step-by-step self-unlocking of God for faith'; but this again is interpreted much too one-sidedly 'from the principle of his rule through the *Heilsgeschichte*'.

[1] Cf. Schrenk, *Studien zu Paulus*, pp. 98ff.; *id.*, *Die Weissagungen über Israel im Neuen Testament*, 1951, pp. 25ff.

[2] This does not hold good, however, in the schematic sense, as is asserted in the picture of Paul that we find in Acts. It is true that in certain cases Paul began his missionary work in the synagogue, but in no case did he make the work among the Gentiles depend on the Jews' rejection of it. For him 'to the Jews first' meant primarily not a temporal sequence but a permanent position of precedence due to special election. A different interpretation is given by Goppelt, *Christentum und Judentum*, pp. 86ff., who transfers to Paul the Lucan presentation, and sees in it a confirmation of the concept of a sequence in the scheme of salvation which he presupposes in the whole of early Christianity.

[3] In I Thess. 2.15f. Paul is obviously using conventional phrases. This is shown by the clear deviation from the theme, and by the excessive importance that is suddenly given to the question of the Jews. We can hardly assume any sharply defined piece of tradition—in particular 'by hindering us from speaking to the Gentiles that they may be saved' (v. 16a) leaves a strongly Pauline impression—but it may be fairly assumed that we have here current phrases of early Christian polemic against Jews. We can see here not only a hint of the pagan anti-Semitism of ancient times, but also in the theologically decisive passages in v. 16b and c an appropriation of traditional Jewish themes, for 16b goes back to Gen. 15.16, and 16c is parallel to an

tidings are taken to those who have hitherto known nothing of God's promise (Rom. 10.16ff.; 11.7ff.). Thus the mission to the Gentiles has become the great and pressing task. Those who are now being called have no share in the particular history of the election of God's people of the Old Testament, but they are nevertheless chosen by God and bow in faith before him. But what can the Gentile mission be for Paul except a singular incitement to the Jews, at last to recognize salvation and seize it? The hard-heartedness of Israel, with whom God himself keeps faith, is only for a certain time, and God's way with the people of the Old Testament covenant has not yet come to an end. The result of this hardness of heart will simply be that the πλήρωμα τῶν ἐθνῶν (the full number of the Gentiles) will come in and receive salvation; and then Israel, too, at the end of this world's history, will reach the aim of its election, make use of its right to priority, and at last participate in the salvation (Rom. 11.25ff.).[1]

---

almost similarly worded passage in *Test. Levi* 6.11; cf. Martin Dibelius, *An die Thessalonicher. An die Philipper* (HbNT 11), 1937³, pp. 11ff., 34ff. The contemplation of the filling up of (the measure of) their sins is an allusion to the idea of judgment, and the difficult 16c must be understood from that point of view. ὀργή thus denotes God's eschatological judgment, as in 1.10. And this judgment of wrath is not merely in the future, but has already come over the Jews, as is made clear by the aorist ἔφθασεν. Therefore the Jews' action described in v. 15 means not only that with their sins they deserve judgment, but that the judgment that has been and is being pronounced on them is becoming manifest in what they do; this also explains the πάντοτε. There remains only the phrase εἰς τέλος, which may mean of itself 'finally', 'to the end', 'for ever', or 'completely'; cf. Arndt and Gingrich, *Lexicon to the NT*, s.v. Because of the context the first meaning need not be considered. Nor must one say that the wrath 'leads to the end', as Dibelius does, *Thessalonicher*, p. 12. The most probable meaning is that the Jews remain under the judgment of God's wrath 'till the end', but the other is also possible, according to which the judgment has already 'completely' come upon the Jews. On the other hand, the meaning 'for ever' must be eliminated, at any rate for Paul, because this would produce a hardly explicable contradiction of the expectation in Rom. 9–11 (but on Mark cf. ch. V 1, pp. 119f.). The basic theme of these chapters in Romans is that the Jews must bear the wrath of God in this present time and experience all its weight; although on the other hand I Thess. 2.15f. is expressly silent about the hope for the Jews, these two texts do not contradict each other. Cf. the thorough researches on the passage in Béda Rigaux, *Saint Paul. Les Épîtres aux Thessaloniciens* (Études Bibliques), 1956, pp. 445ff.; also Georgi, *Kollekte*, pp. 36ff. Ernst Bammel, 'Judenverfolgung und Naherwartung, Zur Eschatologie des Ersten Thessalonicherbriefs', *ZThK* 56 (1959), pp. 294–315, is quite wrong when he tries to demonstrate a 'historico-theological' view held by Paul, leading him at times to an 'intense and immediate expectation' (p. 312).

[1] πᾶς Ἰσραήλ in Rom. 11.26 has been given many meanings; cf. Otto Michel, *Der Brief an die Römer* (KrExKomm IV), 1955¹⁰, p. 250 n. 1; Karl Ludwig Schmidt, *Die Judenfrage im Lichte der Kapitel 9–11 des Römerbriefs* (ThSt 13), 1946², pp. 34ff. Of course, it must not be related to the 'Israel of God' of Gal. 6.16—that is, to the Church; but neither must it be equated with the 'remnant' of Israel spoken of in

The final fulfilment of the history of God's choice has not yet been reached, but the new covenant is already concluded (I Cor. 11.25; II Cor. 3.6ff.), and the real 'Israel of God' is already being gathered (Gal. 6.16).[1] The κλητοί, who accept the gospel, are united in the ἐκκλησία; they are the children of God through faith, who have been baptized in the name of Christ, and have been made members of the 'body of Christ'. In the 'body of Christ' all differences are abolished: 'there is neither Jew nor Greek . . . for you are all one in Christ Jesus' (Gal. 3.28; I Cor. 12.13).[2] Here the eschatological καινότης is already realized. Just as there are no differences in guilt before God, so there is 'no distinction between Jew and Greek' where they call on the name of the Lord and believe in him (Rom. 3.22; 10.12). The theme of election merely points to the different ways that lead in history to this goal; for Jews as well as Gentiles go to meet the glory of God.

Rom. 15.7–33, a chapter to which too little attention is often paid, and probably the last that we have from Paul's hand,[3] expresses again, as in one great summary, the basic ideas of the Pauline view of the mission. In conjunction with the discussion

---

Rom. 9.27ff. and 11.1ff. On the contrary, it relates to the Israelite people of actual history, who are now despising their salvation. But it would be un-Pauline to expect this Israel to be saved at the end of the ages through its mere presence and its physical descent from Abraham. It is rejected simply because it has not believed. Thus the offer of salvation will again be made to Israel, which will again be faced with a decision about belief, and as a believing Israel will attain salvation. As the passage about the πλήρωμα of the Gentiles does not exclude the loss of those who reject the message, so the phrase 'all Israel' does not exclude a real justification which must come through God and a genuine self-giving of the nation. The sentence οὐ πάντες οἱ ἐξ Ἰσραήλ, οὗτοι Ἰσραήλ ('For not all who are descended from Israel belong to Israel', Rom. 9.6) is true not only for the present but also for the future. But if in the case of that first decision about belief it was only a small fraction that accepted the message, it will at some future time be the 'fulness' of the Jews (cf. Rom. 11.12) who will acknowledge their Lord. The purport of the 'all Israel' corresponds to that of the πάντες ἄνθρωποι (all men) in Rom. 5.18 or the οἱ πάντες ('all') in Rom. 11.32.

[1] In relation to this there is Paul's characteristic phrase Ἰσραὴλ κατὰ σάρκα in I Cor. 10.18; cf. Rom. 9.6ff. Similarly the distinction between Ἰουδαῖος ἐν τῷ φανερῷ and ἐν τῷ κρυπτῷ in Rom. 2.28f.; cf. Kuss, *Römer*, pp. 91f.

[2] Cf. Dahl, *Volk Gottes*, pp. 309ff.; also Bultmann, *Theology* I, pp. 308ff. (§34).

[3] It is widely recognized, as a result of New Testament textual criticism, that Rom. 16.1–20; 25–27 does not belong to the original letter to the Romans. The letter to the Philippians, which was formerly thought to have been written during the Roman imprisonment, may rather be put in the time of Paul's imprisonment in Ephesus. Colossians, Ephesians, and the Pastoral Letters can be reckoned as belonging to the post-Pauline tradition.

of the unity of strong and weak in the Church, Paul comes to the unity of the Church composed of Jews and Gentiles. As he has given a Christological basis to the unity of strong and weak (Rom. 14.6ff., 15; 15.3), so here he develops his argument from the fact that Christ, by becoming 'a servant to the circumcised' to show God's truthfulness, fulfils the promises given to the fathers, and so has made God's mercy a reality to the Gentiles. Because the one for whom the Gentiles hope has now come from the root of Jesse, and rises up to rule over them, praise to the Lord and full confession are now heard among the people, and there begins the eschatological glorifying of God, which is the last and the true goal of history.[1] In the mission among the Gentiles, therefore, there is now beginning to happen what should not have happened, according to Old Testament prophecy, till after Israel had received salvation. At this point it can be seen particularly clearly how much the picture has changed.[2] It is Paul the Jew whom God has commissioned with the priestly service of the gospel among the Gentiles, so that he may bring them to God as an acceptable offering sanctified by the Spirit (Rom. 15.16).[3] But this takes place at a time when Israel as a whole is still standing aside. As in the days of Elijah, God has left only a remnant (Rom. 9.27ff.; 11.1ff.), and that small band of 'saints' in Jerusalem, of Israelite origin, takes so to speak as representatives in the midst of Israel the place that that nation should fittingly occupy.[4] Because of Israel's priority, and as a sign of the unity of the Church composed of Jews and Gentiles, Paul takes to that church the collection made by the Gentile Christian churches as an earthly gift in return for the spiritual gifts that the Gentiles have received as joint heirs

[1] Here again we see plainly the depth of Paul's concern for the world, and how this determines his missionary activity; cf. Schrenk, *Studien zu Paulus,* pp. 85ff.

[2] The great transformation by Paul of the traditional picture of the *Heilsgeschichte* and of eschatology is particularly emphasized by Hans Joachim Schoeps, *Paulus,* pp. 231ff.; at the same time he speaks of a basic Pauline misunderstanding of the law (pp. 174ff.). This is not the place to enter critically into this Jewish interpretation of Paul.

[3] Konrad Weiß, 'Paulus—Priester der christlichen Kultgemeinde', *ThLZ* 79 (1954), cols. 355–64, has mistaken the figurative sense of this cultic passage, and tried to represent the Pauline apostolic office as that of a priestly and sacrificial service; this does not do justice to what Paul actually wrote.

[4] It is very interesting to see how Paul combines the theme of the holy remnant with the idea of God's people. God's people is the Church already gathered from Jews and Gentiles; and to it there will one day be added the Israel that is now blind and of which only a 'remnant' has so far accepted the message.

to the promise made to the fathers of Israel (Rom. 15.25ff.),[1] and he appeals for this service to be carried through in the right way, with prayers that it may succeed (Rom. 15.30ff.).

Then, as we are told in Acts 20f., Paul goes to Jerusalem with a large delegation from the Gentile Christian churches and the collection from his mission-field in Asia Minor, Macedonia, and Greece. And this journey to Jerusalem is nothing less than a sign of the Gentiles' eschatological thank-offering and the nations' pilgrimage to Zion. But it is in fact only a sign, for it is not the earthly Jerusalem, but the 'Jerusalem above', to which the eschatological people of God belongs (Gal. 4.21ff.).[2] It is therefore not the temple, but that band of the 'poor' living there in the midst of the still unbelieving Israel, that is the object of the thank-offering.[3] On the other hand, it is in Paul's mind that this visible demonstration of the Gentiles' worship which is already being realized will help to 'make Israel jealous' and so make it at last take hold of salvation. Thus Paul sees himself, as an apostle to the Gentiles, called at least indirectly to the service of Israel.[4] This

---

[1] On the collection and Paul's understanding of it cf. Georgi, *Kollekte*, esp. pp. 128ff. (on Rom. 15.27); for an older piece of research see Wilbur M. Franklin, *Die Kollekte des Paulus* (Diss. Heidelberg, 1938).

[2] Georgi, *Kollekte*, pp. 40ff., 43ff., 126ff., suggests a certain change in the Pauline view, and puts Gal. 4.21ff. into an earlier period; he thinks that through his argument with pneumatics he had to lay greater stress on the historical dimension. I cannot support this thesis, although its possibility cannot in principle be disputed.

[3] Eichholz, *EvTh* 21 (1961), pp. 18f., in stressing, beside the theme of close ecumenical association, the essential unity with Jerusalem as the place of the gospel's origin, has not taken enough account of the character of the collection as an eschatological sign. On the expressions 'the poor' and 'the saints' cf. Georgi, *Kollekte*, pp. 21ff., 126f. In my opinion, however, οἱ πτωχοί is to be understood as a traditional honorary title not only in Gal. 2.10, but also in Rom. 15.26, though it is explained here by the epexegetical genitive τῶν ἁγίων (cf. v. 25).

[4] This calls for another brief observation on Munck, *Paul and the Salvation of Mankind*. He argues that as Jerusalem was regarded as the goal of eschatological perfection, the apostle writes in Rom. 9–11 about an existing problem of his own day, namely about gaining the Jews, which was at last becoming possible (pp. 299ff.); he therefore goes with the Gentile delegation to Jerusalem to proclaim the fulfilment of the Old Testament prophecies and induce the Jews to accept the gospel (pp. 301ff.). But these observations, though partly useful, mean not only that Paul's arguments with Jewish Christianity are unjustifiably blunted but also that the theological importance of Rom. 9–11 is completely misunderstood, even if the polemics against a dogmatic evaluation in respect of the doctrine of predestination may be justified; and lastly the peculiar eschatological fragmentariness evident in Paul's treatment of the theme of the nations' pilgrimage is not taken into account; cf. Georgi, *Kollekte*, pp. 130ff. When Munck, *op. cit.*, pp. 196ff., opposes the view that by this letter Paul is either introducing himself to the Roman church or referring to the conditions in the church there—being rather of the opinion that in the letter to the Romans the apostle is setting out his faith in a manifesto that has grown out of a discussion (following T. W. Manson; similarly Étienne Trocmé, 'L'épître aux Romains et la

expectation of Paul's was not fulfilled; the Jews did not open their minds to the gospel, but used this journey of Paul and his Gentile Christian delegation as an opportunity to take him prisoner, so that all his plans for further missionary work were wrecked. Although this prevented him from completing his journey through the *oikoumenē*, the fact remains that he more than any other before him gave the signal for the gathering together of all the nations on earth.

---

méthode missionnaire de l'Apôtre Paul', *NTSt* 7, 1960/1, pp. 148–53)—it means that the alternatives offered are at least partly false; for it is beyond doubt that Paul wanted to pave the way for his own visit to Rome: 'In the letter to the Romans it is a question of equipping a vital working community', as Schrenk, *Studien zu Paulus*, p. 82, fittingly puts it. The question of the attitude towards the Roman church's problems has recently been taken up again both by Herbert Preisker, 'Das historische Problem des Römerbriefes', *Wiss. Zeitschr. d. Fr. Schiller-Universität Jena*, 1952/3, pp. 25–30, and by Günther Harder, 'Der konkrete Anlaß des Römerbriefes', *Theoe Viat* 6 (1954/8), pp. 13–24; the latter does not ask the troublesome question whether it was Jewish or Gentile Christians who received the letter—a mixed church is rightly assumed—but tries to show in detail how the problems of the letter to the Romans grew from acute situations in the church. But that is by no means convincing. Paul probably knew certain details about the Roman church and turned them to account, as is shown, e.g., by Rom. 14.1ff., where there are a number of special matters that strike us in view of I Cor. 8 and 10; but here, as in the broad development of his thoughts in Rom. 1–11, or in the usual parenesis of ch. 12f., he is concerned to grasp and present the problems as matters of principle, so that there is produced a kind of summary of his decisive theological insights.

V

MISSION IN THE SYNOPTIC GOSPELS AND THE ACTS OF THE APOSTLES

WE do not find anywhere else in the New Testament such a comprehensive presentation of and basis for mission as is given in Paul's writings. That does not mean, however, that there was less interest in mission during the post-Pauline period. We do indeed, as will be shown in a concluding chapter, find a certain separation of sending and gathering, of mission and care of the Church; but the missionary impulses are still very strong in the second half of the first century; and it is very instructive to see how the conceptions of the synoptists, including those in Acts, are determined by the concern for the spreading of the message among Jews and Gentiles.

I. MARK

It is a peculiar and significant fact that the oldest of our Gospels comes from Gentile Christianity. That does not mean that many traditions that go back to early Palestinian Christianity were not taken up and worked into it; but besides these, parts of the tradition that got their present form only in the sphere of Gentile Christianity are also included.[1] No one would take the author of the second Gospel for a Hellenist Jewish Christian, as, however close may be his ties with older views, his theological views are so far advanced beyond Jewish presuppositions[2] that not only his readers[3] but he himself, too, must belong to Gentile Christianity.[4]

[1] This is shown by the account of the transfiguration in Mark 9.2–8, as well as in the miracle narratives of Mark 5.25–34 and 6.47–52; cf. *Christologische Hoheitstitel*, pp. 309ff.

[2] That is clear especially from the title 'Son of God' which dominates his Christology, and which is understood throughout as denoting the essential character of Jesus, and characterizes his supernatural nature.

[3] Cf. the explanation of Jewish customs of purification in Mark 7.3f.

[4] All estimates as to the place of origin are simply conjectures. For the time of origin, the destruction of Jerusalem in AD 70 is to be considered as *terminus a quo* on the basis of Mark 12.1–9; 13.2, 7f.; 15.38. Cf. Adolf Jülicher and Erich Fascher, *Einleitung in das Neue Testament*, 1931⁷, pp. 296ff.; Günther Bornkamm, art. 'Evangelien synoptische', *RGG*³ II, cols. 753–66, esp. cols. 76of.

It is therefore natural that the Gentile mission has an important function. It is true that this has occasionally been disputed;[1] but although the theme is explicitly set out in only a few passages, it nevertheless implicitly dominates the whole presentation of Jesus' life and work.[2]

Mark divided his Gospel into three parts: Jesus' work among the people (1.14–8.26), the teaching that he gave his disciples (8.27–10.45), and the last controversies with his opponents leading on to his death and resurrection (10.46–16.8). Just as his teaching to the disciples forms the central part of the whole Gospel, so the first and third parts have a central section in Jesus' two discourses in chapters 4 and 13. It is only on these lines that we can understand the outline of the Marcan conception.[3]

In the *first part* (Mark 1.14–8.26) Jesus' activity among the people, like that of the Baptist (1.5) is directed first to Israel, especially to Galilee (1.14, 38f.), but already the result of his first appearance in the synagogue at Capernaum is that his fame spread πανταχοῦ εἰς ὅλην τὴν περίχωρον τῆς Γαλιλαίας ('throughout all the surrounding region of Galilee', 1.28). So we are soon told that great multitudes come, not only from Galilee, Judea and Jerusalem, but also from Idumea 'and from beyond the Jordan and from about Tyre and Sidon' (3.7f.). Although Jesus remains in Galilee till chapter 4 inclusive, the horizon is broadened from the beginning, and it is shown that his message reached the Gentiles as well as the Jews.[4] But even by the end of chapter 3 there comes the first fundamental controversy with official representatives of Judaism, and a rejection of Jesus (3.22–30). The parabolic discourse therefore points to the unavoidable separation between 'those outside'

[1] Cf. Kilpatrick's essay, mentioned on p. 71 above, in *Studies in the Gospels* pp. 145ff., which casts doubt, not only on the usual interpretation of Mark 13.10 and 14.9, but also on any fundamental importance of Mark 7.24ff., 11.17, and 15.39. He therefore arrives at the conclusion 'Universalism is absent from Mark' (p. 157). Similarly von Harnack, *Mission und Ausbreitung* I, p. 45 n. 2, had asserted that, apart from 13.10 and 14.9, Mark 'excluded the missionary question altogether'.

[2] Cf. esp. M. Kiddle, 'The Death of Jesus and the Admission of the Gentiles in St Mark', *JThSt* 35 (1934), pp. 45–50; R. H. Lightfoot, *Gospel Message of St Mark*, pp. 55ff., 60ff.; G. H. Boobyer, 'Galilee and Galileans in St Mark's Gospel', *Bulletin of the John Rylands Library* 25 (1952–3), pp. 340ff.; James M. Robinson, *The Problem of History in Mark* (SBT 21), 1957, pp. 64ff.

[3] On this cf. my brief remarks in Ferdinand Hahn, Wenzel Lohff, and Günther Bornkamm, *Die Frage nach dem historischen Jesus* (Evangelisches Forum 2), 1962, pp. 29f. I intend to offer my views on this in more detail later.

[4] We must not think of a coming only of the Jews living in those Gentile regions.

and the disciples (4.11f.), but at the end with the parable of the
mustard seed it also indicates—this is certainly true for the
evangelist—the coming of the Gentiles (4.30–32). It is significant
that, after crossing the lake (4.35–41), Jesus now for the first time
enters Gentile territory (5.1–20)—a step which leads to the
spreading of the news in the Decapolis (v. 19f.). Then Jesus is
once more on Galilean soil (5.21ff.),[1] the followers increase,[2] as
does also the hostility:[3] after the controversy about purification,
supported by officialdom, and after Jesus' repudiation of the
religious Judaism of his time (7.1–13), he again goes into Gentile
country, and comes back to Israelite territory only on his way to
the Passion. He goes 'to the region of Tyre' (7.24) and through
Sidon, and on his way to Galilee he comes to the Decapolis (7.31);[4]
from the country east of the Jordan he crosses into the Dalmanutha
district, where he is at once drawn into another dispute with the
Pharisees (8.11f.), which causes him to cross the lake again to the
north shore to Bethsaida, from where he continues in a northerly
direction to Caesarea Philippi (8.13, 22, 27). Thus the viewpoint
of the whole concluding section of the first part is Jesus' rejection
by the official representatives of Judaism, and a turning to the
Gentiles. That is indeed expressed programmatically in 7.24–30:
although Jesus would like to remain hidden,[5] a Gentile woman
comes to him and asks him for help; Jesus answers that the
children are to be fed first; but 'to the Jews first' already includes
the subsequent turning to the Gentiles.[6] As far as material goes,

---

[1] The journeys across the Lake of Gennesaret (Mark 6.32f., 45, 53) do not lead
to contact with the Gentile population.
[2] The growing pressure of the crowds is stressed from the beginning: Mark
1.32–34, 37; 1.45–2.2; 2.13; 3.7–10, 20; 4.1; 5.21; 6.30–33, 53–56; 8.1.
[3] The controversies begin with the complex of 2.1–3.6; there follow 3.22–30 and
7.1–13, then 8.11f.; 10.2–9 and the conflicts in Jerusalem.
[4] εἰς τὴν θάλασσαν τῆς Γαλιλαίας ἀνὰ μέσον τῶν ὁρίων Δεκαπόλεως ('. . . to the
Sea of Galilee, through the region of the Decapolis'): this disputed indication of
locality needs no correction; cf. Wellhausen, *Markus*, p. 73; Klostermann, *Markus*,
p. 73. The preceding narrative was localized in Tyre, and now Jesus' route leads to
the other famous Phoenician coastal town, and from there into the 'middle' of the
Decapolis. It is already indicating the journey's destination, which is to be reached
in 8.1.
[5] This intention of keeping his incognito occurs again in 9.30f., and is closely
related to the commands not to give away the messianic secret. In each case matters
so stand that Jesus' identity must become manifest; cf. Wilhelm Wrede, *Das Messias-
geheimnis in den Evangelien. Zugleich ein Beitrag zum Verständnis des Markusevangeliums*,
1901 (1963³), pp. 33ff.
[6] It is clear that both stories about feeding the multitude (6.32ff. and 8.1ff.) refer
to the eastern shore; but in 6.33 it is Galileans who follow Jesus there, whereas in

Mark has to rely here on a quite small number of narratives— that of the Gerasenes, of the Syrophoenician woman, and of the deaf-mute (this is localized in the Decapolis); but the purpose that is made clear by the editorial framework is unmistakable: not only does Jesus' work attract the Gentiles, but he himself turns to them.[1]

The *middle part* (Mark 8.27–10.45) is concentrated on the disciples, except for an occasional meeting with the 'crowd'. The localization of Peter's confession in Caesarea Philippi is determined by the tradition, but it may not be without significance for Mark that this decisive event takes place on Gentile soil. Having set out on this occasion the necessity for suffering, Jesus goes back from the Gentile country in the north to Galilee and Capernaum, and then on 'to the region of Judea and beyond the Jordan' (8.27; 9.30, 33; 10.1), 'going up to Jerusalem' (10.32). But this very course enables him to 'give his life as a ransom for many' (10.45), so that in this section, too, which is concentrated on the disciples, the universal aspect, directed to the salvation of all men, is dominant.

In the *concluding part* (Mark 10.46–16.8) there follows, with the Jews' final rejection of Jesus, explicit emphasis on the Gentiles' participation in salvation. First, in 11.1–12.12, Mark has com-

8.1ff. we must probably think of people from the country east of the Jordan. It has often been discussed whether, apart from the editorial framework, these stories themselves with their twelve and seven baskets refer symbolically to Jews and Gentiles; cf. G. H. Boobyer, 'The Miracles of the Loaves and the Gentiles in St Mark's Gospel', *Scottish Journal of Theology* 6 (1953), pp. 8off.; Robinson, *op. cit.*, p. 85; Sundwall, *Die Zusammensetzung des Markusevangeliums*, pp. 49f., supposes a connection with the twelve apostles and the Hellenists' seven deacons. But all this is uncertain. The editorial section in Mark 8.17–21 does not point to an interpretation of that kind, for it is a question there of the Christological secret that the disciples ought to have understood on the basis of the miracles of the loaves. In my opinion, Stoevesandt, *Jesus und die Heidenmission*, pp. 105ff., was right in holding that both the variants of the story give round figures such as are generally favoured.

[1] Marxsen, *Evangelist Markus*, pp. 33ff., has given undue weight to the concentration of the Gospels' presentation on Galilee; he actually asserts: 'The decisive proclamation takes place—always—in Galilee' (p. 39). It may be acknowledged that the localization of individual narratives originates in the sources (p. 45), but it is not apparent that the evangelist immediately corrects the resulting 'inconsistency' and directs Jesus' route back to Galilee (pp. 41ff.). His theory, obtained with reference to Lohmeyer, of the parousia that is expected in Galilee, is entirely problematical (pp. 47ff.). There is nothing to indicate that Mark simply included the neighbouring Gentile northern and eastern districts in the 'Galilee of the Gentiles' (Isa. 9.1; Matt. 4.15) as Lohmeyer assumes in *Markus*, p. 144; similarly Johannes Schreiber, 'Die Christologie des Markusevangeliums', *ZThK* 58 (1961), pp. 154–183, there pp. 171f.

posed a narrative that deserves our attention. However we may judge the connection between the triumphal entry and the cleansing of the temple, there is no doubt that the cleansing of the temple, and the question of Jesus' authority on the one hand, as well as the cursing of the fig-tree and the sayings about the miraculous power of faith and prayer on the other, belonged together in the pre-Marcan tradition.[1] Mark gave a new outlook to the story of the cursing, by relating it to the cleansing of the temple, and he supplemented the question of authority with the parable of the wicked tenants of the vineyard. He therefore understood the cleansing of the temple, the main point of which was for him the passage about the house of prayer for all the nations (11.17), in the light of the preceding parabolic action, as an indication of the judgment on the Jewish sanctuary;[2] and to the question of his authority, which he had at first left unanswered, he added a flat negative: the vineyard is to be taken from the tenants who have farmed it hitherto, and is to be given to others (12.9). As in 7.1ff. and 24ff., the controversy is clearly turned on to the theme of Jews and Gentiles, and now it is brought to bear on the temple in particular.[3] As is shown by the eschatological discourse and the story of the Passion, Mark maintains consistently in the concluding section the correlation of the judgment on the temple and the acceptance of the Gentiles. The saying about the destruction (and restoration) of the temple is taken up three times, and each time put in relation to the Gentiles. Jesus' temple saying which was discussed above appears throughout in Mark (as elsewhere in the New Testament) in a modified form.[4] The evangelist put it in brief first at the beginning of Jesus' second long discourse; in 13.1–4 the scene with the saying about the temple is supplemented by a transition with a question from the disciples, and the Christian apocalypse that was taken over was joined to it (13.5ff.).[5]

[1] That is, Mark 11.15–17, 27–33 and Mark 11.13f., 20–25.

[2] Cf. *Christologische Hoheitstitel*, pp. 170ff.

[3] Mark 11.17 is certainly taken over from the tradition. The evangelist could keep this interpretation in spite of the theme of the destruction of the temple, because what he was especially concerned with was the Gentiles' worship, which was not possible in the Jerusalem temple and within the Judaism that rejected Jesus. Mark 11.17 gives no ground for moving the origin of the Gospel into the period before AD 70. Matthew and Luke have deleted the words πᾶσιν τοῖς ἔθνεσιν, as they did not fit into their setting.

[4] On the temple saying cf. ch. II, p. 37 n. 1.

[5] The evangelist probably took over the temple saying here in a ready-made

As already shown,[1] Mark distinguished, more clearly than did the original version, between a first preliminary epoch and the eschatological events proper. The tradition spoke of the 'desolating sacrilege' (v. 14), probably referring, in accordance with the prophecy in Daniel, to an occurrence in Jerusalem, but certainly not to the destruction of the city and the sanctuary by the Romans. When Mark joins the prophecy of the destruction of the temple to 13.5ff., and in 13.4 has the question asked outright when 'this' is to happen, and moreover what the sign will be that 'these things are all to be accomplished', he is co-ordinating the destruction of the temple with the historical events that precede the eschatological catastrophe, viz. with 7f., whereas he regards the events described in 14ff. as a 'sign' for the completion.[2] That means, therefore, that the interval up to the beginning of apocalyptic events proper is marked by the destruction of the temple as well as by the mission to the Gentiles (v. 10).[3] In 13.2 Mark could not take over the saying about the temple in its old eschatological sense; he related its first sentence to the historical event of the Jewish war, and deleted the later sentence.[4] But he knows it also

---

framework, in connection with v. 1. The introductory genitive absolute, however, is certainly an editorial addition. Besides, the evangelist himself is responsible for indicating the place in v. 3, and for the disciples' question in v. 4.

[1] Cf. ch. III, pp. 69f.

[2] On this passage we must briefly investigate Marxsen, *Evangelist Markus*, pp. 101ff. As already mentioned, he regards the unity of the chapter as the work of the evangelist, who has worked on divergent material (pp. 106, 112). He lays great stress on the phrase 'beginning of the sufferings' in v. 8, and on the inclusion of the events of 5–13 in the eschatological drama (p. 117); but in my opinion this does not hold good for Mark. Verses 5–13 are to be seen against the background of the events of AD 66–70 (pp. 116ff.), and this is true at least of 7f.; it is erroneous to say that neither the first nor the second part of the disciples' question is answered in 5–13, and that the prophecy of the destruction of the temple aims at v. 14 (pp. 121ff.). For it is no longer a matter there of an internal historical occurrence. The argument that 14b summons the Jerusalem church to flee to Pella, Galilee being regarded as the middle of the earth, is quite untenable (pp. 123ff.; but Pella is not in Galilee, and this point is not met by the generalized definition of the idea 'Galilee' on p. 60). On the contrary, Conzelmann, *ZNW* 50 (1959), p. 215, does not assume really eschatological events before 13.24–27, and thinks that Mark intended to relate the whole section 5–23 to history (pp. 215, 216ff.). But it is the double formation of the events before the parousia in Mark 13.5–13 and 14–23 that is the distinguishing feature of this chapter (cf. the double ὅταν δέ in 7 and 14, while the ἐν ἐκείναις ταῖς ἡμέραις in 24 takes up the idea of the shortening of time in 20, and is intended to join 14–23 and 24–27 closely together).

[3] As a further theme the sufferings of the disciples are brought in, as in the middle part 8.27ff.

[4] It is possible that Mark knew the saying about the temple in its original form, but abbreviated and re-shaped it for this context; similarly also Marxsen, *Evangelist Markus*, p. 113.

in that other setting of 14.58, in which the double formation is kept, but for which the text is given a new ecclesiological interpretation.[1] This temple saying stands in some isolation in the trial scene before the Council, and is not carried directly any further.[2] But it is taken up again in the word of mockery in 15.29b: the Jews, who reject Jesus and make merry about what he has said, have no share in the fulfilment of the promise. Thus the presupposition is created for the real climax of the story of the Passion in 15.38f., the tearing of the temple curtain, and the confession of the Gentile centurion. The only editorial intervention is 39. This is shown by the introductory 39a, which expressly refers back to the death in all its circumstances, and in the confession, which introduces into the story of the Passion an entirely new theme, one that is characteristic of Mark; 33 and 38 also belong together as the miraculous signs that form the setting of Jesus' death. However the tearing of the temple curtain may have been understood in the pre-Marcan tradition, in conjunction with 39 it can only be a sign of destruction.[3] Jesus' death, with which the Jews claimed to pronounce judgment on him, was, in fact, the final judgment on Jewish worship and thus on Judaism in general.[4] But simultaneously with this judgment there takes place the acceptance of the Gentiles.[5] With Jesus' death the decision is made about the temple as well as about the Gentiles.

---

[1] On this cf. ch. III, p. 76. The various forms of the saying about the temple in the New Testament show that the early Church had appreciable difficulties with the promise; these arose on the one hand from the actual destruction of the temple in AD 70, but also on the other hand where the Church had given up all connection with the Jewish cult. Whereas in the one case the eschatological promise had to be historicized, in the other it was spiritualized. In John 2.19 there is a christological instead of an ecclesiological interpretation. In so far as the original utterance was kept, it was put into the mouths of opponents as mockery (Mark 15.29b par.) or neutralized by δύναμαι (Matt. 26.61).

[2] It can be seen from vv. 57 and 59 that the saying about the temple in Mark 14.58 is inserted secondarily into the trial scene. It is highly probable that this insertion goes back to Mark himself.

[3] Hauck, *Markus*, p. 190, and Taylor, *Mark*, p. 596, point to the now open access to God (it is a matter there of the inner curtain); but it is much more likely, both in the pre-Marcan tradition and for Mark himself, that the sign indicates calamity (outer or inner curtain), especially as there is interesting later Jewish evidence for this; cf. Billerbeck I, pp. 1045f.; Klostermann, *Markus*, p. 167; André Pelletier, 'La tradition synoptique du "voile déchiré" à la lumière des réalités archéologiques', *RechScRel* 46 (1958), pp. 161–80.

[4] Lohmeyer, *Markus*, pp. 345f., points out the connection with the saying about the temple.

[5] On this cf. Kiddle, *JThSt* 35 (1934), pp. 47ff.; also Lightfoot, *Gospel Message of St Mark*, pp. 55ff.; Robinson, *Problem of History in Mark*, p. 84.

With the confession ἀληθῶς οὗτος ὁ ἄνθρωπος υἱὸς θεοῦ ἦν ('Truly this man was the Son of God') the blood poured out as a ransom for many (10.45; 14.24) is accepted by the Gentiles. And from here there follows the logical foundation of the mission to the Gentiles, as the evangelist has expressed clearly in the editorial passage 14.9: the announcement of Jesus' death and the proclamation of the gospel in the whole world belong indissolubly together.[1]

[1] The literary and historical criticism of the story of the anointing is difficult and controversial. The tradition in Luke 7.36–50 is in my opinion not to be regarded as a variant of Mark 14.3–9 and John 12.1–8 (as it is, for instance, by Julius Wellhausen, *Das Evangelium Lucae*, 1904, p. 31; Bultmann, *Synoptic Tradition*, pp. 20f.), but as an independent tradition which may have been influenced in the anointing theme of 38 fin., 46 by the Bethany narrative. In John 12.1–8, on the other hand, a single theme has been taken over from that story from the Lucan special source in so far as here it is not Jesus' head, but his feet, that are anointed; the drying with the hair is added (3), and this fits in with the wetting with tears (Luke 7.38), but not with anointing. Moreover, there is in the Johannine narrative some influence of the Mary-Martha tradition and the editorial link with the story of Lazarus (1f.), as well as the introduction of Judas in 4 and 6; on this cf. Bultmann, *Johannes*, pp. 316ff. In the basic structure this form of narrative corresponds to the no doubt older form of the tradition in Mark 14.3–9. But what about this narrative itself? It has been asserted at one time or another that it has several points, that it originally ended at 7, 8f. being a later addition that changed the paradigm into a legend; so Dibelius, *From Tradition to Gospel*, pp. 6of.; Bultmann, *Synoptic Tradition*, pp. 36f. On the other hand, Georg Bertram, *Die Leidensgeschichte Jesu und der Christuskult* (FRLANT 32), 1922, pp. 16f., prefers to regard 9 as a more original theme, and 7 and 8 as later insertions. But the close connection of the themes must be noticed. Verses 6f. [*sic*] are already directed at what the woman has done; not without reason is the 'always' contrasted with a 'not always'; and this prepares for v. 8. The story must therefore from the beginning have been brought into line with the uniqueness of the act and have contained an indication of Jesus' death. Joachim Jeremias, 'Die Salbungsgeschichte Mc 14.3–9', *ZNW* 35 (1936), pp. 75–82, has appositely pointed out the archaic features, and shown, moreover, that the later Jewish distinction between 'works of love', among which is the burial of the dead, and 'alms' is assumed. The woman's 'good work' to Jesus is above almsgiving. Verse 9 is more difficult. Joachim Jeremias, 'Mc 14.9', *ZNW* 44 (1952/3), pp. 103–7, has reconsidered the view that he expressed in the former essay, that it is a matter of a secondary addendum; he has pointed to the style of the introductory wording of v. 9, and on the one hand drawn attention to the idea of the 'memory of God' at the last judgment, and on the other hand brought in the eschatological message of victory proclaimed by the angel; similarly in his *Jesus' Promise*, p. 22. But this thesis needs a correction. It is true that the introductory wording and the memory theme belong to the old Semitic tradition; ample material for the 'memory' concept is provided by the same writer, *Eucharistic Words*, pp. 159–65 (IV, 2d; rev. ed., V, 4). But I think it is out of the question that ὅπου ἐὰν κηρυχθῇ τὸ εὐαγγέλιον εἰς ὅλον τὸν κόσμον ('wherever the gospel is preached in the whole world') belongs to it; this passage is a later addition; cf. Stoevesandt, *Jesus und die Heidenmission*, pp. 36f. We see this from the iterative ὅπου, which cannot be understood (with Jeremias, *ZNW* 44 [1952/3], p. 106) temporally ('when'), but follows from the significance of every word in the Greek phrase. As the parallel in Mark 13.10 shows, the terminology of Hellenist Jewish Christianity is adopted here (cf. ch. III, pp. 7off.). The only possible explanation is that the evangelist himself, referring to Mark 13.10 and misunderstanding the original significance of 9b, intended to give a further pointer to the Gentile mission and connect it directly with

But what is the position of the *Jews* in Mark's ideas? According to chapters 1–4 there can be no doubt that many disciples come from Israel. It is not without reason that the πρῶτον ('Ιουδαίοις) is taken up into the Gospel in 7.27a. But the missionary purpose is directed nearly exclusively to the Gentiles. The sending out in Mark 6.7–13 is not limited to Israel, nor does it unmistakably lead beyond Israel; but as with the story of Jesus as a whole, it is merely the beginning of what has been happening ever since, and so it is the basis of the disciples' task after Easter. As Jesus already in his lifetime went out beyond Israel, so with his death every restriction disappears the more completely, and the gospel is preached to all the nations in the world, with no need of any further missionary command to do so.[1] Moreover, we shall hardly go wrong if we suppose that Mark's one-sided emphasis on the preaching of the gospel among the nations was because he felt that by his time the period during which salvation was being offered to Israel had already passed. Jesus himself took account of Israel's right of priority, but with his crucifixion Israel forfeited this. Although in the period after Easter the Church may have turned to Israel with a renewed offer of salvation, the judgment on Israel was in any case settled by the destruction of the temple, and the decision was taken to turn finally and exclusively to the Gentiles. The *heilsgeschichtlich* πρῶτον of Mark 7.27a is replaced by the eschatological πρῶτον of 13.10. Thus Mark understood the πρῶτον 'Ιουδαίοις in the sense of two sequential periods, one of which already belonged to the past. The decision on Israel has been taken, and so the way has become free for the salvation of the Gentiles.[2] Thus Mark develops in his Gospel what was radically

---

Jesus' death. For as this woman's action is associated with Jesus' death, she will be remembered in the whole world; or conversely: because the remembrance of this woman is accompanied by the proclamation of Jesus' death, which has taken place ὑπὲρ πολλῶν, therefore the gospel is going out into the whole world.

[1] It should be noted that in Mark the sending out comes immediately after the rejection in Nazareth (6.1–6). Matthew has it quite differently, with the introductory 9.36ff. before the words of commission; cf. Stählin, *EMZ* 7 (1950), p. 99. Thus, just as the rejection in Jesus' home town is followed by the more far-reaching mission of Mark 6.7ff., so the rejection by Israel is necessarily followed by the preaching of the gospel in the whole world. From this we may consider whether the δεῖ in 13.10 did not contain another meaning for Mark through the correlation—so essential in his Gospel—of the preaching to the Gentiles with the rejection of Jesus by the Jews.

[2] The ἔθνη idea plays no special part in Mark; he adopted it in 11.17 and 13.10, but he did not use it in 14.9. What is said of the Gentiles in 10.42 is illustrated in

expressed in speech already coined and then taken over by Paul in I Thess. 2.15f. Even if I Thess. 2.15f. does not at once exclude what Paul wrote in Rom. 9–11, it is evident from Mark that very different conclusions could be drawn from a thesis of that kind.[1]

2. MATTHEW

Matthew's Gospel is of the greatest importance for the question of the mission in early Christianity. On the one hand it contains the many Jewish Christian elements, which make possible a conclusion *a posteriori* on the particularist view of the mission (discussed above), and on the other hand it adopts (28.18–20) the unit of tradition that is fundamental for the Gentile mission of Hellenist Jewish Christianity. As can easily be seen, Matthew has allowed an important place both to the particularist expressions in his word of commission and to the missionary command at the end of his Gospel. But how did he himself understand the missionary task? How does he weld these two elements into a unity?

It would be well to start, not from chapter 10 nor from the missionary command, but from Matt. 24.14. A comparison with Mark 13.10 shows that Matthew has made an important change in this passage. We shall see from the following analysis that it is inadmissible to regard this form of the saying about the world-wide preaching of the gospel as an old parallel tradition to Mark 13.10,[2] for the editorial marks are too obvious. There are therefore a large number of connecting lines to the rest of the Gospel; and so this verse presents quite a programmatic statement, from which the Matthean view of the mission can be made clear. The pre-Marcan statement of Mark 13.10 has a close connection with the apocalyptic conception of the eschatological discourse. Mark

---

15.1ff., 16ff. In relation to the Passion, the idea is once more used editorially in 10.33, probably in an intentional climax: in 8.31 Jesus is rejected by the Jews, in 9.31 he 'will be delivered into the hands of men', and in 10.33 he will be delivered 'to the Gentiles'.

[1] As an addendum to this section I refer to Manfred Karnetzki, 'Die galiläische Redaktion im Markusevangelium', *ZNW* 52 (1961), pp. 238–72, which carries out a completely erroneous analysis of the historical and editorial aspects, but makes useful references to the Gospel's view of the mission.

[2] Despite Jeremias, *Jesus' Promise*, pp. 22f.

changed nothing of this, although he divided more sharply into periods, and regarded the mission among the nations as a mark of the historical epoch preceding the eschatological events proper. Matthew considerably strengthened this line of thought by deleting πρῶτον and δεῖ; with him it is only the external arrangement in the apocalyptic framework that remains; the word itself has got rid of the features of the apocalyptic way of thinking.[1] It is no longer a matter of ascertaining an eschatological necessity laid down by God, but of Jesus' own promise of what is to take place between his resurrection and return. Like Mark, Matthew speaks of a κηρυχθῆναι, only it must be noticed that with him the verb has a slightly different meaning, for Matthew consistently distinguished between κηρύσσειν and διδάσκειν, the first relating to the message of God's reign and the second to the exposition of the law.[2] It is true that his Gospel speaks of preaching as well as teaching in relation to the people,[3] just as on the other hand there is still preaching among the disciples; yet for Matthew the preaching has primarily a missionary function.[4] It has the character of an announcement and promise of salvation, aiming at the μαθητεύειν which precedes the actual 'teaching'.[5] From this it is made clear that the content of the preaching in Matt. 24.14 is given as τοῦτο τὸ εὐαγγέλιον τῆς βασιλείας ('this gospel of the kingdom'). We must first notice that in general Matthew uses εὐαγγέλιον only in con-

[1] This statement is not invalidated by Matt. 24.14, for, of course, for Matthew the carrying out of the mission remains to the end, though this does not involve his using specifically apocalyptic categories.
[2] Excellently set out by G. Bornkamm, 'End-expectation and Church', in Bornkamm, Barth, and Held, p. 38 n. 1.
[3] On this use of διδάσκειν cf. Matt. 4.23; 9.35; 11.1; 13.54; 22.33. For κηρύσσειν there are many individual texts; see concordance.
[4] It can hardly be by chance that the κηρύσσειν idea does not appear when the disciples themselves are being taught. But it is characteristic that the disciples are present whenever the people are preached to.
[5] In addition to Matt. 28.19, already mentioned above (cf. ch. III, p. 67), the μαθητεύειν idea appears in 13.52 in the phrase γραμματεὺς μαθητευθεὶς τῇ βασιλείᾳ τῶν οὐρανῶν, and in 27.57 in the editorial change in the characterization of Joseph of Arimathea; elsewhere it occurs in the New Testament only in Acts 14.21. That it is a specifically Matthean word is shown by the significance that the idea of following Christ and the theme of discipleship have in this Gospel particularly; cf. Bornkamm, 'End-expectation and Church' in Bornkamm, Barth and Held, pp. 40f. We can see from the close co-ordination of preaching, the calling of the disciples, and doctrine in Matt. 4.17, 23ff.; 4.18ff.; 5.1ff., that the relation of μαθητεύειν and διδάσκειν in Matt. 28.19a, 20a in particular is typically Matthean. As a seal of discipleship, baptism is added in 28.19b. The wording of 13.52, mentioned above, would occur nowhere but in Matthew in this form.

junction with κηρύσσειν.[1] He therefore wants to have the act of preaching the gospel emphasized, and this is fully in line with the very early Christian use of εὐαγγέλιον.[2] If he has added the demonstrative 'this',[3] which is not in the Marcan source, it is a reference to the handing on of the gospel that was preached by Jesus himself, as it appears in Matthew's Gospel.[4]

Moreover, Matthew particularly points out the content of the gospel—it is a matter of preaching 'the gospel of the kingdom'. This had already come in with the Baptist, who was the first to proclaim the nearness of the eschatological reign of God. Jesus took up this message and carried it further; but he is not merely, like John, a man who prepared the way, for with him the fulfilment of the Old Testament promises has come.[5] It was with this message that Jesus entrusted his disciples: according to Matt. 10.1, 7 he bestowed on them the ἐξουσία ('authority') to preach and to cast out demons, and told them to preach, as they went, that the kingdom of heaven was at hand. With that the bridge was thrown across to Matt. 24.14; 26.13; and 28.18–20.

But in this connection we must make clear just what Matthew meant by the βασιλεία idea. There is no doubt about his strongly futuristic interpretation; we need only remind ourselves of the sayings about entering the βασιλεία or about judgment and the accomplishment of salvation. But in contrast to this there are now and again not only isolated *logia* about the presence of the reign

---

[1] Matt. 4.23; 9.35; 24.14; 26.13. The other kinds of usage in Mark are deleted; cf. Mark 1.1, 15; 8.35; 10.29.

[2] In Matt. 24.14 the evangelist is in line with the source in this regard; but in his case greater weight attaches to the joining of 'gospel' and 'preached'.

[3] It stands where the reference is not to Jesus' own preaching, but to preaching by others: 24.14; 26.13. In both passages there are at the same time the passive of κηρύσσειν (differently from 4.23 and 9.35) as well as ἐν ὅλῃ τῇ οἰκουμένῃ (or ἐν ὅλῳ τῷ κόσμῳ).

[4] But the demonstrative 'this gospel' can in no case refer to the 'speech complexes' in Matthew, as is said by Marxsen, *Evangelist Markus*, p. 82. In the preaching of 'this gospel' in 24.14 it is not specially a matter of the content of the eschatological discourse, nor can this thesis be applied in any way to 26.13.

[5] In this context the quotations from the Old Testament are important, because they express the Matthean purpose clearly. The Baptist's preaching in Matt. 3.1–3 takes up Isa. 40.3 with the theme of preparing a way in the desert; on the other hand, in 4.12–17, at the beginning of Jesus' ministry, with the same message of the nearness of God's reign as in 3.2, the messianic text of Isa. 9.1f. is brought in. On this cf. Bornkamm, 'End-expectation', *op. cit.*, pp. 15f. We find also, in relation to Jesus' preaching of the reign of God that has drawn near, the passages with 'the gospel of the kingdom' in 4.23 and 9.35.

of God,[1] but likewise the union of the βασιλεία idea with κηρύσσειν and κηρύσσειν τὸ εὐαγγέλιον. Besides, we have to distinguish in the introductory formulae of the parables between the future ὁμοιωθήσεται (7.24, 26) or τότε ὁμοιωθήσεται ἡ βασιλεία τῶν οὐρανῶν (25.1), where there is in each case reference to a clearly future decision, and the more frequent cases with ὁμοία ἐστιν or ὡμοιώθη ἡ βασιλεία τῶν οὐρανῶν—a distinction that must not be put aside too quickly. The parables in chapter 13, like those of 18.23ff.; 20.1ff.; 22.1ff., namely the parables of the weeds among the wheat, the grain of mustard seed and the leaven, the hidden treasure, the pearl merchant and the fishing-net, but also those of forgiveness experienced and disregarded, of the hiring of labourers for the vineyard and the invitation to the marriage feast, obviously have to do at the same time with present reality. The exposition of the parables in chapter 13 agrees with this. In Mark the interpretation of the parables has only a formal function as pointing to the ἐπίλυσις given to the disciples, but in Matthew the individual features are stressed: the seed scattered on the field with its four kinds of soil is 'the word of the kingdom', the good seed in the parable of the weeds is 'the sons of the kingdom', and the cultivated ground is the kingdom of the Son of man.[2] Of course, the interpretation of the parable of the weeds in particular shows that the winnowing is still to come, and that the final salvation will dawn only with the future βασιλεία τοῦ πατρός.[3] Thus the parables are to be understood, just as in Jesus' preaching, from the point of view of the depicted course of events as a whole; and from the sowing till the reaping, from the common growth of the good seed and the weeds till the gathering and winnowing, they are to be related to the Kingdom of God.[4] According to Matt. 13.10ff., 19a the 'nearness' of God's reign is

[1] Matt. 5.3b, 10b, with the present in the second sentence in contrast to the future of the other beatitudes; later especially Matt. 11.12; 12.28; but also Matt. 18.1, 4; 19.14.

[2] Matt. 13.19 (Matthew only); 13.38, 41 (special material).

[3] The distinction between the reign of the Son of man and of the Father is not consistently followed out in Matthew; the former can take on a future character in 16.28, and on the other hand in many passages the reign of God has a present significance.

[4] Cf. Nils Alstrup Dahl, 'The Parables of Growth' *StTh* 5 (1951 [Lund, 1952]), pp. 132–66. Here we are not to entertain a modern idea of development, or support the idea of a human realization of God's reign on earth; on the contrary, the theme of growth stresses the nature of the miraculous, and signifies above all the realization of salvation in this world; but this must be understood from the point of view of its bearing on the unrestricted future revelation of the reign of God.

understood in the sense that it comes about in the word and in the preaching—that is, in the proclamation to which the συνιέναι, the faith of men, corresponds. So it is possible to speak of the μυστήρια τῆς βασιλείας. This, unlike the singular form in Mark, has no Christological meaning, but relates to the preaching and to the gathering of the Church. Those who are brought together by the call are the 'sons of the kingdom'. Whether, indeed, they enter the Kingdom of God in the last days, however, depends on whether they truly fulfil the will of God;[1] it will appear only on the day of judgment who among these κλητοί '(called') belongs to the ἐκλεκτοί ('chosen').[2] Because the reality of the Kingdom of God is still hidden in the word, 'thy kingdom come' remains the constant prayer of the disciples.[3] Thus the βασιλεία idea in Matthew, in spite of the great emphasis on futurity, must not be explained solely from that point of view.[4]

We come back to Matt. 24.14. ἐν ὅλῃ τῇ οἰκουμένῃ stands in clear contrast to Matt. 10.5f., 23 (15.24), but agrees exactly in essence with 28.19.[5] It is not an adequate explanation to say that whereas Matt. 10 refers only to the sending out of the disciples during Jesus' lifetime 24.14 and 28.19 refer to the period after Easter. For it is quite clear that in chapter 10 the historical situation is

---

[1] In this context one should particularly note Matt. 6.33 with its idea of ζητεῖν, seeking the reign of God.

[2] There is no parallel to Matt. 22.14 in the New Testament.

[3] It is interesting that in Matthew (6.10) this petition in the Lord's Prayer is supplemented by 'thy will be done on earth as it is in heaven'.

[4] Trilling, *Das wahre Israel*, pp. 119ff., has also seen that the futuristic interpretation is not satisfactory, but he quite erroneously regards the idea of God's reign as a general phenomenon ranged above the Old and New Testament. This ignores both the indispensable eschatological element and the purpose of Matt. 13. In Matt. 21.43a the reference is to Jesus' rejected offer of salvation to Israel, not to a previously given reign of God, and an eschatological one at that. We may also point out the sharp break in the *Heilsgeschichte* that Matthew regards as coming with the Baptist; cf *Christologische Hoheitstitel*, pp. 374ff., 379f.

[5] When Harder, *Theol/Viat* 4 (1952), p. 79, says: ' "ἐν ὅλῃ τῇ οἰκουμένῃ" need not mean that the gospel is preached to all nations, but that it is preached to Jews in the whole world', he is unconvincing. Matt. 24.14 cannot be interpreted from 10.1, but should be understood as parallel to 26.13 and 28.18. The οἰκουμένη idea occurs in Matthew in this passage only; but the juxtaposition of ὅλη ἡ οἰκουμένη, ὅλος ὁ κόσμος, and 'in heaven and on earth' in Matt. 24.14; 26.13 and 28.18 is significant, for here it is a question of the whole extent of the Lord's reign; to this there is added πάντα τὰ ἔθνη in 24.14 and 28.19. Otto Michel, art. οἶκος, οἰκουμένη in *ThWb* V, p. 160, supposes that the phrase ἐν ὅλῃ τῇ οἰκουμένῃ is taken over by the evangelist from colloquial Hellenistic Greek. The word οἰκουμένη denotes the inhabited earth, and had acquired in Hellenism an increasingly political and legal sense (*ThWb* V, p. 159 n. 1). This fits admirably here with the legal sense contained in εἰς μαρτύριον πᾶσιν τοῖς ἔθνεσιν (see below).

arranged for the disciples' mission in the time after Jesus' resurrection, as indeed all the longer discourses of the Gospel directly concern the Church. But before the relation of Israel and the world mission can be determined in greater detail, a further observation must be taken into account.

In Matthew the opposition of Jews and Gentiles, without being simply abolished, is in a far-reaching way broken by another view, in which the contrast is between those who believe and those who do not believe the message of Jesus and his disciples. Seen in this light, the ideas in λαός and ἔθνος have undergone a remarkable change. The former is used as early as 1.21 for those who are released from their sins by Jesus, and in 21.43 the latter is applied to the 'nation producing the fruits of the kingdom of God',[1] a clear refusal being given to the representatives of Israel. Thus both these terms are applied to the new people of God, and are used by the evangelist in the same sense as the ἐκκλησία idea, behind which there stands the Old Testament *qāhāl* concept.[2] For this reason even the customary plural use of ἔθνη in some passages loses its conventional sense of 'Gentiles' and is used with the meaning of 'nations'.[3]

Although it is apparent that Israel is largely unrepentant and has called forth judgment on itself,[4] the evangelist and his church regard themselves as inwardly and outwardly tied to Israel.[5] The commissioning words of chapter 10 strongly emphasize the inalienable task of preaching the gospel to God's ancient people. It

[1] Trilling, *op. cit.*, pp. 37ff., has gone thoroughly into the significance of the Matthean form of the parable of the vineyard.

[2] Matthew, however, avoids using terms like 'the true Israel', 'the new Israel', etc. The offer is still made to Israel. The evangelist therefore probably wants nothing said about the new Israel till the eschatological fulfilment dawns with its new order; cf. Matt. 19.28. On the other hand, as Matt. 16.18, 19 show clearly, the *ecclesia* idea is clearly distinguished from the future *basileia*; 'My (i.e. Jesus') church' already belongs to the present reality of God's reign; and this is shown particularly in the authority to bind and loose, but it still stands under the eschatological proviso of the judgment and the accomplishment of salvation. On this cf. G. Bornkamm, 'End-expectation' in Bornkamm, Barth, and Held, pp. 15ff., 45ff.

[3] Of course, in many cases ἔθνη is used quite traditionally in Matthew—we may think merely of 6.32; 10.5b; 20.19, 25. On the other hand, however, it can be recognized in the sense of 'nations' in the pre-Matthean tradition in 25.31–46 (v. 32). For the specifically Matthean application of the idea cf. (besides 21.43) 4.15; 10.18; 12.18, 21; 24.9, and, of course, 24.14 and 28.19.

[4] Cf. Matt. 13.13ff.; 23.29ff., and the Matthean form of the story of the passion; on this cf. Trilling, *op. cit.*, pp. 48ff., 57ff.

[5] Cf. G. Bornkamm, 'End-expectation', *op. cit.*, pp. 21f., and G. D. Kilpatrick, *The Origins of the Gospel according to St Matthew*, 1946, pp. 101ff., 124ff.

is Israel that is offered the Kingdom of God, which has now drawn near, and it is therefore the Israelites who are called in 8.12 'sons of the kingdom'.[1] Matthew lets it be seen particularly clearly that the Church regards itself primarily as the band of disciples from the Jews, as the lost sheep of Israel to whom Jesus has come.

Although it is thus turned towards Israel, Matthew's church is open to the Gentiles. It knows that many Gentiles have shamed the Jews by their faith (8.5ff.; 15.21ff.). It realizes that it has a mission to all nations, and that it must deliver its message εἰς μαρτύριον πᾶσιν τοῖς ἔθνεσιν. The meaning of this much-discussed phrase in Matt. 24.14, similar to one in 10.18,[2] is explained by the whole context of the Gospel. Even in the context of Jesus' first appearance in his ministry, 'Galilee of the Gentiles' is spoken of in the quotation from Isaiah in Matt. 4.15, as well as elsewhere, and shows the fundamental openness of Jesus' gospel to the nations.[3] The parabolic discourse in chapter 13 also opens to view a universal horizon. The Old Testament quotation in 12.18–21 speaks still more clearly of ἀπαγγέλλειν κρίσιν τοῖς ἔθνεσιν ('proclaiming justice to the Gentiles'), and of the Gentiles' hope in his name,[4] the former words being connected with ἕως ἂν ἐκβάλῃ εἰς νῖκος τὴν κρίσιν ('till he brings justice to victory')—that is, with the idea of establishing and carrying out justice in the whole world.[5] In this 'victory' for which the nations hope, one will have to think, not of the resurrection and exaltation of Jesus, but of the συντέλεια τοῦ αἰῶνος ('close of the age'), when all φυλαὶ τῆς γῆς ('tribes of the earth') will beat their breasts, and the ἐκλεκτοί will be gathered in by the angels when the Son of man appears in power and glory (24.30f.). From this we can also explain the expression εἰς μαρτύριον πᾶσιν τοῖς ἔθνεσιν: the κρίσις that is going out over the whole οἰκουμένη and the victory of divine justice assume that all nations

---

[1] In this passage 'sons of the kingdom' means that the eschatological reign of God should be theirs by virtue of their belonging to God's ancient people, that they should have been able to become 'children' = those who belong to and share in salvation.

[2] Cf. Hermann Strathmann, art. μάρτυς,' etc., *ThWb* IV, pp. 508f.

[3] As in Mark, the parable of the mustard seed (Matt. 13.31f.) is to be mentioned, and further the parable of the fishing-net (13.47–50), and that of the weeds among the wheat, with its interpretation which is quite unmistakable in this respect (13.24–30, 36–43). It may be pointed out in this context that Mark 3.7f. is adopted in Matt. 4.24f.

[4] On the form of the text cf. Krister Stendahl, *The School of St Matthew* (Acta Seminarii Neotest. Upsaliensis XX), 1954, pp. 107ff.

[5] On this cf. Gerhard Barth, 'Matthew's Understanding of the Law', in Bornkamm, Barth, and Held, pp. 125ff., 141f.

have been confronted with the gospel; this can take place in the context of judgment as well as through the missionary preaching. The question, therefore, whether εἰς μαρτύριόν τινι has a positive or a negative meaning does not arise here, because both are taken into account;[1] but the decisive aspect remains the validity and nature of the witness with which the gospel is proclaimed before the whole world.

'And then the end will come', we are finally told in Matt. 24.14 —that is, when God will finally confirm and make effective the justice that has already been proclaimed. In view of the gospel which has been preached, there is, of course, to be a separation, not only among Jews but also among non-Jews; it is not for nothing that just before, in 24.9, there is the sentence 'You will be hated by all nations'. Nevertheless the Gentiles as well as the Jews share in God's reign, and the missionary activity is directed to all peoples on the ground of the risen Lord's command.

In this conception as a whole, Matthew can find room for the most diverse traditional material, and has no need to fight shy of the particularist sayings. But all in all, how does he regard the relationship of the mission among Israel and among the Gentiles? Here the pattern 'First—then', such as we know in Mark and Luke, will not do at all.[2] In Matthew each of the two missions, Jewish and Gentile, involves the other. Just as in Jesus' work among Israel the horizon became visible for work among the Gentiles, the same is true for the disciples. They know that they are sent to Israel, and yet they must not lose sight of the world of the nations. Just as the earthly Jesus, who was himself sent to Israel, commissioned them to work among God's ancient people, so the risen and exalted Lord gave the command, as Lord of the whole world, for the mission among all nations. For Matthew it is, so to say, a question of two concentric circles which necessarily belong together, and what he wants to assert in his own way is the priority of the mission to Israel and the permanent obligation towards it—for without Israel as the centre there would indeed be no salvation. This mission, however, is only carried out rightly if at the same time the universal commission is observed by work-

---

[1] That is how Matthew will have understood 8.4 par. Mark 1.44; he has deleted the purely negative use in Mark 6.11.
[2] This is rightly set out by Trilling, *op. cit.*, pp. 114f.

ing among all nations.[1] In this way Matthew succeeds in comprising in a view that is all his own the various older conceptions of the mission.

3 . LUKE

In Luke's Gospel and in Acts the problems are somewhat simpler, for the main ideas come out more clearly.[2]

There is no direct parallel to Mark 13.10; in the eschatological discourse of Luke 21.5ff. the missionary task is not mentioned at all. For Mark's reference to the world-wide preaching of the gospel there is here substituted the probably pre-Lucan remark about the times of the Gentiles being fulfilled (21.24).[3] On the other hand, in 24.47 Luke has a saying that is closely allied to Mark 13.10, but he quotes it as coming from the risen Lord. On the one hand this makes it possible for him to pave the way for the real missionary command at the beginning of Acts, and on the other hand he has thus left out of Jesus' earthly life any direct reference to missionary work among the Gentiles. That by no means implies that Luke's Gospel does not contain plenty of allusions to the salvation that the Gentiles also are to receive; but in contrast to Acts it can, in fact, be said, 'There is a partial krypsis of his universalism while he is writing the Gospel.'[4] That is

[1] In various respects Matthew and Paul meet here, especially with 'to the Jews first', which Paul does not mean temporally either. Similarly, too, G. Barth, *op. cit.*, p. 100 n. 3, as I have seen subsequently. In reference to Goppelt, *Christentum und Judentum*, pp. 178ff., esp. p. 181, Trilling, *op. cit.*, pp. 81ff., offers the completely unsatisfactory apologetic interpretation that to prove his messiahship Jesus had to concentrate on Israel, not being able to send the disciples to the Gentiles till after his rejection. This misunderstands the permanent character of the commission in Matt. 10. Matthew has adhered only piecemeal to Mark's findings on the relation between the mission to the Gentiles and the destruction of the temple; thus in 21.10–46 he completely alters the arrangement, deleting the reference to the Gentiles at the cleansing of the temple; in 26.61 (par. Mark 14.58) he adopts a different form of the saying about the temple; and in 27.51–54 he separates the tearing of the temple curtain from the centurion's confession by inserting other miraculous occurrences. Further, Matthew has quite a different view from Mark of the punishment that Israel incurs by its rejection of Jesus; but this need not be investigated here, as it does not directly concern the problem of the mission.

[2] See particularly the excellent study by Jacques Dupont, 'Le salut des Gentils et le livre des Actes', *NTSt* 6, 1959/60), pp. 132–55, as well as André Rétif, *Foi au Christ et mission d'après les Actes des Apôtres*, Paris, 1953.

[3] I think it very likely that in 21.20a, 21b, 22, and 24 Luke used an additional special tradition.

[4] Cf. N. Q. King, 'The "Universalism" of the Third Gospel', in *Studia Evangelica* (TU 73), 1959, pp. 199–205, the quotation p. 205. Similarly Bosch, *Heidenmission*, pp. 95, 103ff. For criticism see Dupont, *NTSt* 6 (1959/60), p. 138 n. 2.

connected with the fact that the preaching of the gospel among the Gentiles belongs neither to Jesus' earthly activities nor to the eschatological events, but has its place in the period of the Church. Luke therefore logically connects the first saying about it with an appearance of the risen Lord, and does not develop his own view of the mission till he comes to Acts.

But the presuppositions contained in the Gospel must be noticed: already at the end of the introductory narrative, the *Nunc Dimittis* (Luke 2.29ff.) speaks of the σωτήριον τοῦ θεοῦ ('salvation of God') which he has prepared in the presence of all peoples (λαοί), φῶς εἰς ἀποκάλυψιν ἐθνῶν ('a light for revelation to the Gentiles').[1] Then follows the account of the Baptist in 3.3ff., with the quotation from Isaiah (enlarged in comparison with Mark and Matthew), which incorporates not only Isa. 40.4, but also v. 5, of which there has already been a reminder in Luke 2.30, and which says: 'and all flesh shall see the salvation of God'.[2] This sheds light not only on the repeated τὸ σωτήριον τοῦ θεοῦ in Acts 28.28, but also on the πᾶσα σάρξ ('all flesh') of the quotation from Joel in Acts 2.17(ff.). When Jesus first preaches and is repudiated in Nazareth (4.16ff.), with the reference to Elijah's miracle at Zarephath in Sidon and to Elisha's healing of Naaman the Syrian, the Gentiles likewise come into view, as is also the case in 7.1ff. through the recognition of the faith shown by the God-fearing centurion at Capernaum (7.9). The allusions to the salvation that is reaching out beyond Israel are particularly numerous in the so-called travel narrative. This is clear in the editor's setting the scene in Samaria. For although Jesus is rejected in 9.51ff., it is just the stories of the right behaviour of two Samaritans that Luke regards as the scaffolding that supports this middle part (10.25ff.; 17.11ff.).[3] But the lines are drawn out still more clearly: the evangelist follows the sending of the twelve in Luke 9.1ff. with a sending of 70 (72) disciples at the very beginning of the travel narrative in 10.1ff.; of course, both in 9.1ff. and 10.1ff. it is for Luke—unlike Matthew—a matter of events within Jesus' life, and, as is explicitly stated in 10.1, the disciples only touch places

[1] Luke 2.30–32; the allusion is to Isa. 40.5 and 52.10; 42.6 and 49.6 are also brought in.

[2] Rightly emphasized by Dupont, *NTSt* 6 (1959/60), pp. 137f.

[3] On this cf. also Eduard Lohse, 'Missionarisches Handeln Jesu nach dem Evangelium des Lukas', *ThZ* 10 (1954), pp. 1–13, esp. pp. 9ff.

which Jesus himself intends to visit on his way to Jerusalem; but both the setting in Samaria and the figure 70, which corresponds to the number of Gentile nations according to Jewish tradition,[1] indicate activity beyond Israel, and the juxtaposition of the two sendings in chapters 9 and 10 is a preliminary notice of the two-fold mission among Jews and non-Jews.[2] Again, two further passages in the travel narrative, namely 13.28f. (par. Matt. 8.11f.) in the important editorial section 13.22–35, as well as the Lucan version of the parable of the marriage feast (14.16–24) with the twofold bringing in of the guests,[3] point to the salvation that is going to the nations; then Luke concentrates his presentation on Jesus' passion and the eschatological promises, and does not refer to the mission until his account of the resurrection.

The saying that has already been mentioned about preaching the gospel among the Gentiles (Luke 24.47) comes in the risen Lord's instructions to the disciples at the close of the Gospel in 44–49. He refers to the fulfilment of the Scriptures, and opens to the disciples an understanding of the Old Testament. As it is written, Christ had to suffer and rise again, and must also be preached among the Gentiles on the ground of Old Testament prophecy. With this, Luke brings an entirely new line of thought into connection with the words about mission: the early Christian mission is founded, not only on Jesus' command, but also on Old Testament prophecy.[4] Here Luke has indeed adopted the δεῖ from Mark 13.10, but has given it a very different sense, because he has freed it from the apocalyptic setting and transferred it to the pattern of prophecy and fulfilment only. If we ask how, in fact, the phrase 'Thus it is written' (46) must be understood in relation to 47, we must refer to Luke 2.30–32; 3.6. Thus Luke has logically continued the motif that he adopted at the beginning of his Gospel. The noun εὐαγγέλιον, which he often avoids, has been dropped here, too, though he has taken over κηρυχθῆναι . . . εἰς

---

[1] According to Gen. 10; see also the rabbinic texts in Billerbeck II, pp. 604f.

[2] With the second commissioning there are also the words that make a comparison with Tyre and Sidon: Luke 10.12ff.

[3] In any case, this is how the evangelist understands it; how it compares with the parable's original meaning is not the point; cf. ch. II, pp. 35f.

[4] In this, in contrast to Mark, the idea of the rejection of Israel plays no part at all. As Acts expresses it, the killing of Jesus took place through 'ignorance' (Acts 3.17; 13.27).

πάντα τὰ ἔθνη from Mark 13.10.[1] (κηρυχθῆναι) ἐπὶ τῷ ὀνόματι αὐτοῦ μετάνοιαν εἰς ἄφεσιν ἀμαρτιῶν ('that repentance and forgiveness of sins [should be preached] in his name') is new. The μετανοεῖν/ μετάνοια idea is given more weight in Luke than in Mark and Matthew. In general Matthew has used it only where it was provided for him in the traditional material. Mark, however, has intentionally put it in 1.4, 1.15, and 6.12 at the beginning of the preachings of John the Baptist, Jesus himself, and his disciples. Luke joins the idea to Jesus' message,[2] and above all to the missionary preaching.[3] In Luke, when it is joined to 'the forgiveness of sins' on the one hand and to faith and new life on the other hand,[4] it becomes *the* term for conversion.[5] But 'repentance' is just as necessary for the Jews as for the Gentiles.[6] With 'in his [i.e. Jesus'] name' Luke expresses in a special way the presence of Christ,[7] and so this thought fits excellently into v. 47. With the remaining ideas of 24.47–49 Luke is already taking up the theme of the beginning of Acts: v. 49 deals with staying in Jerusalem till the Holy Spirit is poured out; more important are the two ideas of 47 *fin.* and 48, namely the mission's going out from Jerusalem,[8] and the concept μάρτυρες ('witnesses'). As in Matt. 24.14, the Lucan view of the mission is thus expressed programmatically in 24.47(ff.).

The missionary command given before the ascension but related to the time after Pentecost (Acts 1.8), and the further account in Acts, describe in detail what is said in Luke 24.47. Acts 1.8 indicates, with its three stages of Jerusalem/Judea and Samaria/'to the end of the earth', the structure of Luke's second

---

[1] It is remarkable that the connection of Luke 24.47 with Mark 13.10 is generally little noticed.

[2] Cf. the addition εἰς μετάνοιαν in Luke 5.32.

[3] According to Luke, the call to repentance is also characteristic of the Baptist; indeed, this is one of the few features which the picture of John the Baptist has in common with that of Jesus: according to Acts 13.24 the Baptist preached repentance 'before his [Jesus'] coming' (προκηρύξας) to the people of Israel.

[4] With ἄφεσις τῶν ἁμαρτιῶν in Luke 3.3; 24.47; Acts 2.38; 5.31; 26.18, 20; with πιστεύειν/πίστις in Acts 11.17, 18 (εἰς ζωήν); 17.30f.; 20.21; 26.18, 20.

[5] On the predominance of the idea of penitence and the association with ἐπιστρέφειν cf. Conzelmann, *Theology of St Luke*, pp. 225ff.; also Ulrich Wilckens, *Missionsreden*, pp. 178ff.

[6] Besides the passages in Luke's Gospel, cf. for Israel, Acts 2.38; 3.19; 5.31; 13.24; for the Gentiles, Acts 11.18; 17.30; for both, Acts 20.21; 26.18, 20.

[7] Conzelmann, *Theology of St Luke*, pp. 177f., has proved this in more detail.

[8] This 'beginning from Jerusalem' corresponds to 'beginning from the baptism of John' in Acts 1.22, and to 'beginning from Galilee' in Acts 10.37.

work, and this is not contrary to the thematic division of the mission among Jews and Gentiles.[1] With the phrase 'to the end of the earth' the author anticipates the important passage in Acts 13.47 with its quotation from Isa. 49.6, and so interprets the phrase 'to all nations' (Luke 24.47) in the sense of the Old Testament prophecy.[2]

According to Luke's account, the turning-point of the mission comes with the conversion of Cornelius in Acts 10. But in chapters 2–9 the mission to the Gentiles is already prepared in a threefold way. First, the *story of Pentecost*, with its list of Jews and proselytes coming from all nations (2.9–11), and the quotation from Joel about 'all flesh' (2.17), shows that a world-wide horizon is already being opened here; this is underlined by Acts 2.21 (= Joel 2.32), which takes up Isa. 57.19, and again by 2.39: καὶ πᾶσιν τοῖς εἰς μακράν ('and to all that are far off').[3] Those who are gained through the gospel gather first in Jerusalem.[4]

The occasion of the next step is the action against Stephen, and the persecution connected with it (6.8ff.; 8.1). For the result of this is that the scattered *Hellenists* in Judea and Samaria begin to missionize (8.4ff.). The mission in Judea is not described in detail, but its development is summarized in 9.31, where at the same time we are told of the existence of a community in Galilee, where there was religious contact with Judea. On the other hand, the missionizing in Samaria and the conversion of the Ethiopian chamberlain are told in detail in 8.5–40. For Luke this denotes a connecting link and a transitional phase towards the Gentile mission. It is not a question of people who can be called Gentiles in the ordinary sense, but of those who have turned either towards or away from Judaism, and who thus stand in some relation, even if it is a loose one, to Judaism. That is clear in the case of the Samaritans. The fact that after Philip's evangelization Peter and John also go to Samaria is bound up with Luke's view of an apostle. This fact, too, means here the official legitimation of Samaria's conversion to Christianity, which is indicated in 9.31 as having been com-

[1] This shows the connection of Judea and Samaria, for in practice, of course, Jerusalem and Judea (or Samaria) and 'to the end of the earth' belong together, as is seen especially in what follows.
[2] Dupont, *NTSt* 6 (1959/60), pp. 140f.
[3] Cf. Dupont, *NTSt* 6 (1959/60), pp. 144f.
[4] Cf. the collective accounts in Acts 2.41–47; 4.32–37; 5.12–16; 6.7.

pleted. It may be that Luke intentionally left open the chamberlain's religious position,[1] as he is concerned merely to show that
those Gentiles who had hitherto turned to the Jewish faith were
now as a matter of course being reached and won over by the
Christian gospel. But that is not yet a real mission to the Gentiles.

There follows in 9.1ff., as the third stage of the preparation, the
conversion of Paul; and about him we are told in 9.15, 'He is a chosen
instrument of mine to carry my name before the Gentiles and
kings and the sons of Israel', a theme that will be taken up again
later. The overcoming of this persecutor of the Christians at the
same time brought peace to the hard-pressed churches (9.31).

The transition to the Gentile mission was carried out on express divine instructions through Peter as the apostles' representative. The importance for Luke's outlook of the narrative of the
conversion of Cornelius, and its justification in Acts 10.1–11.18, is
well known.[2] Even the Apostles' Conference, which the Judaistic
agitators made necessary (15.1ff.), merely re-adopts and streng-
thens the decision made in Caesarea; and thus Peter's task, as it is
presented in Acts, is fulfilled.[3] Acts 11.18 expresses the fundamentally new perception, 'Then to the Gentiles also God has
granted repentance unto life.' Not till after this are we given the
account in 11.19ff., according to which the Hellenists who had
been driven out of Jerusalem preached in Antioch 'to the Greeks
also', and converted them to the Lord. This missionary work was
now legitimized by Barnabas, the emissary of the Jerusalem
church, and it was he who brought Paul from Tarsus to Antioch
to the missionary work of the church there.[4]

With the sending out of Barnabas and Paul (Acts 13.1ff.) there
begins a new period in the history of early Christianity. Not only
is the door now opened to the mission 'to the end of the earth', but
after that basic stage in Acts 2–9 and the great turning in Acts 10,
the mission is placed in the hands of the 'second' generation; for
according to the Lucan definition of the apostolic status in Acts

---

[1] On Acts 8.26–39 cf. ch. III, p. 62 n. 2.
[2] Cf. Martin Dibelius, 'The Conversion of Cornelius' and 'The Apostolic Council' in *Studies in the Acts of the Apostles*, pp. 109ff. and 93ff.; Haenchen, *Apostelgeschichte*,
pp. 301ff. On the traditional material in Acts 10.1–11.18 cf. above ch. III, pp. 51ff.
and 54 n. 3.
[3] Cf. Dupont, *NTSt* 6 (1959/60), pp. 146ff.
[4] According to Acts 9.26ff., Barnabas also introduced the newly converted Paul
to the apostles in Jerusalem.

1.22, neither Barnabas[1] nor Paul belongs to the ἀπόστολοι.[2] The 'missionary' activity of the ἀπόστολοι, on the contrary, has been confined to Jerusalem,[3] the evangelizing of Samaria falling to Philip, though it was, as one might say, completed afterwards by Peter and John. But it becomes a different matter in 11.19ff. and 13.1ff.; from then onwards the mission is entrusted to the 'post-apostolic' Church, at the beginning of which there stands no less a figure than Paul, who in a first victorious march takes the gospel as far as Rome.[4] In principle, however, the Church's early period is concluded, and a transitional period is opened, in which the author of Acts himself stands, and which will last till the coming of the events of the last days. Luke has thus with a bold grasp claimed Paul, the missionary to the Gentiles, for his own epoch, and seen in him the great prototype for the Church's missionary activity. The apostles indeed set to work on the mission and put it on the right lines, but Paul showed how the missionary mandate could be carried out and made to achieve its end.

According to Luke's account, three considerations bearing on Paul's mission to the Gentiles are of decisive importance:

(*a*) Both Paul and the early Church, which preached salvation to the Jews in Jerusalem and Palestine first, and only then went to the Samaritans and Gentiles, felt the sequence of the Jewish and Gentile missions in the scheme of salvation to be valid.[5] Paul is not free to go to the Gentiles till he has preached to the Jews of the Diaspora and they have rejected the message.[6] This is expressed programmatically in Acts 13.46f. with the quotation from Isa. 49.6, partly reproduced already in Luke 2.32 and Acts 1.8. It is repeated twice in 18.6 and 28.25–28.

---

[1] He is mentioned first in Acts 4.36, and then again in 9.27.

[2] On the problem of the Lucan idea of apostleship cf. Günter Klein, *Zwölf Apostel*, esp. pp. 202ff., on this the criticism by Haenchen, *Apostelgeschichte*, pp. 676ff.

[3] In my opinion it is incorrect to say that Luke does not regard them as missionaries.

[4] In Acts 14.4, 14 Barnabas and Paul are 'apostles' only in the sense of the ἀφορίζειν of 13.1ff. They are therefore classed as ἀπόστολοι ἐκκλησιῶν or ἐκκλησίας such as are mentioned in II Cor. 8.23.

[5] One should notice particularly the πρῶτον in Acts 3.26.

[6] So in Acts 13.16–41 there is a further missionary speech to the Jews! This sermon, so closely related to the speeches in chs. 2, 3, and 10, is to show that Paul preaches the gospel among the Jews in the same way as do the 'apostles'.

(*b*) The preaching to the Gentiles presupposes, not the covenant with and the promises to the fathers, but the care of the Creator.[1] At the same time it remains true, in relation to Jews and Gentiles, that what they have done through 'ignorance'—in the one case the killing of Jesus, in the other the worship of idols[2]—can be forgiven, that the law that even the fathers could not bear shall not be laid on 'the neck of the disciples'[3]—from now on only the decisions of the Apostolic Decree are authoritative[4]—and that conversion and faith stand under the sign of the coming judgment.[5]

(*c*) As can be seen from Paul's speeches in his defence (22.12–21 and 26.14–20), his personal commissioning as missionary to the Gentiles was effected by the present Lord himself, who appeared to him near Damascus and in the temple at Jerusalem. As Luke, in contrast to Paul himself, regarded this call as clearly separate

---

[1] Acts 14.15–17; 17.22–31. These discourses to Gentiles, which are very characteristic of Lucan theology, uphold the principle of using connecting links, which has a great effect on later views, and give the sermon in the Gentiles, from the point of view of the relationship of God and men, an essentially different motivation from what was usual in the earliest period of Christianity. Certainly, God's creative action had its settled place there, too, starting from Jesus' own preaching; but this was inseparably connected with his saving activity, and it nowhere has a propaedeutic function. In this passage not only has an assimilation to later Jewish propaganda been made—Luke may have gone back in this to certain tendencies in later Hellenist Jewish Christianity, as Dieter Georgi rightly supposes (orally)—but an important preliminary stage has been reached in the missionary understanding of the Christian world in the second century (the Apologists). Acts 14.15–17 is only a preparatory sketch of the sermon to the Gentiles that is not developed in detail till the Areopagus speech of 17.22–31; on this cf. Wilckens, *Missionsreden*, pp. 86ff., 178ff., which at the same time sets out the connection with the pattern of the older missionary sermon recognizable in I Thess. 1.9f. and Heb. 5.11ff. (pp. 8off.). On the peculiarity of the Areopagus speech we need only refer to Martin Dibelius, 'Paul on the Areopagus' in *Studies in the Acts*, pp. 26–77; Walther Eltester, 'Gott und Natur in der Areopagrede' in *Neutestamentliche Studien für R. Bultmann* (BZNW 21), 1957², pp. 209–27; *id.*, 'Schöpfungsoffenbarung und natürliche Theologie im frühen Christentum', *NTSt* 3 (1956/7), pp. 93–114; Wolfgang Nauck, 'Tradition und Komposition der Areopagrede', *ZThK* 53 (1956), pp. 11–56; Haenchen, *Apostelgeschichte*, pp. 466ff.; Conzelmann, *Apostelgeschichte*, pp. 97ff.; also Rudolf Bultmann, 'Anknüpfung und Widerspruch' in *Glauben und Verstehen* II, 1952, pp. 117–32, esp. pp. 125ff. (ET, 'Points of Contact and Conflict' in *Essays Philosophical and Theological*, 1955, pp. 135–50, esp. pp. 142ff.).

[2] Cf. Acts 3.17; 13.27 with 17.30. There is added to this the concession to the Gentiles, that they were even able to worship the real God ἀγνοοῦντες(!).

[3] Acts 15.10f. This view of the law contrasts sharply with Paul's own wrestling about the law; on this cf. the excellent exposition by Philip Vielhauer, 'Der Paulinismus der Apostelgeschichte', *EvTh* 10 (1950/1), pp. 1–15, esp. pp. 5ff.

[4] Acts 15.20, 29; 21.25; on this in detail cf. Haenchen, *Apostelgeschichte*, pp. 390f., 410ff.

[5] Acts 17.31; for the connection with the understanding of the mission cf. Dupont, *NTSt* 6 (1959/60), pp. 152ff.

from the resurrection appearances, he was able to put Paul on the
threshold of his own time.[1] But the continuing work of the
Gentile mission is not only under the direct guidance of the Lord
and of the activity of the Holy Spirit, but is at the same time part
of the fulfilling of the Scripture according to which 'the salvation
of God' must be preached to the Gentiles.

Thus the large structure of Luke's conception stretches from
Luke 2.30; 3.6, across 24.47, as far as Acts 28.28. It can be seen
from this to what a degree he finds in the mission to the Gentiles
the dominating theme. Because of his view of the scheme of
salvation he does, indeed, assume a graduated development, so
that the universal preaching of the gospel according to Old Testament prediction is only indirectly indicated during Jesus' lifetime,
and is not carried out, even in the early Church, till after a certain
transitional period.[2]

[1] This is not invalidated by the speech at Miletus in Acts 20.17ff. Haenchen,
Apostelgeschichte, p. 529, has rightly pointed out the importance of the prediction
of suffering in this speech; this, indeed, is instead of a narration of the end of Paul's
life. But not only the apostle but also the Church will have to face suffering from
without (29) and from within (30). As a rule this parallelism is not observed. True,
this speech is presented as the departing Paul's will and testament, but not in the sense
that here one period is ending and a new one beginning; and it is not in the least the
case that 'legitimate successors in office' in the sense of *successio apostolica* are being installed here for the time to come (despite Klein, *op. cit.*, pp. 178ff.).

[2] It should be beyond dispute that here Luke takes into account the actual historical course of events in a schematized and condensed form.

VI

THE PROBLEM OF THE MISSION IN THE REST OF THE POST-PAULINE TRADITION AND IN THE JOHANNINE WRITINGS

We still have to indicate how the missionary concern of the second half of the first century found expression outside the synoptists and Acts. The real missionary epoch came to an end with the death by martyrdom of the two apostles Peter and Paul. The intensity of the mission, indeed, did not slacken—as is shown by the theological conceptions discussed above, and also by the fact that the Christian message was zealously spread abroad, far beyond the hitherto existing sphere of the Church—but the structure of the missionary work underwent a marked change, as we shall show briefly.

1. MISSION AND CHURCH

What makes the changed situation clear is that the work of the mission, which was directed outwards, and the work of developing, consolidating, and caring for the churches, became distinct, one may perhaps even say to some degree separated. Of course, it is not to be denied that already in Paul the missionary sermon can be distinguished from the preaching to existing churches; but in that case it is at first a matter rather of shifts of emphasis than of problems that are fundamentally different.

The churches of the initial period were in principle open to all who came into contact with the preaching, and in their life and work they were prepared to win other people for the Christian faith. We find an instructive example in Paul's remarks (I Cor. 14) about the church service: the church service must certainly conduce to the edification of the church itself, 'edifying' (οἰκοδομεῖν) being for Paul the real criterion of the right ordering and practice of Christian assembly; but the church service must also guarantee that the ἰδιῶται and ἄπιστοι, those who are on the fringe and those

who disbelieve, may be won over.[1] They are to be convinced by
prophecy, so that 'the secrets of his heart are disclosed; and so,
falling on his face, he will worship God and declare that God is
really among you' (I Cor. 14.23–25).[2] In the early days, too, the
celebration of the Lord's Supper was quite different from its
later form;[3] of course, there is a warning against unworthy participation: εἴ τις οὐ φιλεῖ τὸν κύριον, ἤτω ἀνάθεμα ('If anyone has no
love for the Lord, let him be accursed', I Cor. 16.22); but according to the *Didache*, which preserved various old traditional
material, the real formula of invitation reads: εἴ τις ἅγιός ἐστιν,
ἐρχέσθω· εἴ τις οὐκ ἔστι, μετανοείτω· μαραναθά (10.6).[4] A somewhat
later stage can be recognized where a clear distinction is laid down
between those who are admitted to the Lord's Supper and those
who are not; again the *Didache* provides us with evidence: 'Let no
one eat and drink of your eucharist except those who have been
baptized in the name of the Lord' (9.5a).[5] The reason given in
this passage is 'For on this the Lord has said, "Do not give dogs
what is holy" ' (9.5b).[6] But already in Revelation this principle is
expressed still more pointedly: at the end of the book, leading up
to the celebration of the Lord's Supper, John says: ἔξω οἱ κύνες
('Outside are dogs', 22.15); this means that we can point to about
AD 96 as the first time when we know the Lord's Supper to have
been celebrated esoterically[7]—a practice that later led to the distinction between the *missa catechumenorum* and the *missa fidelium*.[8]

[1] In connection with I Cor. 14, therefore, we must not merely say 'that the
church assembly is thus on occasion also open to non-Christians' (Lietzmann,
Korinther, p. 73).
[2] Cf. Günther Bornkamm, 'Die Erbauung der Gemeinde als Leib Christi' in
Das Ende des Gesetzes, pp. 113–23; id., 'Glaube und Vernunft bei Paulus' in *Studien zu
Antike und Urchristentum*, pp. 118–37, where it is pointed out (pp. 133ff.) that Paul
attaches special importance to prophecy as a λαλεῖν τῷ νοΐ ('speaking with the mind')
in relation to the edification of the Church as well as in relation to those who are
outside it.
[3] Cf. Günther Bornkamm, 'Das Anathema in der urchristlichen Abendmahls-
liturgie' in *Das Ende des Gesetzes*, pp. 123–32; my *Christologische Hoheitstitel*, pp. 100ff.
[4] 'Being holy' is here equated with πιστεύειν.
[5] Bornkamm, *Das Ende des Gesetzes*, pp. 125f.: 'The explicit instruction, however,
clearly assumes that this regulation was not a matter of course.'
[6] Matt. 7.6 occupied an important place in all the ancient Church's Lord's Supper
paranesis. The words 'dogs' was at first intended purely figuratively in this context,
but it was quite early taken over with the traditional Jewish meaning of Gentiles—
now, the unbelievers.
[7] The next witness is Justin, *Apol.* I, 66, 1 (about 150).
[8] Cf. *Const Apost.* II, 57, and VIII, 6; with the latter passage cf. also the text best
preserved in Coptic, Hippolytus' *Apostolic Tradition* 19.1 (ed. and trans. B. S.
Easton, 1934, p. 43; ed. and trans. G. Dix, 1937, p. 30).

What we see in the Church's life in relation to the divine service is symptomatic of the epoch. It is well known that not only the political situation with its incipient persecutions, but also the danger to the churches through false doctrine and fanaticism, necessarily induced efforts towards a stronger consolidation of the churches. On this we need only remember the speech (Acts 20.18–35) that Luke puts into Paul's mouth on the latter's departure from Miletus. The consequence is that on the one hand the churches are given a stricter organization, and that on the other hand much more weight is laid on preaching within the Church, particularly on parenesis.[1] As far as church order is concerned, the transition from the earlier Church guided charismatically to the one organized institutionally can be followed quite well through the emergence of the office of presbyter. This development is important and significant,[2] even though the transition from a precedence that was at first understood in a more patriarchal way to an official position with legally determined duties may have been fluid and gradual.[3] Luke in Acts, and similarly the Pastoral Letters, try to connect the change to presbyterial order with Paul himself. In Jerusalem the presbytery had been introduced earlier; for the churches in the Hellenist areas the change from the Pauline to the post-Pauline period was probably decisive in this respect, although Paul himself cannot be brought into connection with it. The development is also recognizable in the Letter of James and the First Letter of Peter; and in the Pastoral Letters we can already see beyond it the emergence of a single episcopate.[4] The shift of emphasis in preaching on to the tasks and problems within the Church is clear in the same way. It is only on these suppositions that the exclusive interest in the parenesis, as in James, or the broad homiletic development of confession proceeding from the Old Testament and with the cultic service in view, as in Hebrews, becomes intelligible.

[1] It is characteristic of Paul that in his argument with heretics, which was necessary even in his time, he does not refer to the official leadership of the Church, as he regards the parenesis as being entirely within the framework of the preaching of salvation (e.g. cf. Rom. 12.1f.; 13.11–14).

[2] Cf. Günther Bornkamm, art. πρέσβυς, πρεσβύτερος, *ThWb* VI, pp. 651–83, esp. pp. 664ff.

[3] Cf. Hans Frh. von Campenhausen, *Kirchliches Amt und geistliche Vollmacht* (BHTh 14), 1953, pp. 82ff.

[4] Cf. James 5.14; I Peter 5.1–4; I Tim. 5.17, 19; Titus 1.5, and also I Tim. 3.1ff.; Titus 1.7ff. The Pastoral Letters are to be understood in the first place as orders.

The concentration on the life and strengthening of the churches is so strong that it is now largely impossible to speak of an understanding of the mission, in the sense in which the phrase has so far been used and was characteristic of the oldest Christianity.[1] Of course, the mission's task is not in dispute, but it is a thing by itself, needing its own style of preaching and a corresponding form of writing, such as we meet in the greatly changed internal and external conditions, say from the second century onwards, in the apologetic literature of the ancient Church.[2] As the *Pastoral Letters* clearly show, the existence of Gentile Christian churches and the preaching of the gospel throughout the world is assumed as a matter of course;[3] a real missionary purpose, however, cannot be recognized. Christ's saving work, too, is understood as being in essence universal: he came into the world to save sinners, and he desires all men to be saved and come to the truth;[4] the message is of 'the appearing of our Saviour Jesus Christ, who abolished death and brought life and immortality to light through the gospel' (II Tim. 1.10). But the question of Israel and the Old Testament *Heilsgeschichte* plays no part at all. It is hardly by chance, therefore, that the confession of God as the giver of all life *(ζῳογονῶν τὰ πάντα)* is co-ordinated in the ordination parenesis of I Tim. 6.13 with the confession of Christ, who testified before Pontius Pilate, so that the doctrines of creation and salvation are thus put into relation to each other, as they were by Luke in the Areopagus speech.

If in the Pastoral Letters the concentration on the Church is

[1] Heinrich Greeven, 'Die missionierende Gemeinde nach den apostolischen Briefen' in *Sammlung und Sendung* (Festschrift H. Rendtorff), 1958, pp. 59–71, investigates the lines of thought that bear on the Church's missionary responsibility in the assumed separation of the Church and the world; he shows that the Pauline letters already provide material for this, but in my opinion a clearer distinction should be drawn between the Pauline and the post-Pauline view, with their important divergence.

[2] There is no doubt that, side by side with the defence and justification of Christian faith and life, the recommendation of Christianity by its apologists also played an important part; cf. von Harnack, *Mission* I, pp. 372ff. This was accompanied by a not inconsiderable influence on the part of Jewish propaganda, and also by the assimilation to current literary forms and popular philosophical thought, so that in many respects we can see the beginning of the end of the primitive stage of Christian writing; on this cf. Franz Overbeck, *Über die Anfänge der patristischen Literatur* (reprinted in *Libelli* XV), 1954.

[3] Cf. I Tim 3.16; II Tim. 4.17. Paul is regarded as the authoritative apostle to the Gentiles, who has left his testament to the present generation; cf. II Tim., esp. 4.17, but also I Tim. 2.7.

[4] Cf. I Tim. 1.15; 2.4; 4.10.

due mainly to the danger of false doctrine, in *I Peter* it is due to persecution. The Christians are harassed to the limit of their endurance, and all missionary activity is denied to them;[1] so the emphasis falls all the more strongly on how the Church stands with regard to salvation, and thus on the parenesis. But it is very characteristic that while this persecution is going on the commission in relation to the world is not lost sight of: the upright conduct of Christians is required on the very ground that someone or other may be won over in this way,[2] but above all because it is through discipline and steadfastness that one can witness rightly for the gospel. As in the Pastoral Letters, the thought here proceeds from the creation,[3] and there is likewise a strong emphasis on the universality of Christ's saving work, including his sermon to the 'spirits in prison'.[4] In I Peter a special part is played by baptism as the means of rescue from perdition and of the entry, already effected, into the new life.[5] Here, too, the eschatological expectation is much more insistent than in the Pastoral Letters, for instance: the testimony given before the Gentiles under persecution—the readiness to respond to anyone 'who calls you to account for the hope that is in you' (3.15)—serves to confront the unbelievers and the persecutors with their future judge. The parenesis in this letter is therefore supported by the reason 'that in case they speak against you as wrongdoers, they may see your good deeds and glorify God on the day of visitation' (2.12). And in the same way the summons to accept suffering willingly, and not to refuse to testify, ends with the injunction to 'do it with gentleness and reverence; and keep your conscience clear, so that, when you are abused, those who revile your good behaviour in Christ may be put to shame' (3.16).[6] In this New Testament

[1] The letter probably belongs to the time of the persecution by Domitian; on the question of the time of origin see the cautious discussion in Karl Hermann Schelkle, *Die Petrusbriefe/Der Judasbrief* (Herders Theol. Komm. z. NT XIII/2), 1961, pp. 7ff.

[2] ἄνευ λόγου (I Peter 3.1f.). The theme of irreproachable behaviour towards those outside the Church is also known to the older early Christian parenesis; cf., e.g., I Thess. 4.12; I Cor. 10.32; but in I Peter it has an importance all its own.

[3] Again Israel and the Old Testament history of election play no part.

[4] Cf. Werner Bieder, *Grund und Kraft der Mission nach dem 1. Petrusbrief* (ThSt 29), 1950, pp. 3ff., 12ff.

[5] *Ibid.*, pp. 18ff., 24ff.

[6] It seems to me beyond doubt that in I Peter 2.12 the eschatological day of judgment is meant, although this question is left open in most commentaries; but cf. Schelkle, *Die Petrusbriefe/Der Judasbrief*, p. 72, who brings the eschatological interpretation into the foreground, and is of the opinion that the other interpretation

writing, as in Mark 13.9; Matt. 10.17f., and also in Phil. 1.7, 12–14, 19f., we can see that, in the existing situation relating to persecution and judgment, the idea of 'testimony' is given greater weight. But we can speak of an understanding of the mission only in a modified way.[1] This line of thought, which is recognizable in I Peter, is continued later, especially in the Acts of the Martyrs.

It is interesting to compare this with *II Thessalonians*. This letter also assumes the situation of persecution, as is shown particularly in 1.3–12. But not only has the missionary aspect virtually disappeared;[2] the confrontation with the world has an entirely different sense from I Peter and also from Paul's writings. Central to the thought is the 'judgment of God', which will come upon all those who are now oppressing the Church, and who, as requital for what they are now doing to it, will receive their punishment, just as the Christians, on the other hand, will participate in the future salvation because of their acceptance of the faith and their sufferings.[3] This is connected not least with the noticeable re-Judaizing of the theological expressions and with the dependence on apocalyptic writings, where there is the same kind of one-sided turning towards the elect, while the Gentiles remain as the *massa perditionis* quite outside the scope of salvation. Moreover, the Revelation of John adopts, at least from chapter 15 onwards, a similar attitude, although in 14.6f. it has also taken up the call

---

is true only in conjunction with the eschatological one. At first sight, matters do not seem so clear on 3.16; but this passage must be read in its context, which goes on as far as 4.6, and in 4.4f. leaves no doubt as to the eschatological outlook. This does not exclude the idea of conversion through the testimony of Christians in conduct and suffering, though this is not the real purpose of the two declarations. For a one-sided relating of the passage 2.12 to conversion, see Edward Gordon Selwyn, *The First Epistle of St Peter*, 1947[2] (reprinted 1958), p. 171; Bieder, *op. cit.*, pp. 8f.

[1] Thus far Bieder's one-sidedly stressed concept of the mission and the 'missionary service' (*op. cit.*, pp. 6ff., 16ff. and 29f.), is only conditionally useful for I Peter. It is true that the task in respect of the world, and the Church's commission, were seen clearly; but there is no longer any question here of missionary action. Apart from the very indirect function in 3.1f., this Church has no possibility of 'missionary service' in the real sense. In the passive character of its trials in persecution, and in the testimony that it gives, something of the missionary commission is carried out, in so far as the Church's whole existence is determined by the missionary function; but the distinction should not be too hastily obliterated.

[2] Perhaps the passage in II Thess. 3.1 modelled on Paul may be quoted, but cf. only the conjunction with v. 2.

[3] Cf. the excellent study by Herbert Braun, 'Zur nachpaulinischen Herkunft des zweiten Thessalonicherbriefs', in *Studien zum Neuen Testament und seiner Umwelt*, 1962, pp. 205–9; on the previous Jewish history of this view cf. the inquiry by Wolfgang Wichmann, *Die Leidenstheologie* (BWANT IV/2), 1930.

from heaven to the Gentiles for repentance. In view of the general attitude of II Thessalonians, therefore, we can hardly expect the theme of the Gentile mission to be taken into account at all. Cullmann, however, has now put forward the thesis that the puzzling ὁ κατέχων (τὸ κατέχον) in the apocalyptic sketch 2.1–12 must be related to the preaching of the gospel that had to be carried through by the apostle before the end.[1] But this exposition is no more satisfactory than any other interpretation of a phenomenon within history.[2] Strobel has recently shown, with the support of plentiful evidence, that the expression goes back to an old peculiarly apocalyptic Jewish idea, in which God's own wish and the plan of salvation that he has laid down are expressed in a form that is mysterious, but defined and therefore intelligible to initiates.[3] Thus II Thessalonians is evidence, to a much greater degree than I Peter and the Pastoral Letters, for the separation of mission and Church in the post-Pauline period.[4]

2. THE LETTERS TO THE COLOSSIANS AND EPHESIANS

The documents most closely connected with the authentic Pauline letters are the Letters to the Colossians and the Ephesians. It is easy to recognize that the apostle's missionary commission is here observed and even emphasized. But what we have to do is to find out how the missionary idea was changed theologically. The problem has recently been carefully investigated by Eduard

[1] Oscar Cullmann, 'Le charactère eschatologique du devoir missionnaire et de la conscience apostolique de St Paul', *RHPhR* 16 (1936), pp. 210–45; *id., Christ and Time*, ET 1962², pp. 164ff.; *id.*, 'Eschatology and Missions in the New Testament' in *The Background of the NT and its Eschatology* (in honour of C. H. Dodd), 1956, pp. 409–21; adopted by Munck, *Paul and the Salvation of Mankind*, pp. 36ff.

[2] Particularly frequently interpreted to mean the State or a mythical figure; cf. Rigaux, *Thessaloniciens*, pp. 259ff.

[3] August Strobel, *Untersuchungen zum eschatologischen Verzögerungsproblem auf Grund der spätjüdisch-urchristlichen Geschichte von Habakuk 2.2ff.* (Suppl. to NovTest II), 1961, pp. 98ff., esp. pp. 106f.

[4] It is difficult to date II Thessalonians; it may have been written at the latest in the middle of the nineties. It can be seen in various ways that in Asia Minor a strong apocalyptic current lasted till into the second century, as in general the Pauline mission field there was marked at the end of the first century by various un-Pauline currents; on this cf. Walter Bauer, *Rechtgläubigkeit und Ketzerei im ältesten Christentum* (BHTh 10), 1934, pp. 81ff. On the other hand, I Peter, which is also connected with Asia Minor (cf. the opening words), rather shows certain Pauline traits; according to 5.13 the letter probably originated in Rome; cf. Jülicher and Fascher, *Einleitung*, pp. 196f.

Schweizer;[1] his observations can be accepted and in a certain direction carried further.

Although Colossians and Ephesians are close to Paul, an essential shift of emphasis is shown by the structure of their thought as a whole. The transition from Hellenist Jewish Christianity, to which Paul notwithstanding all the differences belongs, to Hellenist Gentile Christianity is here completed. Of course, Paul, particularly in his soteriology and ecclesiology, took up significant non-Jewish Hellenist elements to set out the universality and immediacy of salvation; but fundamentally his concepts were determined all along by historical thinking that was intelligible only from Jewish presuppositions. In Colossians and Ephesians things are quite different. In spite of the influence of traditional ways of thought, for example, spatial categories clearly predominate here over temporal. The contrast between heavenly and earthly reality plays a decisive part, and the whole universe in its origin, nature, and aim is kept in view as a matter of course. Paul supplemented the Jewish and Jewish Christian ways of thought with the Hellenist outlook, so as to be able to reveal the eschatological fragmentariness of historical reality.[2] But in a precisely opposite way, Colossians and Ephesians have to strive, while allowing for the weight of the cosmic declarations, to set out and maintain the historicity of salvation. The ontological explanation that suggests itself here is by no means appropriate, because it is opposed to the consistent historical understanding both of Christ's saving action and of the reality of the Church's salvation. The concern is the same as in Paul's writing—only, so to speak, with the plus and minus signs reversed: the universal dimensions of redemption through Christ are to be expressed in a mode of thought intelligible to Hellenists.[3]

---

[1] Eduard Schweizer, 'Die Kirche als Leib Christi in den paulinischen Antilegomena', *ThLZ* 86 (1961), cols. 241–56; cf. *id.*, 'Übernahme und Korrektur jüdischer Sophia-theologie im Neuen Testament' in *Hören und Handeln* (Festschrift für Ernst Wolf), 1962, pp. 330–40, esp. pp. 331ff.

[2] Already rather different in Gentile Christianity before and contemporary with Paul; e.g. cf. the hymn quoted in Phil 2.6–11.

[3] Cf. Eduard Schweizer, *Erniedrigung und Erhöhung bei Jesus und seinen Nachfolgern* (AThANT 28), 1962², pp. 145ff.; further, Günther Bornkamm, 'Die Hoffnung im Kolosserbrief. Zugleich ein Beitrag zur Frage der Echtheit des Briefes' in *Studien zum NT und zur Patristik* (Festschrift E. Klostermann, TU 77), 1961, pp. 56–64, esp. pp. 58ff. I do not feel so certain whether the temporal-eschatological concept is so completely eliminated and is only echoed in traditional phrases; just as the writer

Eduard Schweizer has pointed out admirably that, as presuppositions of this deutero-Pauline conception, two other elements must be taken into account besides the real Pauline tradition. On the one hand there is the pattern of *Epiphany-Christology*, developed with concepts of the Wisdom literature—a pattern 'that with the contrast between "once" and "now" separates the time of hidden things from the time of God's revealing action'.[1] This 'pattern of revelation' certainly comes from Hellenist Jewish Christianity;[2] it was adopted by Paul on occasion (I Cor. 2.7ff., 10), and occurs, moreover, in the post-Pauline doxology of Rom. 16.25–27; it also has a central place in Colossians and Ephesians. On the other hand, a cosmologically sketched Christology is taken up, which is clearly recognizable in the hymn on which Col. 1.15–20 is based. However, we should analyse Col. 1.15–20 against its background in terms of comparative religions,[3] it is certain that the writer of Colossians did not adopt the hymn without correction, as it expresses an outlook (not free from danger, and largely detached from Jewish presuppositions) on Christ as the Creator and Reconciler of the universe ('all things in heaven and on earth').[4] Now, it is instructive that the Gentile Christian hymn I Tim. 3.16 takes up in a modified form a Christology that is likewise cosmologically determined, in which, besides the epiphany of Christ in the flesh, 'preached among the nations' and 'believed on in the world' are

---

of Colossians strives to hold fast to historicity within his way of thinking in spheres so, too, he may have taken account of the outlook of the *Heilsgeschichte* and of eschatology, as is shown by the centrally placed declaration in 3.4 (cf. also 1.21–23).

[1] E. Schweizer, *ThLZ* 86 (1961), col. 247.

[2] Thus Nils Alstrup Dahl, 'Formgeschichtliche Beobachtungen zur Christusverkündigung' in *Neutest. Studien für R. Bultmann* (BZNW 21), 1957², pp. 3–9; there pp. 4ff., distinguishing this from the related 'soteriological pattern of contrasts' that confronts the perdition of the 'once' with the state of salvation of the 'now'. Günther Bornkamm, art. μυστήριον, *ThWb* IV, pp. 809–34, esp. pp. 825ff., has shown that this pattern of revelation, in its structure and its connection with the mystery theme, goes back to apocalyptic presuppositions.

[3] Ernst Käsemann, 'A Primitive Christian Baptismal Liturgy', *Essays on New Testament Themes*, ET 1964, pp. 149–68; James M. Robinson, 'A Formal Analysis of Col. 1.15–20¹, *JBL* 76 (1957), pp. 270ff.; E. Schweizer, *ThLZ* 86 (1961), cols. 241ff.; id., *Erniedrigung und Erhöhung*, pp. 102ff.; Hans Conzelmann, 'Der Brief an die Kolosser' in *Die kleineren Briefe des Apostels Paulus* (NTD 8), 1962², pp. 135ff.; Harald Hegermann, *Die Vorstellung vom Schöpfungsmittler im hellenistischen Judentum und Urchristentum* (TU 82), 1961, pp. 88ff.

[4] Schweizer, *ThLZ* 86 (1961) col. 253, supposes that the ascension was here regarded as a plain physical happening and a decisive fact of salvation, through which earth and heaven were reunited and the broken unity of the cosmos was restored.

mentioned as historical events.[1] For the writers of Colossians and Ephesians joined the universal cosmic declarations on Christ's saving work to the preaching of the gospel among all nations and, beyond that, to the Church's existence in the world.

So far, Colossians and Ephesians have been regarded as a certain unity, but now we have to differentiate. In *Colossians*, as regards the preaching of the gospel, two points of view overlap in a remarkable way. First, some passages speak freely of the preaching of the gospel in the whole world (as we often find in Paul's letters); so, for instance, in the prologue, Col. 1.5b, 6, and in 1.23b (cf. 1.21–23). But a pronouncement with quite a different stress appears in 1.26 in conjunction with the thought of the mystery that has now been made manifest, where attention is directed solely to the Church. According to this passage, the 'mystery' has been 'made manifest to his saints'; it is to them that God chose to make known 'how great among the Gentiles are the riches of the glory of this mystery, which is Christ in you'. Nor must it be overlooked that just before, in v. 25, it is said, obviously in tension with v. 23, that Paul has become a διάκονος of the ἐκκλησία 'according to the divine office which was given to me for you, to make the word of God fully known'. Lastly, we must notice the remarkable expression in v. 28, where καταγγέλλομεν ('proclaim') is associated with νουθετοῦντες ('warning') and διδάσκοντες . . . ('teaching every man in all wisdom'), that is, with expressions that denote instruction within the Church,[2] just as the added sentence ἵνα παραστήσωμεν πάντα ἄνθρωπον τέλειον ἐν Χριστῷ ('that we may present every man mature in Christ') can probably only be understood to mean that the members of the Church in particular are to be made 'mature in Christ'.[3] Here we may grasp the writer's real purpose. What does it mean for his understanding of the mission? Obviously the preaching among the Gentiles is regarded as a necessary but subordinate fact. The reality and the task of the Church

---

[1] On the details of this little hymn cf. Jeremias, *Die Briefe an Timotheus und Titus* (NTD 9), 1949[5], pp. 2of.; Martin Dibelius and Hans Conzelmann, *Die Pastoralbriefe* (HbNT 13), 1955[3], pp. 49ff.; E. Schweizer, *Erniedrigung und Erhöhung*, pp. 104ff., 155f.

[2] One might refer, e.g., to Col. 3.16; but cf. also the concordance. Ernst Lohmeyer, *Der Brief an die Kolosser* (KrExKomm IX/2, 1961[12], p. 87 n. 2, is not right in saying 'here νουθετεῖν seems to have to do with μετάνοια, and διδάσκειν with πίστις'; however, he was the first to feel the section's problem.

[3] This is supported by Col. 2.1(ff.) as by 4.12; but cf. also 1.22, 23a.

chosen out of the Gentiles is determined primarily by the fact that *it* is the bearer of the mystery amid the Gentile nations. In it there is realized God's will for salvation; it must be kept firm in its salvation, and must grow and be taken on to perfection.[1] The Gentile mission still remains a function of the Church, but from the existing Church one can at the same time look back to the mission and the great turning-point, in the story of salvation from 'once' to 'now'. Thus it has in any case an intermediary significance, with its outlook on the ἐκκλησία idea, just as the historical dimension of the reality of salvation is determined less by the missionary idea than by the explanation of the concept of the Church. It is hardly by accident that the hymn is already corrected by the ἐκκλησία concept (v. 18); and the whole of the further line of thought, including the argument with the false doctrine, is dominated by it. Eduard Schweizer's thesis—that what is said historically in Colossians about Christ's importance and penetration of the world implies reference to the mission—must therefore be supplemented by adding that the historical dimension is expressed here, not only by the thought of the mission, but above all by that of the Church. Missionary activity among the Gentiles is a preliminary stage, whereas the decisive penetration of the world and the leading of it to its goal belong to the historical existence of the Church. Of course, mission and Church are inseparable and form an inner unity; for just as Paul is the bearer of the mission to the Gentiles, so in the same way he is the one who has cared for the preservation of the Church in the right faith and for the strengthening of the service entrusted to it. If this is the right interpretation, we can see a very instructive change in regard to Paul's understanding of the mission. Of course the missionary activity goes on, but it is not the sign of the present time. The Lord's presence in this world is being accomplished by the existing Church among the Gentile nations. The Church's main task lies in its right existence as a Church, and its main service to the world lies in its existence and growth towards its Head.

---

[1] E. Schweizer, *ThLZ* 86 (1961), cols. 247f., considers whether the missionary idea might not be the *Sitz im Leben* for the theme of growth; but I do not regard this as likely, for the use of this theme in Colossians (1.6, 19; 2.19) and Ephesians (2.21; 4.15f.) and also in Paul's letters (I Cor. 3.6f.; II Cor. 10.15) and in I Peter 2.2 nowhere stands in relation to the mission, but to the inner growth of the Church or of individual Christians. Only in Acts 6.7; 12.24; 19.20 is it otherwise.

A short comparison of Colossians with the doxological addendum in *Rom. 16.25-27* is enlightening. There, too, the theme of the mystery that was once hidden and has now become manifest plays a decisive part. But the purpose is different. The statement is not about the reality of the Church, but about the accomplishment of the Gentile mission. Thus far this text, notwithstanding all other differences, is quite close to Paul's point of view: the mystery is disclosed and εἰς ὑπακοὴν πίστεως εἰς πάντα τὰ ἔθνη γνωρισθέντος ('made known to all nations . . . to bring about obedience to the faith').[1]

The guiding thoughts of Colossians are taken farther and enriched by certain new elements in *Ephesians*. The world picture in spheres is even more dominant,[2] and the de-eschatologizing is carried farther.[3] Here, too, however, a certain temporal and historical element is preserved, which holds fast to the unique act of redemption and to the final fulfilment of salvation; under Christ's lordship the whole universe will one day obtain its unity, which is now really and visibly present in the Church. Even more than in Colossians, ecclesiology is the real centre of the theological statement, and the writer takes an essential step beyond the conception of Colossians. We see this from what is said about the predestination of the Church in 1.3–12, from the arguments about the unity of the Church, resting on Christ's reconciling action, in 2.11–18, from the definition of the apostolic office in 3.1–13, and from the opinion, variously expressed in these texts, of the Church's function in relation to the cosmos. The problems of the introductory hymn may be allowed to rest, only it may be remarked that here already, in connection with statements on the Church, the writer speaks (1.10) of God's will ἀνακεφαλαιώσασθαι τὰ πάντα ἐν τῷ Χριστῷ (' to unite all things in Christ'). Then in 22b,

---

[1] The thought of the mystery revealed to the nations, and calling them to obedience in faith, is bound up with the idea, which is by no means Pauline, that this declaration is issued through (Christian) prophetic writings, commissioned by the eternal God. In the same way the preceding sentence takes up the thought—probably traceable to the Jewish apocalyptic tradition—of the mystery 'kept secret for long ages'. Cf. in detail Michel, *Römer* pp. 349ff.; Erhard Kamlah, *Traditionsgeschichtliche Untersuchungen zur Schlussdoxologie des Römerbriefs* (Diss. Tübingen, 1955, typewritten); notice by the author in *ThLZ* 81 (1956), col. 492.

[2] For Ephesians' world picture cf. Franz Mußner, *Christus, das All und die Kirche* (Trier Theol. Studien 5), 1955, pp. 9ff. In conjunction with this important work, see Ernst Käsemann's review in *ThLZ* 81 (1956), cols. 585–90.

[3] Cf., e.g., the passage about exaltation in Eph. 1.20ff., and on this *Christologische Hoheitstitel*, pp. 131f.

23 we read: καὶ αὐτὸν [sc. Χριστὸν] ἔδωκεν κεφαλὴν ὑπὲρ πάντα τῇ ἐκκλησίᾳ, ἥτις ἐστὶν τὸ σῶμα αὐτοῦ, τὸ πλήρωμα τοῦ τὰ πάντα ἐν πᾶσιν πληρουμένου. This means unmistakably that salvation and final complete unity are accomplished over and through the Church.[1] We therefore come here to the same attitude of the Church towards the world as in Colossians. Again it is through the edification and growth of the Church that the aim, μέτρον ἡλικίας τοῦ πληρώματος τοῦ Χριστοῦ ('the measure of the stature of the fulness of Christ', 4.13b), is attained, as also the Church's most important service to the world is that in it the riches of the grace and manifold wisdom of God should become visible for all ages and powers.[2] But here it is quite characteristic that the declarations about the edification of the Church are not, as in Colossians, bound up directly with those about the mission. Paul does not appear here as the διάκονος who has to preach the gospel 'to every creature under heaven', and at the same time as the διάκονος τῆς ἐκκλησίας (Col. 1.23b, 25). We are told in Eph. 3.8f. that he has to preach the gospel to the Gentiles, but the concept 'Gentiles' has undergone a vital change, and is now in principle related only to those Gentiles who are accepted into the body of Christ, and to whom the mystery and the unsearchable riches of Christ are made known; thus the expression may go over at once into the designation of the Church's function in relation to the powers (3.10).[3] But Paul's service to the Church, described here, is also understood otherwise than in Colossians; it is true that, according to 4.11, the apostle has one office among others,[4] but his own particular service is defined by saying that 'his holy apostles and prophets by the Spirit' (3.5) have become recipients of the mystery of Christ, and that only through their mediation do the Church and discernment of the reality of salvation exist. In this sense Paul has the

[1] It would not be possible to give a translation of Eph. 1.22b, 23 that would do full justice to all the shades of meaning in the text. For an explanation in detail cf. Heinrich Schlier, *Der Brief an die Epheser*, 1957, pp. 89, 99. Käsemann, *ThLZ* 81 (1956), col. 587, has rightly emphasized that the concept of Christ as the head stands in contrast to the idea of the all-embracing unity; here we feel the effect of the Old Testament thought of subordination. On the idea of the edification of the universe by the Church, cf. again Heinrich Schlier, 'Die Kirche nach dem Brief an die Epheser' in *Die Zeit der Kirche*, 1956, pp. 159–86, there pp. 168ff.

[2] Cf. Eph. 4.13, and also 2.7; 3.10.

[3] Cf. the phrase 'you Gentiles' (which is characteristic of Ephesians) in 2.11; 3.1; the idea is used in essentially the same way in 3.6, 8 (otherwise only in 4.17 in a traditional manner of expression). The same idea underlies 1.13(f.); 6.19f.

[4] Eph. 4.11(ff.), varying what is said in I Cor. 12.28.

task of bringing to light what the οἰκονομία τοῦ μυστηρίου is, namely the Church's reality and unity (3.9; cf. v. 6). It is not without reason that the οἰκονομία idea is used in 3.2, 9, but now not one-sidedly in the sense of the office, as in Col. 1.25, but from the point of view of the revelation of the μυστήριον, in view both of the apostolic office and of the mystery's 'content' that is now being realized through the apostolic office:[1] the unity of the Church of Jews and Gentiles. With this a theme is taken up again that was dealt with at some length in Eph. 2.11–18 and again summarily formulated in 3.6.[2] It would be wrong, however, to suppose that Ephesians, in contrast to the rest of the post-Pauline tradition, would discuss here the problem of the Jewish and Gentile missions and of Israel's priority in the scheme of salvation; in Eph. 2.12, 15a these are mentioned only in passing. There is retained from the Pauline conception only that one element according to which there are no longer any distinctions between Jews and Gentiles in the Church—on the contrary, they are all united in the one body of Christ.[3] In this sense Col. 3.10f. also spoke in passing of Jews and Gentiles. Otherwise this consideration serves to set out the reconciliation between God and the world, abolishing at the same time all contrasts, both in this-worldly matters and in the scheme of salvation.[4] For by the death of Christ the wall of partition, hostility, is broken down, and the two (τὰ ἀμφότερα) have become one. With his death Christ 'came and preached peace to you who were far off and peace to those who were near' (2.17).[5] The special point of the whole argument in 2.11ff., especially in 14–18, is that it speaks of a unity that is already realized in Christ. With his death unity is already given, and the one σῶμα, 'the one

---

[1] Cf. Martin Dibelius and Heinrich Greeven, *An die Kolosser, Epheser, an Philemon* (HbNT 12), 1953³, p. 74.

[2] This definition of the μυστήριον according to its content is new in relation to Colossians. But Eph. 1.9f. shows that the mystery also has to do with the ἀνακεφαλαίωσις of the universe, and this assertion is to be understood as the more comprehensive, while agreeing essentially with the conception of Colossians.

[3] Cf. ch. IV, p. 107, above.

[4] It is characteristic of Ephesians how in this particular passage the ideas about cosmic spheres are bound up with those about time and history. If the former serve to express the universality of what happens in salvation, the latter serve to hold fast the actual earthly component of the saving action and of the present reality of salvation.

[5] εὐαγγελίζεσθαι in Eph. 2.17 has no real missionary dimension; on the contrary, the mere fact of Christ's coming and founding peace is a 'preaching' and speaks for itself. A different view in E. Schweizer, *ThLZ* 86 (1961), cols. 247f.

new man', is already here, just as, according to the proem, we
are all now chosen 'in Christ'. In Jesus' death and act of reconciliation, therefore, the Church's nature is determined and settled in
advance. But the concrete realization comes about only through the
apostles. It is to the apostle himself that 'the stewardship of God's
grace'[1] (οἰκονομία τῆς χάριτος τοῦ θεοῦ) is revealed. And therefore
the one Church of Jews and Gentiles is exclusively founded on
the apostle and his one gospel. It can hardly be by chance
that in 2.20 the concept of the foundation emerges. The apostle
remains the basis of the Church; he has taken the gospel to the
Gentiles and thereby created the one Church in the world.
Through him the Church has come into existence, and through his
actions the soteriological turning of the Gentiles from 'once' to
'now' has been completed (2.1ff., 1.1ff.). Now the Church is here,
and through it the ages and powers learn divine wisdom (3.10f.).
With this the apostolic and the fundamental missionary functions
become an entity *sui generis*, distinguished from the Church's
possession of the present reality of salvation. Thus the mission's
intermediary character, which was already noticed in Colossians, is
present here, too, and is even more pronounced, because the fundamental preaching to the Gentiles, as well as the revelation of the
mystery of salvation, shares in a definite way in the uniqueness of
Christ's saving action, or, one may say, corresponds to it. But as
regards Ephesians we must not simply speak of 'one after the
other' and of the mission as a thing of the past; one can rather say
with regard to Ephesians' spatial concept that it is a question of
'one over the other'. 'One over the other' means for Ephesians a
lasting presence. As Christ's saving action in the gospel is present,
so the apostolic office on which the Church is founded, and the
missionary function in the gospel, are something living. But all
this has in view the reality of the Church's salvation, and is 'subordinated to it' as the foundation on which the living growth of the
structure and the ἀνακεφαλαίωσις of the universe can be completed.

   With this conception, the main features of which agree in
Colossians and Ephesians, that very characteristic and distinctive
mark of the post-Pauline period, the separation of mission and
Church and the concentration of theological utterances on the
ecclesiological problems, is perhaps most clearly illuminated. For

---

[1] Cf. Schlier, *Epheser*, pp. 147f.

here the missionary task is not regarded as something that takes place externally, nor is it left on one side or perhaps intentionally ignored; on the contrary, it is to be defined in its relation to the Church's existence. It thus acquires a position that is at once introductory and subordinate, because according to this deutero-Pauline view the Church's essential quality lies in its existence as a widely visible witness to the reality of God's salvation, while on the other hand it is in its missionary relation that the concept of the Church is seen and determined.

3. JOHN'S GOSPEL AND LETTERS

The view of mission held in the Johannine writings is a very controversial subject. On the one hand it is said that there is behind it a Church 'that has no fundamentally missionary outlook', but separates itself rigidly from the world and regards itself as in contrast to it;[1] and on the other hand John's Gospel is referred to as a 'missionary work', whether for Israel or for the world.[2] The question needs to be examined, and it is advisable not to form an opinion too quickly, but to take into account the main Johannine lines of thought, and to determine on that basis the co-ordination of the missionary ideas.

It is comparatively seldom that *John's Gospel* makes real statements about mission. But not only are utterances directly about the missionary task frequently adduced, but various indirect conclusions are drawn. In particular, the writer's closeness to the manner of thought and expression current in his environment is pointed to, and it is said that this is so marked that it can be explained only by missionary interest.[3] It has even been asserted that there are only two possible explanations: either that John's Gospel has been completely overgrown by foreign ideas, or that

---

[1] K. G. Kuhn, 'Problem der Mission', *EMZ* 11 (1954), p. 167.

[2] Karl Bornhäuser, *Das Johannesevangelium eine Missionsschrift für Israel* (BFchrTh II/15), 1928; Wilhelm Oehler, *Das Johannesevangelium eine Missionsschrift für die Welt*, 1936; id., *Zum Missionscharakter des Johannesevangeliums* (BFchrTh 42.4), 1941; Albrecht Oepke, 'Das missionarische Christuszeugnis des Johannesevangeliums', *EMZ* 2 (1941), pp. 4–26.

[3] Thus especially Oepke, *EMZ* 2 (1941), pp. 6ff., who assumes interest in the synagogue, the Samaritans, John's disciples, Dionysus, the healing gods, inspired men, mysticism and gnosis, and even the Church as it had hitherto existed, from missionary motives. Oepke thinks the attitude of varying adjustments and parryings to be genuinely missionary. Similarly Oehler, *Missionsschrift*, pp. 23ff.

'the approximation of the language and style to those of the environment' serves 'more or less consciously the missionary aim.'[1] But this antithesis is not satisfactory. For this way of understanding the early Christian message may well also have arisen within an existing Church.[2] One might perhaps draw conclusions *a posteriori* as to how these particular Christians were reached by the mission; but the decisive fact is that the Church tried, through ways of thought and expression that were partly determined by its environment, to define its own position in the world and face to face with the world.[3] It is quite wide of the mark to suppose that this Gospel has to be understood particularly from its outlook towards Israel.[4] What it really addresses is the world,[5] only we must not at once think of a missionary purpose,[6] because otherwise the missionary theme would be bound to dominate much more strongly among the topics treated. The primary outlook on the Church, which has already been noted, is also shown

---

[1] Oehler, *Zum Missionscharakter*, pp. 11f.

[2] Oehler, *Zum Missionscharakter*, pp. 12f., points this out in passing; in particular he takes chs. 15 [*sic*]-17 out of the 'missionary document' as a 'church sermon'; nor does he reckon the supplementary ch. 21 as part of the missionary document. Cf. his *Missionsschrift*, pp. 31ff.

[3] It may be mentioned in passing that John's way of thinking is not exclusively Hellenist, but also contains Semitic elements; the connections with the comparative study of religions are not discussed.

[4] Despite Bornhäuser, *op. cit.*, esp. pp. 138ff., who tries to distinguish between 'all Israel', to whom the missionary document is directed, and the 'Jews' = Pharisees and scribes, who he thinks are the enemies not only of Jesus but also of Israel. There is, it is true, a certain difference in the use of 'Israel', 'Israelite' and 'Jew', but it is not practicable to confine the last one to 'fanatics of the Torah', especially as John specifically names the Pharisees as official representatives of Judaism beside the 'Jews'; the sole criterion of the positive or negative judgment of those belonging to the Old Testament people of God is the attitude to Jesus. According to Oehler, *Zum Missionscharakter*, pp. 70ff., it is a matter of downright polemical writing against the Jews, a wish to gain converts being shown only towards the Gentiles. He thinks that although the positive side repeatedly gains the upper hand in the polemics, and the Jews' numerous hesitations have an apologetic aim, yet according to 12.37ff. the Jews' unbelief is a settled fact—a state of affairs that would not be allowed to appear in a missionary work directed to Israel. Earlier, Wilhelm Heitmüller, *Das Johannes-Evangelium* (SNT IV), 1918³, pp. 16, 17f., described the Gospel as 'a work against the Jews, both offensive and defensive', and on the other hand as 'a piece of propaganda addressed to the Gentiles, especially the Greeks'.

[5] Oehler and Oepke are undoubtedly right in this respect.

[6] Oehler, *Zum Missionscharakter*, pp. 14ff., sees in the Christology, in the description of what salvation means ('life'), and in the concept of faith, decisive missionary elements; in pp. 58ff. and 91ff. he also points to the function of the dialogue, whereby misunderstandings are to be removed and difficulties overcome, and also to the formation and arrangement of the material; in particular he would explain the evangelist's free treatment of Jesus' discourses by the needs of the missionary situation (pp. 111f.).

both in John's Gospel and in the Letters. That is not simply to
assert that the thinking here is completely non-missionary, for the
exact relation of Church and mission must first be determined.

John's Gospel is distinguished by its emphasis on the *universalism of salvation*. The comprehensive scope of Jesus Christ's saving
action is brought out time and again. It is a question of salvation
for the whole world: Jesus is 'the Saviour of the world' (4.42).
'For God so loved the world that he gave his only Son, that
whoever believes in him should not perish but have eternal life'
(3.16). The Logos that became flesh is 'the Lamb of God, who
takes away the sin of the world' (1.29). He is 'the light of the
world' (8.12; 9.5; 12.46), 'the true light that enlightens every man'
(1.9).[1] But where John speaks of light, this also involves darkness.
Darkness is the world parted from God, 'this world' that lives in
sin and falsehood and is subject to death. Into this darkness there
shines the light. Salvation is again bestowed on the lost world, but
the darkness has not grasped the light (1.5):[2] it will not renounce
its own powers. Everything is therefore concentrated on the
mutual opposition of light and darkness. The Johannine *dualism*,
however, is no radical dualism that is founded in cosmology, for
the whole world is God's creation (1.3); nor is it a dualism of
decision in the sense that man has two possibilities and can decide
freely; for human decision cannot be dealt with as something that
is immanent,[3] and there are not simply two opposing contrasts:
dualism is determined by the fact that Jesus, as the Son of God,
did not come to judge but to save (12.47ff.), that by his coming he
has overcome the 'ruler of this world' (12.31; 16.11), and that he
has 'overcome the world' (16.33).[4] He has made manifest the truth
through which falsehood perishes, and has brought the life that
overcomes death.[5] Although the world tries to assert its own
powers, it will pass away; even if it summons all its resources
to resist salvation, the issue has long since been decided against

[1] Here and in what follows no attempt is made to give a complete list of the
relevant passages; it is a question merely of the main lines of the Johannine outlook.
[2] Bultmann, *Johannes*, pp. 26ff., has shown that even as early as John 1.5 the
reference is to revelation in history.
[3] Cf. Bultmann, *Theology*, §42 (II, pp. 15ff.).
[4] Bultmann does not sufficiently take this point of view into account.
[5] On the significance of ζωή as the most comprehensive term for the gift of salvation, see especially Franz Mußner, *ZΩH. Die Anschauung vom 'Leben' im vierten
Evangelium unter Berücksichtigung der Johannesbriefe* (Münchener Theologische Studien
I/5), 1952, esp. pp. 48ff., 144ff.

it.[1] As the world does not accept the life and light that have become manifest in Jesus and are meant unreservedly for everyone, salvation has itself become its judgment (3.17ff., and cf. 5.21ff.). Thus the world proves that its nature comes, not from God, but from the devil.

John's references to *predestination* must not be taken, any more than those on dualism, out of their soteriological context. For they are nowhere in contrast to the call to and readiness for faith, just as they do not annul the universality of the offer of salvation. But on the one hand they emphasize that in relation to faith there is no question of any work of man's in the sense that he can appeal to it before God,[2] and on the other hand they indicate that unbelief is not due merely to man's unwillingness, but that behind it a mystery is concealed that is beyond human grasp. How very much everything is concentrated on faith is also shown in John's attitude towards *Israel*. Of course, he knows about Israel's peculiar position, and he emphasizes that salvation comes from the Jews (4.22).[3] But the real Israelite acknowledges Jesus (1.47), as indeed Moses and the Old Testament testify to Jesus (5.45f.; 5.39);[4] when the Jews decline to accept him they forfeit their special position, as they have moved over to the side of the world which is hostile to God.[5] For the decisive criterion is not descent from Abraham, but the ἐκ τοῦ θεοῦ εἶναι which is shown in faith (8.30ff.). Thus it is not Israel's priority that is stressed, but rather the fact that the act of redemption took place 'not only' for this nation (11.51f.); Jesus has other sheep as well, who are not of this fold

[1] Cf. I John 2.8b.

[2] On this cf. Bultmann, *Theology*, §43 (II, pp. 21ff.), drawing attention to the numerous passages in which predestinary expressions are directly joined to invitations to faith. In this connection there also belong the sayings that no one can come to Jesus unless the Father 'draws' him (6.44), and that God has 'given' him his own (6.37; 17.2, 6f., etc.).

[3] The difference between Old Testament and New Testament revelation is also stressed; cf., e.g., 1.17. Bultmann, *Johannes*, p. 139 n. 6, p. 292, regards John 4.22 and the related passage 10.16 as editorial insertions; but I cannot feel sure of this. On this cf. Strathmann, *Johannes*, pp. 88f., 167; Barrett, *John*, pp. 198, 312f.

[4] In John 1.35ff. the Old Testament titles are adopted. The designation 'King of Israel' ('of the Jews') in 1.49, 12.13, and the passion narrative is certainly not entirely due to the tradition.

[5] The condemnation of the unbelieving 'Jews' is no doubt partly determined by the situation after AD 70; cf. Goppelt, *Christentum und Judentum*, pp. 251ff.; Eduard Lohse, *Israel und die Christenheit* (Kl. Vandenhoeck-Reihe 102), 1960, pp. 26f. All the disputes with the Jews are concentrated on Jesus' divine sonship; cf. Bultmann, *Theology*, II, p. 5 (§41.1).

(10.16). When Jesus speaks for the first time of his 'going away' there arises, in one of the misunderstandings that are typical of the Fourth Gospel, the question whether he will 'go to the Dispersion . . . and teach the Greeks' (7.35f.). When the Greeks in Jerusalem come and want to see him there is a reference to his being 'glorified', which according to the Johannine view is associated with the crucifixion: the grain of wheat has to die, so as to bear much fruit (12.20ff.). Nevertheless it is not now the Greeks, in contrast to the Jews, for whom salvation is meant. Rather is it those who believe—πᾶς ὁ πιστεύων (3.14f., 16)—among both Jews and Greeks, who obtain salvation.[1] It can even be said that Jesus gives his life for 'his sheep' (10.11), that he will gather the children of God who are scattered abroad (11.52); and the question is raised by the undiscerning disciples why he manifests himself only to them and not to the world (14.22ff.). But these statements about the universality of salvation, and about a direct relationship to believers, are not mutually exclusive, but condition each other. Universality is itself an expression of the unlimited claim that God makes on his whole creation, and makes clear the inclusive character inherent in those sayings that relate to the disciples. But on the other hand there is no salvation that could be detached from acceptance in faith. Consequently, wherever there is salvation, and salvation is granted to anybody, there is the question of separation, of the world's κρίσις.[2] The separation of the believers from the world that is hostile to God is completed. They remain in the world, but they are 'sanctified', singled out (17.15ff.). They are Jesus' 'friends', 'his own' (15.13f.; 13.1, cf. 10.3, 4; 12), who as such have to prove themselves in the world, but at the same time are especially given his help (17.9ff.). John

[1] By their unbelief the Jews have become representatives of the world, but that does not finally settle the problem of the Jews for John; a decision has indeed been made, but salvation is still offered to the whole world, and it can be grasped in faith. John's view is not simply that of Mark, according to which the Jews have abandoned their claim and the gospel now goes to the Gentiles. Anton Fridrichsen, 'La pensée missionnaire dans le Quatrième Évangile' in *Arbeiten und Mitteilungen aus dem neutestamentlichen Seminar zu Uppsala* VI (1937), pp. 39–45, thinks that salvation, which John thought of all along as universal, was realized by Jesus' death and the resurrection first in and for Israel, whereas after the exaltation it is given to other people too through the disciples. But in John the death and exaltation are far too closely intertwined for any such distinction; salvation has been decided on for Jews and Gentiles in the (incarnation and) 'exaltation' of the Son of God, and through faith it becomes effective for both.

[2] Cf. Bultmann, *Theology*, §45 (II, pp. 33ff.).

does not describe them as the people of God (ἐκκλησία), but as the flock that is cared for by Jesus as the Good Shepherd (10.1ff.), as the community in which those who are separated from the world are all 'one' (11.52; 17.20).

The different lines run together in John in the way indicated: the offer of salvation is to all men, and would include everyone, but salvation itself exists only in separation from and in contrast with the ways of this world. Notwithstanding its universality, the Christian message is unfolded in its relationship to believers, and the status of the Christians in face of the world is explicitly stressed. John's Gospel is therefore by no means to be understood as a missionary document; on the contrary, it is directed to a Christian Church, and this, moreover, is in accordance with the literary form of the Gospel. That does not prevent the Church's missionary service from being taken into account as well. The explicit words of commission are correlated in several ways, and should be understood in this special context. We are told, not only of the sending of the disciples, but above all of the sending of Jesus, and moreover of the sending of the Baptist and the Spirit. According to the concluding words, John's Gospel seeks to establish faith, and to assure believers of eternal life (20.30f.). Eternal life, however, consists in nothing else but the knowledge of the one true God and of him whom he has 'sent' (17.3). Jesus' divine sonship rests in his being sent by the Father (10.36).[1] Here in particular 'sending' means that Jesus came down from heaven (6.38) and goes away out of the world (16.28). What is decisive in the idea of sending is not primarily the description of this way,[2] but the thought of authority that is bound up with it. Jesus' claim to having been sent by God causes the Jews to interfere against him (7.28-30; 10.36). In the sense of authorization it can also be

[1] In John all the Christological statements are directed towards the idea and concept of the divine sonship, the title of sovereignty now being understood no longer in the original messianic sense, but on the premises of the Christian recasting that took place in the sphere of Hellenist Christianity. There the thought of the sending, together with declarations about Jesus' divine sonship, arose comparatively early, and had already appeared in Paul (Gal. 4.4; Rom. 8.3). It represents the first tendency towards and transition to statements on pre-existence. It must not be explained as a matter of course from mythological contexts, but is to be understood primarily as coming from the Old Testament idea of authorization; it need not be disputed that influences of another kind increasingly make themselves felt, Cf. *Christologische Hoheitstitel*, pp. 315ff.
[2] So already Phil. 2.6-11.

said of the Baptist that he was sent by God (1.6). And because of this legal element the idea of μαρτυρία is joined to that of sending. The testimony relates to what has been 'seen' or 'heard' (3.32).[1] Thus the Baptist, who is commissioned by God, testifies to the light, to the one who comes after him (1.8; 3.28). Jesus, on his part, has 'come into the world to bear witness to the truth' (18.37); he bears witness, as the one who has come from heaven, to what he has seen—that is, not earthly but heavenly things (3.11f.). In a certain sense he must also bear witness to himself, but he can do so because he is not alone, but because he and the Father are one (8.13ff.; 10.30). Thus with his testimony he does not stand alone; both the works that God has given him and also the 'Scriptures' bear witness to him (5.31ff.). And after he has gone away the Paraclete will likewise bear witness to him (15.26). Sending[2] therefore means that Jesus did not come of his own accord (7.28; 8.42), but came into the world to do the Father's will (4.34; 5.30; 6.38f.)—that is, to do the works entrusted to him (9.4; 10.36f.), and to say what was given him to say (3.34; 12.49). Sending therefore also means that he does not seek his own glory but that of the Father (7.18), and that everyone who believes in him and accepts his words believes at the same time in the Father who sent him (5.23f.; 12.44f.).

What Jesus has done on earth is only a beginning. The *Paraclete*, the Holy Spirit, who is sent to the disciples, teaches them everything, and continually reminds them afresh of what Jesus himself has said (14.26; 15.26); indeed, only he will guide them into all truth and will declare to them what he will take from 'what is mine' (16.7, 12–15).[3] But the Paraclete is not only a special gift to

[1] Oehler has rightly stressed in *Zum Missionscharakter*, pp. 25ff., the legal character of μαρτυρεῖν, μαρτυρία (against Strathmann, art. μάρτυς, etc., *ThWb* IV, pp. 502ff.). But he has stressed one-sidedly the fact of eyewitnesses, and this does not correspond to the Johannine purpose. Bultmann, *Johannes*, pp. 30(f.) n. 5, also lays weight on the forensic character.

[2] The ideas ἀποστέλλειν and πέμπειν occur side by side. Karl Heinrich Rengstorf, art. ἀποστέλλω, *ThWb* I, pp. 403f., has rightly drawn attention to the fact that these are marked by a certain regularity in the use of one or the other: thus, e.g., for God the phrase ὁ πέμψας με is always used. But it will not do to assume that ἀποστέλλειν means that Jesus' authority is founded in God's authority, while πέμπειν expresses God's participation in Jesus' work. The latter assumption founders at once on the fact that πέμπειν is repeatedly used in speaking of Jesus' subjection to God's will; moreover, the two words are closely related to each other and are clearly synonymous and interchangeable in John.

[3] With this ἐκ τοῦ ἐμοῦ λήμψεται the uniqueness of the revelation is meant to be kept, as in 14.26; cf. Bultmann, *Johannes*, pp. 443f.

the disciples; the Spirit will also convince the cosmos 'of sin and of righteousness and of judgment', and that takes place only through the call to faith, the message of the Christ-event, and the proclamation of judgment on the ruler of this world (16.8–10).[1] Thus Jesus continues his work in and on the world, and it is in the realm of this activity of the Spirit that the *disciples* find their task in relation to the world.[2] John has no doubt whatever that the message is to be handed on (4.28ff.); the disciples are promised that they will do the works that Jesus does—in fact, that they will do greater works than he, because he goes to the Father (14.12ff.). But there is also explicit mention of their sending, and a statement that whoever receives them receives the sender himself; this is certainly an old principle, but in the whole context of Johannine thought it gets its special significance (13.16, 20). As the disciples act in his authority, so they have to witness for him, both to his works and to his words (4.39; 15.27).[3] The high-priestly prayer, which is permeated from the beginning by the theme of the sending of Jesus, puts the commission of the disciples in direct correspondence to that of Jesus: 'As thou didst send me into the world, so I have sent them into the world' (17.18). The risen Lord's sending commission is, then, in the context of John's Gospel merely a confirmation of this (20.21–23). But it now becomes clear why, contrary to the other early Christian tradition, the sending commission is joined to the bestowal of the Spirit. The work of the disciples is to be joined even more directly to that of the exalted Lord himself, so that both are seen as one. It is the eschatological harvest, in which the sower and reaper rejoice together, although they are separate (4.35ff.).

Thus it cannot be said that the missionary element in John's Gospel has become insignificant or plays only a quite subordinate part. But it is fitted into the Gospel's whole concept, and is subjected to quite definite presuppositions. In particular, a mission

---

[1] See in detail Bultmann, *Johannes*, pp. 432ff.

[2] Strathmann, *Johannes*, p. 224, quite rightly points to the disciples' missionary preaching, which was carried out with the Spirit's help.

[3] Witness-bearing is not confined to the first generation, but is for all times. We see this from the fact that Jesus' words and works can be repeated and continued—that is 'witnessed to' again—by the disciples. Of course, it is a witness that comes from faith and is directed to faith, but it must not on that account be deprived of its legal structure. It is a question of truth that is held fast through faith in contrast to all falsehood.

exists only where the disciples are conscious of their contrast to the world, and have drawn the necessary conclusions from this. But as the universality of Christ's saving action determines the message, so the Church has to witness to the victory of the light over the darkness that still asserts itself although it is overcome, and it also has to advance beyond its own sphere. God's eschatological benefits are not for it only, but for everyone. But the sending of the disciples not only arises from separation from the world; it also aims at this separation. It is turned to the world and at the same time contrary to it. However explicitly the missionary idea is here set out, the way in which the Church is understood provides a clear preliminary sign by which the missionary task took on a character substantially different from that of the earliest Christian period.

The *Letters of John* show a different picture from that of the Gospel. They are of great interest, because here it becomes plain how easily, in the conception of John's Gospel, the view could be one-sidedly narrowed on to the Church and its existence in the godless world. The docetic heresy, which became so menacing, broke out within Christianity itself, showing that the world is to be encountered even in its own ranks. The Church therefore has to be further strengthened in its own Christian status, and above all be placed on the only serviceable basis of faith. Thus the problem of the tradition now becomes highly urgent. What was 'from the beginning' becomes the norm of criticism.[1] There is no doubt that the Letters of John come from the same circle as the Gospel, but it is hardly probable that they were written by the same author; in particular, we can well recognize a later stage in I John, which has been termed, not without reason, a 'Johannine Pastoral Letter'.[2] It becomes plain that it was written at a later period than the Gospel; the change we can see in comparison with the Gospel is to be inferred not only from changed situations, but from the fact that the comprehensive scope of the horizon is no longer maintained. Only in standard Christological turns of speech is the universal claim still kept. Thus 2.2 reads: 'And he is the expiation

---

[1] We find this $\dot{\alpha}\pi'$ $\dot{\alpha}\rho\chi\tilde{\eta}s$ already in John 15.27, but in the Gospel it has no sort of dominating function. Cf. on the other hand I John 1.1; 2.7, 13, 14, 24; 3.11; II John 5f.

[2] Cf. Hans Conzelmann, ' "Was von Anfang war" ' in *Neutest. Studien für R. Bultmann* (BZNW 21), 1957², pp. 194-201, esp. pp. 200f.

for our sins, and not for ours only, but also for the sins of the whole world'; 3.8b speaks of God's Son having appeared 'to destroy the works of the devil'; and in 4.9 it is said that God sent his Son into the world 'so that we might live through him'; and this is expanded in v. 14 to the statement that he is 'the Saviour of the world'.[1] Although the universal element derived from Christology is still kept, the other range of sayings, which relates the work of salvation directly to the believers, is much more strongly emphasized. The words 'you' and 'we' run through almost the whole of I John; they are the words with which the writer either addresses the Church or includes himself with it, and which also define the numerous participial expressions. In the proem, which, somewhat in connection with John 1.1ff., speaks of the manifestation of $ζωή$ in the flesh, we read: $ἀπαγγέλλομεν ὑμῖν$. The declarations about light and darkness are directed, not primarily to the contrast between God and the world, but to the Church, which knows that the darkness is passing away (I John 2.8), and that it must not itself live in darkness. Because God is light, it must walk in the light (1.5ff.), and because God is love, there can exist for it nothing but brotherly love (3.11ff.; 4.7ff.).[2] It must not, however, love the world (2.15ff.), but must prove itself to be the band of those who are born of God and therefore overcome the world (3.9; 5.4). The believers stand in the eschatological hour of the apostasy against which they, in possession of the *chrisma*, the Holy Spirit, must stand firm (2.20ff.). Thus they already stand in the world as God's children, knowing that they will one day be like him and be able to see him as he is (3.2). The focus is therefore only on those who have taken hold of salvation

[1] That the wording of I John 2.24 and the similar passage 4.10b belong here has been contested by Rudolf Bultmann, 'Die kirchliche Redaktion des ersten Johannesbriefes' in *In Memoriam Ernst Lohmeyer*, 1951, pp. 189-201, there p. 201. But even if these passages were eliminated, there would still remain universal lines of thought in the other Christological statements; indeed the shift in contrast to the Gospel would be still more obvious.

[2] The theme of mutual love already emerges in John 13.34; 15.12, 17, and is surprising in view of Jesus' understanding of the love of one's neighbour. But the inclusive character of mutual love must not be overlooked. On the other hand, however, the theme of mutual love is strongly emphasized in I John by the fact that it speaks expressly of love of one's brother and separates this from love towards the world, so that in this passage, too, a shift of emphasis is unmistakable. In the world ruled by darkness true love exists only where God's children are; and so love is thought of as a characteristic of the Church as a whole. Cf. Rudolf Schnackenburg, *Die Johannesbriefe* (Herders Theol. Komm. z. NT XIII/3), 1953, pp. 102ff.

and life and are freed from the power of Satan. We cannot be certain of any real missionary interest in any passage in I John; rather do we get the impression that stress is to be laid, not on taking the message outside, but on drawing an even more rigid line between the Church and the world. Here it is worth noting that in the argument on heresy expressions are used that come from the missionary sphere: ἐξ ἡμῶν ἐξῆλθαν, ἐξεληλύθασιν εἰς τὸν κόσμον (I John 2.19; 4.1; II John 7), which, however, are now used in conjunction with the apocalyptic concept of the antichrist (I John 2.18, 22; 4.3; II John 7). Almost more important is what is said in III John, for the messengers whom the 'elder' sent out, and who accept nothing from the heathen, but are to be lodged and cared for by the churches, are obviously missionaries.[1] It thus appears that missionary service has not simply died out in the Johannine sphere. But the argument with the heretics shows that here another missionary movement has come into being, against whose false doctrine a clear attitude must be taken up from the outset so as to defend the existing Church. And this in its turn shows how inconsiderable the missionary impulse is, and how far apart the Church and the mission have actually gone.[2] The Church's function and existence are no longer understood from the missionary point of view. If John's Gospel was still able to hold together both the Church's essential nature and independence and also the task of the mission in a definite co-ordination, this undivided view soon broke up, and the problem of the Church took the stage.[3]

The picture given us by the post-Pauline and the Johannine tradition is comparatively homogeneous. What is surprising is that the synoptists have preserved in such a high degree the missionary concern of the early days. This may be largely due to the shaping of the traditional material, which for the most part came from that period. It is not difficult to see that Matthew and

[1] Cf. Günther Bornkamm, art. πρεσβύτερος, *ThWb* VI, p. 671 n. 121.
[2] Moreover, the mission's activity abroad is probably now used in no small measure to combat heresy.
[3] K. G. Kuhn's thesis, *EMZ* 11 (1954), pp. 167f., mentioned at the beginning of this section, is thus confirmed as regards the Johannine Letters. In John's Gospel, however, there must be more marked differentiation. Without doubt there is no question of a 'missionary document', whether for Israel or for the world; but the unmistakable universalism of salvation is combined there with a clear recognition of missionary service, however much the contrast with the world and the concentration on the Christian Church are emphasized.

Luke viewed the Church as an independent unit. But it was only John who created a Gospel that developed the message of salvation primarily in its relation to the Church, while taking up the missionary theme, which the synoptists made to predominate, only in quite definite co-ordination. We have recognized something similar in some deutero-Pauline letters also. But the other early Christian writings that have been investigated here, not least I John, show how strong the tendency then was for Church and mission to become more independent of each other and for the missionary task to recede into the background.

CONCLUSION

WE see from a detailed consideration of the early Christian evidence how earnestly the first Christians endeavoured to understand the commission that Jesus had entrusted to them, and to perform their missionary service in the right way. In the New Testament, therefore, we do not find a conception that is in all respects uniform. What we do see, however, is that all the different lines converge, and that the New Testament's understanding of the Christian mission is held together by two fundamental questions which, however differently they might be answered, the early Church found unavoidable: the question of Jews and Gentiles, of Israel's priority and of the equally unquestionable universality of salvation; and the question of the unity of mission and Church. These basic questions also demand an answer today, and there can be no doubt in which direction the whole of the New Testament evidence points us, even if we meet different expressions of opinion on isolated occasions.

The New Testament's understanding of mission cannot be understood apart from the background of the Israelite concept of God, and of the promise, given in the Old Testament, of the salvation of the nations in the last days, although in the Old Testament there is no going out to the nations and no command to undertake a mission. Judaism's religious propaganda and efforts to proselytize in the time of Jesus represent only an external preparation for the early Christian mission, without being itself a mission in the real sense. What is decisive for the missionary service of early Christianity is the work and message of Jesus. The Kingdom of God which has drawn near begins to be realized with his appearing, the new people of God is gathered, and in spite of the concentration on Israel, the Gentiles do not remain untouched by it. With the command to missionize and the conveying of his own authority, Jesus brings the disciples into his eschatological work.

After Jesus' resurrection, the disciples, urged by the Holy Spirit, carried his message and work further. But difficulties at once arose. Israel's priority was to be guarded, but the universality that had been unmistakable in Jesus' work had to be firmly adhered to. Could the Gentiles simply be received into the Church on the basis of their faith, or had their time not yet come? Could a real Gentile mission be undertaken at all by men, or was not this reserved for God himself according to the Old Testament understanding? At first the acceptance of Gentiles had certainly been more or less an exception, but quite soon the so-called Hellenists began a systematic mission to the Gentiles, and in doing this they appealed less to the commission of the earthly than to that of the exalted Lord, who had already assumed the royal office in heaven in the last days, and was therefore the ruler of the whole world. They regarded the coming of the Gentiles not as an event in the completion of the last days, but as the sign of the time and history that still endured and that had been determined in relation to the *eschaton*. The controversy was intensified by the appearance of the Judaizers, who demanded the circumcision of all Gentile Christians. The Apostles' Conference brought clarification and the final acknowledgment of the Gentile mission without legal conditions, and at the same time Israel's priority was confirmed. But the fact that the difficulties were not really settled, but broke out in another place, is shown by the Apostolic Decree which was decided on subsequently, and by which, in spite of concessions unacceptable to Paul, complete community between Jewish and Gentile Christians was to be achieved, and thus the decision of the Apostles' Conference for the Gentile mission was to be confirmed.

How very much the problem of Jews and Christians had become the main problem of the Christian understanding of mission in the initial period is shown by the whole theology of the apostle Paul. His commission to go to the Gentiles, the idea of crossing the whole world as the messenger of the gospel, and the knowledge of freedom from the law, are for him inseparable from service to Israel. Even if all men in the same way are under sin and need redemption, and in the Church itself all distinctions between Jews and Gentiles are abolished, yet the fact remains that Israel has experienced election of a special kind in its history, and that because of God's faithfulness the salvation that is now rejected will one day come to this Israel. The only result of the temporary delusion can be that now the Gentiles also share in salvation. At the same time, the idea of Israel's priority was not understood everywhere like this, as we see from the evangelist Mark, who regards Israel as having abandoned its right to priority with its rejection of Jesus. But both Matthew and Luke try in different ways to make clear the necessity of the mission to the Jews and the lasting precedence of Israel, while the mission to the Gentiles has long ceased to be a problem to them.

When the decision in favour of the Gentile mission had been taken the question of Jews and Gentiles quickly receded after Paul's time, and in part of the later New Testament writings it is no longer taken into account at all. Instead of that the second fundamental problem, which had not become acute in the earliest period, comes to the fore: the determination of the relation between mission and Church. With the consolidation of the churches that already existed, and the concentration on internal structure and development, the missionary preaching, as a work that was directed outwards, became a more independent function; a certain separation is unmistakable. This is a question, not merely of practical necessity, but rather of an internal shift of emphasis. For Christianity no longer understood its service primarily from the point of view of its missionary task, but from that of its existence as a Church amid the world. The missionary element was therefore increasingly related to and co-ordinated with ecclesiology, and this could lead to an essential deepening of the concept of the Church, while at the same time involving the danger of narrowness.[1] The state of the mission work may have contributed to this: churches were established in almost the whole of the known *oikoumenē*, the gospel had been carried through the world in a great triumphal march, and the consciousness had grown that a first decisive step had been completed. On the other hand, the difficulties and vexations, which became more and more apparent, showed how necessary it was for the Church to maintain its character as a Church. It never gave up the universal claim of the gospel, or set limits to the spreading of the glad tidings, but saw its commission from a different angle. The questions that were so characteristic of the second and all later generations now came to the fore, and the mission repeatedly had to be comprehended afresh from the point of view of its unity with the Church.

[1] This is shown on the one hand by Colossians, Ephesians, and also John's Gospel, and on the other hand by the Pastoral and Johannine Letters.

Finally, the results of the inquiry into the New Testament view of the mission give rise to some questions that concern the present understanding of the mission.[1] The 'great century' of recent missionary history belongs to the past, and today it is not difficult to recognize that there converged at that time a number of external and internal presuppositions that made possible a missionary activity of that kind throughout the world.[2] Meanwhile the situation has changed fundamentally; this has been expressed by saying that today the mission not only has problems but has itself become a problem.[3] The commission remains, but besides the question of carrying it out, it was and is necessary to think out entirely afresh its theological basis. In our day it is widely agreed that only a biblical foundation for mission is legitimate, and that nothing else can provide the theological basis of all missionary work.[4] This is not so self-evident as it may sound, for the missionary theory of the nineteenth century took very different paths.[5] Certainly, with the demand for a biblical basis for the mission an important and necessary switch-over has been undertaken,[6] but this has not decided anything in detail about a practical development of missionary theory and a carrying through of the missionary command in accord with the gospel.

For the New Testament the mission is determined by two facts: the one is the knowledge that the eschatological hour has dawned,

[1] For the time about 1900 we may refer to the comparison by Heinrich Weinel, *Die urchristliche und die heutige Mission* (Religionsgesch. Volksbücher IV/5), 1907.
[2] Cf. Kenneth Scott Latourette, *A History of the Expansion of Christianity*: vol. 4, *The Great Century, 1800–1914: Europe and the United States of America*, 1941, chs. 2–3; Hans Werner Gensichen, 'Missionsgeschichte der neueren Zeit' in *Die Kirche in ihrer Geschichte*, 1961, pp. 30ff.
[3] Walter Freytag, 'Strukturwandel der westlichen Missionen' in *Reden und Aufsätze* I (ThBüch 13.1), 1961, pp. 111–20.
[4] Cf., e.g., Walter Holsten, *Das Kerygma und der Mensch. Einführung in die Religions- und Missionswissenschaft* (ThBüch I), 1953, pp. 120ff.; Johannes Blauw, *Gottes Werk in dieser Welt. Grundzüge einer biblischen Theologie der Mission*, 1961, pp. 7ff.
[5] We may mention the past-master of missionary knowledge, Gustav Warneck, *Evangelische Missionslehre* I, 1897[2], who tried to give an ecclesiastical, historical and ethnological foundation for the mission as well as its biblical, dogmatic and ethical basis. On the different foundations of the mission cf. Walter Freytag, 'Vom Sinn der Weltmission' in *Reden und Aufsätze* II (ThBüch 13.2), 1961, pp. 207–16, esp. pp. 209ff.
[6] This also holds good in respect of Roman Catholic missionary theory; cf., e.g., Thomas Ohm, *Machet zu Jüngern alle Völker*, pp. 69ff., where the sources of missionary theory are discussed, and there is a discussion of the Scriptures and also of the *traditio apostolica et divina* up to the Papal missionary decrees and the provisions for propaganda, and further, as 'subsidiary sources', of the *ratio naturalis*, the *auctoritas philosophorum* (in the sense of the *philosophia perennis*), and the *historia humana*.

bringing salvation within reach and leading to its final completion, and the other is the commission that they had received from Jesus Christ and his authorizing them to preach the glad tidings that concerned everyone. Whatever divergences occurred in details, these two elements never constituted a problem for early Christianity. The eschatological aspect of missionary service was discussed thoroughly at the International Missionary Conference at Willingen in 1952 and at the World Council of Churches at Evanston in 1954, and it was laid down that 'In the theology of the mission no one will now be able to go back behind Willingen'.[1] It was again recognized that Christ as the world's *hope* is the basic starting-point for all the Church's missionary service.[2] The mission has sometimes previously had an eschatological foundation in that fanatical sense that by a feverish staking of resources on the spreading of the gospel the Lord's return could be brought about, or—assuming a definite date for the end of the world—all the activity was to be concentrated on the mission before that event; but a mission is not a fanatical undertaking. There is a 'mission in view of the end' in the sense of the obedient service of the Church of Jesus Christ in its 'existence between the times, between Jesus' resurrection and return, between the world's reconciliation and its redemption'.[3] Mission already belongs, as can be clearly seen in the New Testament, to the events of the last days; nevertheless it has its place in present time and history. It is 'Christ's reign looking towards the end'.[4] Missionary preaching testifies to the 'Now' of salvation, which can be nothing other than the ever new promise that we are moving towards God's coming world, from which we may already draw our life.[5] Only this can give meaning to the history of our world, and in this we

[1] Hans Jochen Margull, *Theologie der missionarischen Verkündigung. Evangelisation als oekumenisches Problem*, 1959, pp. 24ff., 39ff. (quotation from p. 38).
[2] Cf. the lecture at the World Council of Churches, Evanston, 1954, by Edmund Schlink, 'Christus—die Hoffnung der Welt', *ThLZ* 79 (1954), cols. 705–14, now in the author's volume of essays: *Der kommende Christus und die kirchlichen Traditionen* 1961, pp. 211–20.
[3] Walter Freytag, 'Mission im Blick aufs Ende' in *Reden und Aufsätze* II, pp. 186–98, there p. 187. Cf. also Karl Hartenstein, *Die Mission als theologisches Problem*, 1933, pp. 13ff.; *id.*, 'Mission und Eschatologie', *EMZ* 7 (1950), pp. 33–42.
[4] Freytag, *op. cit.*, II, p. 190.
[5] Margull, *op. cit.*, pp. 294f., speaks of 'hope in action', which is quite appropriate in the sense indicated above, but can easily be misunderstood. Margull himself tries to convey this 'definition' more fully, and in any case it must be clearly stated what this hope is, and of what kind the 'action' can or cannot be.

have the incentive for the mission.[1] 'Without the mission, history is nothing but human history, whose progress consists at the most in the intensification of its catastrophe. But if we know of the coming kingdom, we cannot rejoice at the promise without proclaiming it.'[2] But there would be no mission if Jesus Christ had not appeared on earth. The Christological basis of mission is inseparable from the eschatological.[3] For the whole New Testament there is no missionary preaching and activity that does not involve making known the Christ-event in the whole world and proclaiming to all mankind the salvation that has become manifest in Christ. The view directed towards the end is possible only because Jesus preached with unique urgency the message of God's latter-day reign, and commissioned his disciples to carry this very message into the world. Given such an eschatological horizon, the sending by Christ is plainly constitutive for the New Testament view of the mission, whether the sending was attributed to the earthly or to the exalted Lord. It is Christ alone who gave the authority with which the gospel can be carried forth to all mankind. Thus the sending of the disciples is grounded in the sending of Jesus himself by the Father. Moreover, the authority of Jesus' disciples does not rest simply on a word of command once given, by which we should be bound as if by a law; it is at the same time the present authority given to us by the Holy Spirit, on whose power Jesus' witnesses may always rely.

Mission as a function entrusted to Christianity has never been without problems, as we already see in the New Testament. It is true that the question of Jews and Gentiles, which was such a burning one in the Church's earliest period, receded into the background as a direct missionary problem, owing to the decision taken by the great majority of the early Christians in favour of the

---

[1] The 'indicating' and the 'fulfilling' characteristics of gospel preaching and missionary activity—on this cf. Blauw, *op. cit.*, pp. 118ff.—should present no contrast.

[2] Freytag, 'Sinn der Weltmission', *op. cit.*, II, p. 216.

[3] On recent discussion cf. Margull, *op. cit.*, pp. 45ff. Georg F. Vicedom's work, *Missio Dei. Einführung in eine Theologie der Mission*, 1958, esp. pp. 12ff., which favours an ultimately trinitarian starting-point for the mission, has not, in my opinion, taken sufficient account of the predominant eschatological and Christological orientation of the New Testament pronouncements on the mission. The claim to a missionary theology on a trinitarian basis was previously made by Wilhelm Andersen, *Auf dem Wege zu einer Theologie der Mission* (Beitr. z. Missionsw. u. evang. Religionskunde 6), 1957, pp. 35ff.

Gentile mission.[1] But this involves several fundamental questions of our Christian existence, which must not be ignored: there is the question of the Old Testament as the book of the promise; there is the question of the relation of the Church of Jesus Christ to the Israel that has not yet acknowledged its Lord; and there is the question of right practice with regard to law and freedom, a problem that in a different way is acute in the mission among peoples whose background is not that of our western ecclesiastical tradition.

The most harassing question in all modern missionary history has been the uneasy relation between Church and mission. The missionary work undertaken by the pietism and the revival movement of the eighteenth and nineteenth centuries was to a considerable degree in broad contrast to the existing churches, and a man like Louis Harms, who about 1850 wanted to regard the Hermannsburg mission as a function of his Hanoverian state church, met with considerable difficulties.[2] It is helpful to us to see that even in the New Testament there was argument about the co-ordination of Church and mission. The unhappy divergence has to be overcome again and again through the necessary unity of Church and mission, which cannot be abandoned. For there is 'no other Church than the Church that was sent into the world. And there is no other mission than that of Christ's Church'.[3] The World Council of Churches at New Delhi in 1961 showed that this unity of Church and mission has been seen more and more clearly in our own time, and that practical conclusions have been drawn. It was decided there that the World Council of Churches and the International Missionary Council should be amalgamated.[4] Bishop L. Newbigin of South India, who sketched the previous history and the scope of this union, pointed out that it was conditioned by the nature of the gospel itself, mission and church unity being 'two sides of the same reality, or rather two ways of

[1] On this cf. Heinrich Schlier, 'Die Entscheidung für die Heidenmission in der Urchristenheit' in *Die Zeit der Kirche*, 1956, pp. 90–107; he has, however, strongly systematized.

[2] On this cf. Holsten, *Das Kerygma und der Mensch*, pp. 150f. On the importance of the missions of the different churches in the later nineteenth century cf. Gensichen, 'Missionsgeschichte', pp. 37ff.

[3] Blauw, *op. cit.*, p. 136.

[4] Preparations for this had been made by the International Missionary Conferences from Jerusalem 1928 onwards; cf. Andersen, *op. cit.*, pp. 11ff.; Gensichen, *op. cit.*, pp. 52ff.

describing the same action of the living Lord who wills that all men should be drawn to himself'; just as all mission presses towards union, so there can be no use of the word 'ecumenical' that excludes the missionary dimension.[1]

It ought to be self-evident that the unity of mission and Church does not mean merely a correlation and supplementing, or perhaps a provisional missionary stage followed by a church stage. Nor, on the other hand, may we undertake a complete equalization of Church and mission, as this might too easily involve the loss of the missionary concern and impetus.[2] It is a question of an essential unity of Church and mission, in which, although they are necessarily involved in each other, various tasks and functions are necessary. For the Church in all its doings is affected by its missionary mandate, without in every case taking a real missionary initiative; and on the other hand all missionary action is nothing less than action by the Church. In other words, the Church has in any case a missionary character, and possesses *ipso facto* a missionary dimension, just as on the other hand every missionary activity has an ecclesiological basis.[3] The Church's

[1] Lesslie Newbigin, 'The Missionary Dimension of the Ecumenical Movement' in *The New Delhi Report*, ed. W. A. Visser 't Hooft, 1962, p. 4; more fully in a German translation in *Neu-Delhi 1961*, ed. W. A. Visser 't Hooft, 1962, pp. 535-42, esp. p. 536. Cf. also Walter Freytag, 'Mission und Ökumene', *Reden und Aufsätze* II, pp. 115-24.

[2] The leaning towards identification has been expressed particularly clearly in dialectical theology; cf. the well-known essay by Karl Barth, 'Die Theologie und die Mission in der Gegenwart' (1932) in *Theologische Fragen und Antworten (Ges.Vorträge* III), 1957, pp. 100-26; on this cf. Blauw, *op. cit.*, pp. 122ff., who quotes Bishop Neill's remark 'If everything is mission, nothing is mission.' On Karl Barth's present position, cf. his *Kirchliche Dogmatik* IV/3.2, 1959, pp. 999ff. (ET, *Church Dogmatics* IV/3.2, 1962, pp. 872ff.).

[3] Thus, e.g., Lesslie Newbigin, in *One Body, One Gospel, One World*, 1958, pp. 21, 43, distinguishes between 'missionary dimension' and 'missionary intention', and suggests that all the life of the Church has a missionary dimension, but that the mission is not always a primary intention. In a different way a broad current of Dutch theology has tried to take up the unity of mission and Church with the idea of the 'apostolate'. This idea was introduced into the discussion, with reference to B. M. Schurman and O. Noordmans, especially by Hendrik Kraemer; cf. especially his book *The Christian Message in a Non-Christian World*, 1938. It took form later in the Church Order of the Nederlandse Hervormde Kerk of 1948 (in force since 1951), where Article VIII expressly mentions the Church's apostolic commission; apart from conversational interchange with Israel and the mission's work among the nations of the non-Christian world, it speaks here at the same time of work among those who are alienated from the gospel, and of the 'Christianizing' of society. On this cf. W. Holsten, *op. cit.*, pp. 152f.; Evert Jansen-Schoonhoven, 'Der artikel "Vom Apostolat der Kirche" in der Kirchenordnung der Niederländischen Reformierten Kirche', in *Basileia* (Festschrift für W. Freytag), 1959, pp. 278-84. This view is developed still further theologically by A. A. van Ruler; cf., e.g., his essay 'Theologie

position in the world has therefore in any case, as is clearly shown by some of the later New Testament writings, a missionary aspect. Only where this is completely misunderstood can the ecclesiological view of the mission be regarded as a wrong approach.[1] But the recognition of the unity of mission and Church cannot be abandoned, and must help us, not only to understand the mission in the right way, but also to determine rightly the Church's nature and mandate in relation to the world.

The Church in the world is always confronted with a particular situation, which is not the same today as in the time of early Christianity. The question as to this situation and the special kind of missionary service for which it calls from the Church is not simply external and sociological, but also theological.[2] But the situation is not the same, either at all times or in all places. The gospel has been carried through the whole world; churches have arisen in almost all countries, and the task of both Church and mission has to be seen as it presents itself from time to time. Such problems already existed for the early Church. The gospel had then been preached through the whole of the known world in a first triumphal march, churches had arisen and new questions repeatedly sprang up; for the situation was not the same throughout, and moreover it changed appreciably in the short period of early Christian history. The early Church did not evade this, and

des Apostolates', *EMZ* 11 (1954), pp. 1-21. Apart from the problems of the specifically Dutch conception of 'theocracy'—on this cf. K. H. Miskotte, 'Naturrecht und Theokratie', in *Die Freiheit des Evangeliums und die Ordnung der Gesellschaft* (BEvTh 15), 1952, pp. 29-72—a difficult question arises: How far is it appropriate, from the New Testament point of view, to speak of 'apostolate' in connection with the mission, for there is no doubt that the word is used there for a function that existed only once and could not be repeated. It may be regarded as the decisive gain of this article of the Dutch Church Order that it sets out the indissolubility of Church and mission, and also the eschatological horizon of the Church's commission.

[1] This must be asserted in particular with reference to J. C. Hoekendijk, 'Die Kirche im Missionsdenken', *EMZ* 9 (1952), pp. 1-13. In his opinion the ecclesiological interest in connection with the mission is 'a sign of spiritual decadence'. The danger that he sees in particular is that the world may cease to be the world and may become the Church's outfield. 'People pursue ecclesiology in the second generation; in the first generation, in times of revival, of reformation, and of missionary advance, people study Christology, think eschatologically, live doxologically, and speak of the Church without stress and with a certain ingenuousness, as of something that a seven-year-old child knows of, thank God' (p. 2). There is no need to deny that the danger of such ecclesiological narrowness may emerge, but we ought not to make that a starting-point. On this cf. also Andersen, *op. cit.*, p. 28; Hans Werner Gensichen, 'Grundfragen der Kirchwerdung in der Mission', *EMZ* 8 (1951), pp. 33-46.

[2] Cf. Margull, *Theologie der missionarischen Verkündigung*, pp. 162ff.

the palpable divergences of many New Testament passages (however much common ground there might be in their basic structure), especially the contrast between the earliest and the later views, must also be understood from this point of view. Seen in that way, not only can the New Testament tell us of the right basis for mission; it can also help us in one way or another in our present-day problems.

If, in conclusion, we try to define mission by referring directly to the New Testament, we may put it like this: Mission is the Church's service, made possible by the coming of Christ and the dawning of the eschatological event of salvation, and founded in Jesus' commission. The Church goes in confidence and hope to meet the future of its Lord, with the duty of testifying before the whole world to God's love and redemptive deed.—Mission in this sense is just as mandatory for the Church in our greatly changed world as in the first days of Christianity. The missionary task already presents itself in our immediate environment, which is largely detached from the Church. Yet the missionary task necessarily involves going out beyond the territory that the message has already reached.[1] The whole of mankind, which has in recent times been overtaken by so much external and internal distress and lives in slavery to the present way of life, must be told the glad tidings, and so receive that true freedom that is unfettered by legal bonds.

---

[1] Cf. K. Barth, *Kirchliche Dogmatik* IV/3.2, p. 1002 (ET, p. 874).

INDEX OF AUTHORS

The following works appeared shortly after the German edition of this book: Georg Strecker, *Der Weg der Gerechtigkeit. Untersuchungen zur Theologie des Matthäus* (FRLANT 82) 1962; Reinhart Hümmel, *Die Auseinandersetzung zwischen Kirche und Judentum im Matthäusevangelium* (BEvTh 33) 1963; and Walter Schmithals, *Paulus und Jakobus* (FRLANT 85) 1963. The first two of these works would have had to be noticed in Chapter Vb, and the last would have had to be discussed critically in connection with Chapters III and IV.

INDEX OF REFERENCES

OLD TESTAMENT